Til Kim
fra Jan   28/9/09
Nato i Oslo i
Takk for vennskap og
samarbeid!

New Security Challenges Series

General Editor: **Stuart Croft**, Professor of International Security in the Department of Politics and International Studies at the University of Warwick, UK, and Director of the ESRC's New Security Challenges Programme.

The last decade demonstrated that threats to security vary greatly in their causes and manifestations, and that they invite interest and demand responses from the social sciences, civil society and a very broad policy community. In the past, the avoidance of war was the primary objective, but with the end of the Cold War the retention of military defence as the centrepiece of international security agenda became untenable. There has been, therefore, a significant shift in emphasis away from traditional approaches to security to a new agenda that talks of the softer side of security, in terms of human security, economic security and environmental security. The topical *New Security Challenges series* reflects this pressing political and research agenda.

Titles include:

Jon Coaffee, David Murakami Wood and Peter Rogers
THE EVERYDAY RESILIENCE OF THE CITY
How Cities Respond to Terrorism and Disaster

Christopher Farrington *(editor)*
GLOBAL CHANGE, CIVIL SOCIETY AND THE NORTHERN IRELAND PEACE PROCESS
Implementing the Political Settlement

Kevin Gillan, Jenny Pickerill and Frank Webster
ANTI-WAR ACTIVISM
New Media and Protest in the Information Age

Andrew Hill
RE-IMAGINING THE WAR ON TERROR
Seeing, Waiting, Travelling

Andrew Hoskins and Ben O'Loughlin
TELEVISION AND TERROR
Conflicting Times and the Crisis of News Discourse

Janne Haaland Matlary
EUROPEAN UNION SECURITY DYNAMICS
In the New National Interest

Michael Pugh, Neil Cooper and Mandy Turner *(editors)*
CRITICAL PERSPECTIVES ON THE POLITICAL ECONOMY OF PEACEBUILDING

Brian Rappert
BIOTECHNOLOGY, SECURITY AND THE SEARCH FOR LIMITS
An Inquiry into Research and Methods

Brian Rappert *(editor)*
TECHNOLOGY AND SECURITY
Governing Threats in the New Millennium

New Security Challenges Series
**Series Standing Order ISBN 978-0-230-00216-6 (hardback) and
ISBN 978-0-230-00217-3 (paperback)**

You can receive future titles in this series as they are published by placing a standing order. Please contact your bookseller or, in case of difficulty, write to us at the address below with your name and address, the title of the series and the ISBN quoted above.

Customer Services Department, Macmillan Distribution Ltd, Houndmills, Basingstoke, Hampshire RG21 6XS, England

European Union Security Dynamics

In the New National Interest

Janne Haaland Matlary
*Professor of International Politics,
Institute of Political Science
University of Oslo,
and the Norwegian Defence Education Command,
Norway*

palgrave
macmillan

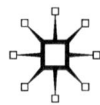

© Janne Haaland Matlary 2009

All rights reserved. No reproduction, copy or transmission of this publication may be made without written permission.

No portion of this publication may be reproduced, copied or transmitted save with written permission or in accordance with the provisions of the Copyright, Designs and Patents Act 1988, or under the terms of any licence permitting limited copying issued by the Copyright Licensing Agency, Saffron House, 6-10 Kirby Street, London EC1N 8TS.

Any person who does any unauthorized act in relation to this publication may be liable to criminal prosecution and civil claims for damages.

The author has asserted her right to be identified as the author of this work in accordance with the Copyright, Designs and Patents Act 1988.

First published 2009 by
PALGRAVE MACMILLAN

Palgrave Macmillan in the UK is an imprint of Macmillan Publishers Limited, registered in England, company number 785998, of Houndmills, Basingstoke, Hampshire RG21 6XS.

Palgrave Macmillan in the US is a division of St Martin's Press LLC, 175 Fifth Avenue, New York, NY 10010.

Palgrave Macmillan is the global academic imprint of the above companies and has companies and representatives throughout the world.

Palgrave® and Macmillan® are registered trademarks in the United States, the United Kingdom, Europe and other countries.

ISBN-13: 978–0–230–52188–9 hardback
ISBN-10: 0–230–52188–6 hardback

This book is printed on paper suitable for recycling and made from fully managed and sustained forest sources. Logging, pulping and manufacturing processes are expected to conform to the environmental regulations of the country of origin.

A catalogue record for this book is available from the British Library.

Library of Congress Cataloging-in-Publication Data

Matlary, Janne Haaland.
　　European Union security dynamics in the new national interest / Janne Haaland Matlary.
　　　p. cm.—(New security challenges series)
　　Includes bibliographical references and index.
　　ISBN 978–0–230–52188–9
　　1. Security, International – European Union countries. 2. National security – European Union countries. 3. European Union countries – Military policy. I. Title.

JZ6009.E94M38 2009
355'.03304—dc22   2008035172

10 9 8 7 6 5 4 3 2 1
18 17 16 15 14 13 12 11 10 09

Printed and bound in Great Britain by
CPI Antony Rowe, Chippenham and Eastbourne

In memoriam *my mother*
Ada Johanne Haaland, 1926–2007

Contents

List of Abbreviations	x
Acknowledgements	xii
Epigraph	xiii
Introduction	1

Part I Security Policy in Europe

1 Post-National Security Policy in Europe — 15
- From nation-state to 'service-state' in Europe — 17
- From existential, territorial threat to diffuse risk — 19
- Implications for non-state actors in security policy — 23
- The state may lose its monopoly on military force — 26
- Driving forces of internationalisation — 29
- Multilateral legitimacy — 31
- The return of security interests: Doing good and fighting terrorism — 36

2 EU Security and Defence Policy: Legitimacy and Capability — 40
- EU legitimacy for the use of force — 41
- EU military capabilities — 46
- European Capabilities Action Plan (ECAP) — 49
- Headline goal 2010 — 50
- EDA — 51
- The civilian headline goals for 2008 — 53
- Gendarmerie force — 53
- Institutional capacity building — 54
- Planning Cell instead of headquarter — 55
- EU operations — 57
- NATO's role — 58
- Relations between NATO and the EU — 60
- How are decisions made in the EU? — 61

3 EU Security Dynamics: The New National Interests — 68
- The *new* national interests in security policy — 73

	Realist models of the ESDP	77
	Constructivist and institutionalist approaches	79
	The EU: Soft power – therefore ethical power?	84
	Indirect power: The shaping of institutions	86
	Exercising power in the ESDP	89

Part II EU Security Dynamics: Pursuing National Interests

4	**Playing the Great Game: France, Britain, and Germany**	97
	Grand strategy in Europe	99
	France	101
	The evolution of French strategic thinking	104
	Britain	110
	From unilateral to multilateral force deployments	117
	The main political dynamic: *Directoire* inside the EU	120
	The battlegroups	125
	The EDA and defence industry 'pooling'	130
	Conclusions	134
5	**Playing the Two-Level Game: France, Britain, Germany**	138
	Two-level games played	138
	Domestic political processes	143
	Weak governments: Italy and Germany	146
	Italy	146
	Germany	149
	Strong governments: Britain and France	159
	Britain	159
	France	162
	Weak state elites must play two-level games	164
	Strong state elites sometimes play two-level games	165

Part III Incurring Security Policy Dependencies?

6	**Coalitions of the Able: The Pooling of Military Capacity in the ESDP**	169
	Military integration in Europe	171
	Integration in the battlegroups	173
	Integration through procurement and planning?	174
	Military capacities: Who depends on whom?	176
	The political process: Does it create integration?	184

7	Coalitions of the Willing: The Pooling of Sovereignty in the ESDP	188
	EU as an arena or an actor?	190
	In bello decision-making matters increasingly	192
	Coercive diplomacy: Another area of core logic	195
	EU strategic culture: A contradiction in terms?	202
	Capability, legitimacy, but no political will	204
	Conclusion: A French model for the EU?	206

Notes	213
Bibliography	218
Index	229

Abbreviations

ABC	Atomic, Biological, Chemical (Weapons)
ACT	Allied Command Transformation
AU	African Union
AWACS	Airborne Warning and Control System
CA	Comprehensive Approach
CFSP	Common Foreign and Security Policy
DCAP	Defence Capabilities Action Programme
DCI	Defence Capabilities Initiative
DG	Directorate-General
DST	Direction du Surveillance territoire
ECAP	European Capabilities Action Plan
EDA	European Defence Agency
EDTIB	European Defence Technological and Industrial Base
EGF	European Gendarmerie Force
EMU	Economic and Monetary Union
EP	European Parliament
EPC	European Political Cooperation
ESDP	European Security and Defence Policy
ESS	European Security Strategy
EU	European Union
EUMC	EU Political and Military Committee
EUMS	European Union Military Staff
FPP	Foreign Policy Prerogative
IAEA	International Atomic Energy Agency
ICISS	International Commission on Intervention and State Sovereignty
IO	International organisation
ISAF	International Stability and Assistance Force
NAC	North Atlantic Committee
NATO	North Atlantic Treaty Organisation
NPM	New Public Management
NRF	Nato Response Force
OEF	Operation Enduring Freedom
PGM	Precision-Guided Missiles
PMC	Private Military Company
PSC	Political and Security Committee

PSO	Peace Support Operations
QRF	Quick Reaction Force
QMV	Qualified Majority Voting
R2P	Responsibility to Protect
R&T	Research and Technology
RMA	Revolution in Military Affairs
ROE	Rules of Engagement
RRF	Rapid Response Force
RUSI	Royal United Services Institute
SHAPE	Supreme Headquarters Allied Powers Europe
SITCEN	Situation Centre
SPD	Sozial-Demokratische Partei Deutschland
TEU	Treaty on European Union
UAV	Unmanned Aerial Vehicle
UN	United Nations
UNDP	United Nations Development Programme
UNPROFOR	United Nations Protection Force
UNSC	United Nations Security Council
USSR	United Soviet Socialist Republics
WMD	Weapons of Mass Destruction

Acknowledgements

The author gratefully acknowledges a grant from the Norwegian Ministry of Defence for support for this project. In 2006, the Ministry funded a report on the European Defence and Security Policy (ESDP) and its political dynamics on which this book is based. Thanks also to research assistants Majken Thorsager and Kim Angell, both of the Department of Political Science, University of Oslo, for valuable assistance in connection with this study. John Taylor proof-read the whole manuscript in meticulous detail, and Gemma D'Archy Hughes of Palgrave Macmillan was very helpful, especially when circumstances made it impossible for me to finish this book as quickly as I had planned. In addition, gratitude is expressed for very useful contributions and comments from various diplomatic and military sources in Oslo, London, Paris, Washington, Munich, and Brussels. I wish to thank the British ambassador in Norway, David Powell, for arranging interviews in the British Ministry of Defence. Any errors remain the responsibility of the author.

Epigraph

'France and England will never be powers comparable to the US or the Soviet Union. There remains to them only one way of playing a decisive role in the world; that is to unite to make Europe. Europe will be your revenge.'
Konrad Adenauer to the French Foreign Minister Chr. Pineau on the eve of the British stand-down over Suez, in Pineu, C. (1976), *Suez 1956*. Paris: Robert Laffont. p. 71.

'Politicians are motivated primarily by the desire to avoid blame for unpopular actions ... incentives to avoid blame lead politicians to adopt a distinctive set of political strategies, including agenda limitation, scapegoating, "passing the buck" and defection.' Weaver, K. (1996). The Politics of Blame Avoidance. *Journal of Public Policy*, 6(4): 371–98.

Introduction

This book explores the security dynamics in the EU, especially the role domestic politics has come to play in EU security policy after the cold war. As long as threats were existential to the state – as in traditional inter-state wars, security policy remained insulated from domestic pressures and public discussion. This was the case in the long cold war period and in previous wars where war meant war, and peace – the absence of war. Domestic actors played scant role in security and defence policy throughout these decades because it was eminently important to retain national unity in the face of an external enemy. The potential use of military force was not an option, but a necessity.

After the cold war, however, European states typically engaged in wars of a new type, mostly optional ones that concern terror and/or humanitarian and human rights abuse. These new wars engage military power along with political power; they are not about winning in a traditional sense, and the threat picture that elicits the military response is often indecisive and diffuse. In this setting, the EU has developed its own European Security and Defence Policy (ESDP) with remarkable speed and ambition, particularly in the period 1998–2008.

This book argues that state leaders – in this case prime ministers, presidents, foreign ministers, and their representatives – take advantage of the multilateral EU level of politics in order both to influence their domestic political level as well as draw on this level so as to influence EU politics. State executives play what are referred to as 'two-level' games, and security policy in the EU is driven largely by the national interests of states. However, these national interests are not the traditional, static geopolitical interests that used to characterise security policy. Today, they are much more flexible, and concerned with general foreign policy standing rather than with security in any clear-cut sense.

The study of EU politics is often classified in two categories. On the one hand, intergovernmentalists argue that *fixed* national interests dictate and determine EU policy, hence with little or no influence by EU actors and institutions on states. On the other hand, institutionalists and integration scholars of various kinds argue that there is explanatory power in the EU itself, that states are influenced by the way politics unfolds in the EU. Applied to security studies, the intergovernmentalist approach seems most fruitful as foreign policy in the EU belongs in the so-called Pillar Two where the decision-making is in the hands of the Council of Ministers. The cooperation that occurs in the EU foreign policy area is often referred to as a 'pooling' of sovereignty. This means that states agree to cooperate, but that this cooperation is reversible although it may occasionally entail obligations. In the following, I investigate what is specifically meant by sovereignty 'pooling' in the area of security. I argue that the new national security interests benefit from multilateral 'pooling', although the latter also entails irreversible elements because military capabilities today are scarce and increasingly integrated across borders. No state, not even the most powerful, can undertake extensive international military operations on its own. As is also argued in this book, in optional wars and missions the national government no longer *wishes* to act alone. The less existential and territorial the conflict, the less involved the nation-state wishes to become. It is not useful to interpret the security dynamics of the EU in the familiar intergovernmentalist versus integration-scheme. This is a rather fruitless exercise, as argued in Chapter 3. Rather, the security dynamics of the EU, such as those of NATO, concern the *offset of domestic constraints and interests between the national and international levels*. Governments need multilateral support and risk/cost-sharing for optional wars, and the EU learns and internalises policy from missions undertaken. This is valuable experience which amounts to capacity-building and political credibility in a policy field where concrete results count more than anything else. The EU development of the ESDP over the last ten years – from 1998 to 2008 – is indeed remarkable. However, its success is largely due to the *new logic of domestic-multilateral interaction* that influences all foreign policy in Europe today, including security policy.

This main political dynamic can be modelled on Putnam's two-level metaphor (1988) applied to security policy. It seems clear that the traditional Foreign Policy Prerogative (FPP) is gone in all European states but France and Britain. Formally, the president of the French Republic alone decides on the deployment of French forces, and the same applies in Britain. Yet one of the first proposals Prime Minister Gordon

Brown made was to vest in Parliament some of the decision-making concerning using military force, thus abolishing the centuries-old FPP. But in states such as Germany, the decision to deploy military force requires elaborate legitimation and public support, and once deployed, own losses have instant impact on the executive's ability to maintain an operation. In *post-national* wars run by *post-national* publics, support is fragile and a military culture is lacking.

In these times of 'optional wars' there is considerable pressure from domestic actors and public opinion. Security policy undergoes what we call 'de-securitization' (Buzan and Wæver, 2003). It becomes a policy area like normal policy, subject to pressures like most policies. It remains true that security policy is a special area, but today this is true in an almost ironic sense, as it is a policy area where parliamentarians are rarely able to win much in public opinion.

The main political dynamic in EU security policy is directly tied to the post-national situation in Europe: *The more optional the war, the weaker the support achieved*, and hence the need for 'negotiating' between the domestic and the multilateral levels on the part of the state executive. Further, *the more dangerous the mission, the more contested it becomes*. Taken together, this means that an optional war that is dangerous equals wavering and weakening public support. All politicians recognise that they cannot expend national soldiers and officers such as they could in former times, because children are fewer and therefore much more precious, because the wars fought are optional, and because the modern Western view of war is that the institution of war itself is largely unacceptable. As we move from humanitarian missions of peacekeeping into very dangerous wars in places like Afghanistan and Iraq, the domestic political stakes are much higher. Which government can survive major losses in an optional war in a society that no longer understands the risks of war?

For these reasons it is quite clear that the *legitimacy* for using force is extremely important, and that the conduct of war, once legitimated, must be as 'humane' as possible. The public is bound to play a key role. *The last truly traditional foreign policy area – war – is now 'normalised' as part of domestic discussion*. This general development, most pronounced in Western Europe, has a major impact on both the EU and NATO.

In sum, this fundamental change makes for *new security policy dynamics* in Western nations, particularly in Europe. The relevance of the domestic policy level becomes very important, if not the most important factor, in decision-making. This is a radically new thing: security policy was always a province for the elite, the few who had special insights and special mandates. Now everyone takes an interest: NGOs, the media, the clergy, women's groups, and so forth. War always means drama, and the press is in theatre in a new way, using global media to disseminate news in real time. 'Whoever coined the phrase "the theatre of operations" was very prescient. We are conducting operations now as though we were on stage, in an amphitheatre' comments General Sir Rupert Smith (Smith, 2005, p. 284).

A government thus has to deal with all the *normal elements* of politics in the security and defence field today. This happens in a context where war is asymmetric, involving terrorism, the killing of civilians, barbarism in the form of genocide, and where war does not start or stop when politics cease and borders end. It is a dramatic fact that all the parameters of war as we have known it from Napoleon to the end of the cold war, have now changed.

Given the new importance of the domestic level for security and defence policy, what are the political dynamics at work? Foreign policy analysis as well as the more specialised security studies field are not usually concerned with domestic factors. The dominant theory of security studies – realism – rules out the importance of domestic factors altogether, dismissing them. States are thought to be unitary actors pursuing a geopolitical interest where self-help and relative power counts. The realist view is that states always pursue security because they are always threatened in an anarchic world. Thus, the state's interests are given, and take pre-eminence over all other political interests because they concern the very survival of the state.

Today's optional wars are of another kind than the existential state-to-state war. As security and defence policy has become normalised, so has the political process. Where can we find analytical frameworks that help in the study of these new security dynamics? In the international relations literature, there is still very little emphasis on domestic determinants of foreign policy even if they now impact heavily also on security policy. Peter Gourevitch (1978) called for an 'inside-out' approach, and Andrew Moravcsik (1991, 1993) developed his intergovernmental model by opening up the 'black box' of the state. But the most sophisticated theorist of the domestic–international foreign policy dynamic is Robert Putnam. In his renowned article about two-level games from 1988, he outlines how government executives use their exclusive access to both levels to gain advantages on both. When a minister emerges from a EU ministerial meeting, he addresses his national press and tells them how he has advanced national interests. If his interests were not favoured, he is able to argue that 'the EU made me do it'; that is, to blame the EU. Unpopular decisions can always be blamed on the relevant international organisation – such as the argument that NATO obligations mean that German troops be contributed to some optional war or that the EU is a liberal regime that allows 'the Polish plumber' to threaten French jobs, as was a major argument in the French run-up to the referendum which said 'No' to the constitutional treaty in 2006.

At election time, European leaders often blame the EU for issues that they themselves have supported in the EU, thus using a cheap populist technique which may nonetheless be effective. In the French presidential election campaign both candidates opposed and criticised EU policy on national champions as well as the fiscal discipline imposed by the European Central Bank, knowing full well that their own parties had supported both policy decisions. In sum, national politicians use and misuse the EU and other international organisations as and when it appears opportune.

Putnam defines several policy dynamics. Policy pressure from the international level can be used to change policy domestically, as the government binds itself to international obligations and can argue that it is bound to implement them at home. Also, domestic constraints can be used to get one's way in the international organisation – in fact, the more bound one is, the more one may gain because other states that want to reach an agreement and have larger scope for negotiation may be forced to concede much more than they would normally do. The government elite can play both levels of policy to their advantage, as we shall see in this book. In security and defence policy, governments can blame the international level when things go wrong; they can share risk and cost, and they can use the second level to effect changes at home. In neutral states like Sweden and Finland, the EU has been used to change the meaning of neutrality as one example of how the international level impacts on the national level (Græger et al., 2002).

The dynamics of two-level game politics are largely unexplored in the political science literature in terms of application, and we therefore do not know very much about the explanatory value of this theory. Intuitively, when we observe the interaction between the national and the international levels, it seems that politicians play two-level games a lot. Putnam called his model a 'metaphor', and suggested that it be used as a basis for empirical testing and application. This naturally requires operationalisation and further elaboration. In the following chapters I take up this challenge, intending to see how far two-level games go towards describing and explaining EU security dynamics: The aim is to contribute to the limited empirical knowledge in this area. It is rather odd that so little academic work has been done along these lines. Koenig-Archibugi's work is an exception (2004a, 2004b). He makes a preliminary study of the ESDP with this framework as his point of departure, albeit with a much more 'sinister' twist to it, suggesting that state executives actually *collude* in order to overcome bothersome domestic opposition.

But EU security dynamics are not exhausted by two-level games. There is another very important dynamic at work, one that I argue is the more important in the French and British case. It is what we can term the 'great power game'. There exists a distinct model and strategy of how an ESDP should develop in the policies of both these states, expressed in their long-term strategic thinking. This strategic-level security policy remains constant, I argue. The French and the British models are distinctly different, and remain so, thereby *limiting the scope* of EU policy in the security field. After the election of President Sarkozy, however, these strategic visions have become more similar. Both France and Britain now desire a close relationship with the United States and both states want the Europeans in general to share much more of the military burden in international operations.

Also at the tactical level, these states change their national interests during the period of investigation. They both realise that influence can only be had through engagement and contributions to the EU, and more importantly, they realise that national-level great power politics is no longer an option. Britain and France thus share a number of important security interests that explain why the ESDP got seriously under way after 1998. These common interests are the 'new' national interests. My argument is that they concern the need for multilateral legitimacy, the military needs for multilateral sharing of capacities in international operations, and the strong interest in effecting military modernisation in Europe. It is suggested that France and Britain hang together in mutual dependency in the ESDP: neither state can realise this policy without the other. Paradoxically, because the two states differ in their 'great game', they are bound together in the ESDP: France cannot be left alone in the ESDP because that would endanger the primacy of NATO in the European security architecture, the Britons think. On the other hand, the French conclude that Britain cannot be allowed to dominate the ESDP as that would ensure that the EU would rank as a second-order security organisation. Both states are therefore *bound to participate* in all ESDP initiatives in which one of them engages in order to shape, constrain, or counteract the former.

In this book, I advance the thesis that EU security dynamics is dominated by the pursuit of such new national interests which arise in a situation of a post-national security paradigm. These new national interests have to do with multilateral settings, sources of legitimacy, and the 'pooling' of military capabilities.

First, governments must place premium value on force protection of their own soldiers because the public will not accept large losses in non-existential or 'optional' wars. The less existentially dangerous is the threat, the fewer losses democracies will accept. Also, democracies, as such, are risk-averse. This induces governments to seek *multilateral risk-sharing*.

Second, their defence budgets have shrunk and continue to shrink after the cold war. Governments today can no longer afford balanced defence structures and must integrate with other states. Governments therefore depend increasingly on multilateralism in military procurement, maintenance, and deployment. No state can field all the capabilities that are needed for a long-term stabilisation operation. This is naturally truer the smaller the state, and induces governments to develop *multilateral military cooperation*.

Third, governments will seek to transfer blame if needs be. The United States and Britain experience this problem today over Iraq. There is no international organisation to blame, no UN or NATO on whom to place the blame. The safety of being part of a coalition, preferably nested in an international organisation, is very important in today's wars that are rarely won. Even own losses can be transferred to an organisation to some extent. The press reports that International Stability and Assistance Force (ISAF) or NATO suffered losses, not that Canada nor Britain did. The risk-averse nature of Western publics extends to political risk-aversion. If the military operation leads to military and political failure, governments prefer to blame an international organisation. They therefore *seek to vest foreign policy in a multilateral setting*.

Fourth, governments today have few, if any, security interests of their own. States are not pitted against states in zero-sum competitive games in security, but fight against enemies that are *common*, be they terrorists or others. There is therefore no point in single state security policy. Only via common fronts can Western states undertake credible defence. They therefore have no incentive to go it alone. *Multilateral security action is in their true national interest.*

Fifth, states cannot fight without legitimacy. This is a new issue in the sense that multilateralism itself today seems to be the provider of legitimacy. Multilateralism has no clear definition, and scholars are unable to provide much clarity regarding the concept as an empirical category (Ruggie, 1993). It refers to a formal set-up for cooperation between two or more states where an international organisation is formed. But it can also refer to informal cooperation, such as in a so-called coalition of the willing. States have always justified their use of force, but have done so as states alone. Today, even great powers seek multilateral legitimacy. Legitimacy is tied to formal multilateralism: the most legitimate is a UN mandate and an operation undertaken by NATO, the African Union (AU), the UN, or the EU, but sometimes there is no such mandate. Yet some degree of legitimacy is had through the multilateral organisation that deploys the force. This is a new and controversial development, but one that makes the EU the more important in security terms. *Only military action undertaken by many states, ideally under UN, NATO, or EU auspices, is regarded as legitimate.*

Sixth, states enjoy world power status when they are in the EU. Apart from the United States, the EU is the most important Western power on the world stage. Small EU states that otherwise would not have much leverage internationally are now able to be represented diplomatically all over the world, and partake in EU power. Thus, *the EU acts as a force multiplier for the single state in general foreign policy terms.*

Seventh, states use the EU to forge issue linkages. A state strong in one field will enhance its participation in this field in order to gain general standing in the EU and thus be able to compensate for weakness in other areas. Both France and Britain are strong military actors, and therefore enhance their role in the ESDP with this tool. *Military contributions have an effect on the general standing of a state in the EU.*

Eighth, the security architecture of Europe – the question of how NATO is likely to evolve in relation to the EU – remains a key one which demands that all states concerned with this seek participation in the security policy of both organisations in order to influence their development. Here, the major powers – France and Britain – have different models in mind, hence different strategic interests, but in the 1990s France returned to NATO and Britain became active in the ESDP. Common to both states is that they are 'doomed' to participate in both the EU and NATO *because influence equals participation, and in the military field, equals contribution.*

These eight reasons for multilateral security policy are common to all Western states, but major powers, such as those of this study – France, Britain, and Germany – are less dependent on multilateralism for some of them than are smaller states. The point is, however, that *also major powers depend on multilateralism.* This is the newness of traditional national security interests explored and analysed in this book. I show how the dynamics of EU security policy are driven by these new national interests, and how the resulting multilateral security policy also entails interdependencies between states themselves and provides some institutional role to EU actors.

Thus, in this book I explore this new national interest in multilateral security policy. In so doing I first analyse competing explanations of EU security policy. They largely fall in two camps. One is the category which can be termed 'strategic security interests'; the other 'two-level game interests'. The states analysed in this book – the great military powers France and Britain, and the lesser military power Germany – have different preference hierarchies. France and Britain share a key interest in pursuing strategic political visions – the great game – whereas Germany's main preference is to play two-level games to offset domestic constraints. However this may be, it remains true that the main EU security dynamic in this field is that of great power politics. The protocol on 'structured cooperation' in the new Lisbon treaty is retained after renegotiation of the rejected Constitutional Treaty, allowing two or more states to initiate practical military cooperation. This is the decision rule that drives the hard end of the Common Foreign and Security Policy (CFSP), as seen in the battlegroups and in the creation of the European Defence Agency (EDA). Moreover, the EU security policy initiatives that are created are always only an addition to 'real' security policy in its traditional sense. The British reservation to the reform treaty is very clear on this: territorial defence is an untouchable. The reservation regarding the United Nations Security Council (UNSC) permanent membership and national sovereignty speaks for itself: there is no British willingness to change the parameters of traditional territorial security policy. The same holds for France. EU security policy is only concerned with crisis management, and there is no 'competition' with the national level and national sovereignty in this respect. Both France and Britain retain their vetoes in the UNSC and have a national nuclear deterrent – one that Britain has recently decided to renew. Like EU diplomacy in general, EU security policy appears to be a supplement. Yet 'pooling' does not imply that one can return to a state of national security policy in political terms. In this book I seek to show in which ways 'pooling' binds the state, even great powers.

The model of European security policy dynamics that emerges from the analysis in this book can be summarised as follows: Security policy after the cold war is mostly driven by domestic factors and interests where some governments are more powerful than others – France being an example of a strong government; Germany of a weak. In the multilateral EU setting, strong governments can excel in influencing, but weak governments can offset domestic powers. The more contested is the threat picture, the more controversial security policy becomes. As an example, the case of ISAF shows how German domestic factors have now come to dominate the security policy process completely. Generally, the international security situation matters less for domestic security policy than domestic factors. The EU serves as a force multiplier as well as a legitimator vis-à-vis domestic audiences.

This model takes the domestic, the international, and the intermediary arena of the EU into account. Most theories of the EU neglect the role of domestic politics. This is also very true of most theories of security policy. In our analysis we combine these three levels. Theoretically, we assume that interests are rational in the sense that policy-makers will seek political survival at home, influence abroad, and the resolution of security issues in theatre, in that order of preference. The 'normalisation' of security policy is of paramount importance to this model, but as we shall see, is particular to EU-Europe. The 'optional' character of this security policy implies that legitimacy plays a much greater role than in existential wars, and that risk-aversion becomes much stronger. Both these factors make multilateralism much more important to European governments.

In Chapter 1, the state of security policy in Europe is discussed. After the cold war, there is a paradigm shift in this field. The existential threat of the former USSR has gone, and threats are diffuse and vague to the average citizen. Security and defence policy has therefore become 'normalised' and subject to disagreements like any other policy area. This makes for difficult decisions by governments. They have to sustain wars where their own citizens risk and sometimes lose their lives, and they have to maintain increasingly expensive defence budgets in times that are characterised by relative peace. European publics are post-national, largely thanks to the successful integration of the EU, and cannot be expected to understand the security issues that still typify international politics.

Thus, the paradigm shift in European security policy is a very important basis for understanding why and how EU politics in this field has developed. In this chapter we show why two factors are of particular importance for understanding EU dynamics in this field: one is the need for a pooling military resources in a time of decreasing defence budgets; the other is the need for multilateralism as legitimacy for the use of force. Not even major states deploy alone any more. They all seek the protective political shield of political risk-sharing They further seek participation in the EU in order to be able to invoke its demands at home – they need to be able to play 'two-level games', as it were.

In Chapter 2, we discuss EU security and defence policy and how it relates to post-national security policy characteristics. First, we look at the capacities, military and institutional, possessed by the EU. We then discuss the policy basis for the ESDP, which is also post-national, namely the concept of human security. But only if capacities, political will, and legitimacy basis coincide, will the result be effective policy. In Chapter 3, we present the main argument of the book – the security dynamics of the ESDP and the concept of new national interests in the area of security and defence policy. In a criticism of contending approaches, such as realism and its balance-of-power argument as well as constructivist institutionalism, we show that neither approach explains why Britain and France have chosen to develop the ESDP. In fact, the claim that balance of power concerns drive EU security developments remains unfounded, as the United States supports this development. Yet this assumption, based on a rather automatic realist reflex amongst security policy scholars, is a common one in the literature. Likewise, much EU literature assumes that EU processes explain what is termed 'integration' in this policy field. But when we look closely at the policy initiatives undertaken, they are all traceable to national interests of great powers. Thus, the assumption that there are 'path-dependencies' at work in the ESDP or that institutional processes matter, is as unfounded as is the realist thesis.

Instead, we find two major dynamics at work. The first is the 'great power interdependence' which is analysed in depth in Chapter 4 where France and Britain both share interests but also have divergent interests, and also incur dependencies on each other. The driving forces here are what we term 'new' national interests. The second dynamic is the two-level game metaphor whereby governments offset domestic constraints on their security and defence policy, analysed in Chapter 5. Here, particularly weak governments need the second level of international politics, that is the EU-level. Germany is such a state. Only through internationally binding commitments is it able to develop a security policy that involves international deployments. But also France and Britain increasingly need this dynamic. Although they are strong states in the security and defence policy area – retaining much of the traditional FPP – their publics increasingly matter in this field.

In Chapters 6 and 7, we turn to the interdependencies that the ESDP entails. Is 'pooling' sovereignty irreversible? Formally not so, naturally, as even EU membership can be given up, but in political terms? The degree of military integration in Europe is a major new factor that contributes to the real need for cooperation of a lasting character. As we shall see, even great powers must find partners in both weapons procurement as well as maintenance, training, and of course, deployment. But also the political importance of legitimacy – domestic support for deployments – is by now a very important factor, if not the most important. Public support waxes and wanes with own losses, developments in war, cost, and domestic power plays. This makes it almost impossible to plan for long-term engagements on the part of governments. The only way to ensure some backing for such engagements is through multilateral action.

Part I
Security Policy in Europe

1
Post-National Security Policy in Europe

The EU has shown remarkable ability to develop security policy in recent years; it has emerged as a security actor in a very short time, also in a military sense. The EU has a policy for crisis management and has adopted several measures to improve capability, develop common research and procurement, and has published an embryonic paper on strategic thinking, the European Security Strategy (ESS). In addition, it has now deployed in several missions. Hence, a *post-national* security and defence policy is emerging; both private actors and international organisations conduct military operations. We are in a transition phase in Europe, but it is clear that this represents a paradigm shift.

Security policy refers not only to military issues, but also to non-military security issues, and can be usefully defined as the policy addressing whatever poses a threat. But the threat need not be existential. Defence refers to the military component of security policy, although the proper name is really 'the military tool'. There is no longer a traditional stationary defence meaning to the term in Europe. It now refers to the defence of whatever is life-threatening to own citizens and state interests – and sometimes to 'strangers' as well – at home or abroad, but not to territorial defence in the traditional sense of averting an invasion. Vedby-Rasmussen (2007) points out that we now live in risk societies rather than threat societies, and that security policy concerns risk management rather than defence. This changes this policy field, away from the state and its territory towards multilateral settings. Managing risk is a global matter when the enemy may be a terrorist group on the other side of the world which may strike inside European states or far away.

Security further refers to the promotion of state interests – those of foreign policy proper. The connotations we have with regard to the concept of 'defence' constrain our understanding of the new situation where the military tool is used actively and in limited manner for political purposes. Paradoxically it is used with *more* political strings attached today (force projection and use limited by political and media objectives) than previously, while it is used actively and *offensively* as well.

Thus, in Europe, defence and security policy undergo paradigmatic change along many dimensions. The nation-state model of defence in Europe is disappearing. Taking Diesen's (2005) typology as a point of departure, we can discern the *Kabinettkriege* of the seventeenth century and the subsequent Napoleonic paradigm, which has lasted until the present in Europe. The latter is characterised by conscription, defence of national territory, loyalty to the nation, and a *raison d'être* based on existential survival of state and nation. This kind of defence and security policy amounted to the total, existential defence of state and nation: the state could therefore ask the ultimate loyalty unto death, from its citizens. Its parameters were the defence of national borders, citizen-soldiers, legitimacy in 'King and Country' – the nation; and the threat was existential. The Weberian state underpins this paradigm. The definition of the state is vested in defence; the state has the legitimate monopoly on the use of force inside and outside its borders.

After the cold war, this picture has changed. Today the situation is entirely different. General Sir Rupert Smith puts it bluntly 'War no longer exists' (Smith, 2005, p. 1). He adds the important qualification: 'War as battle in the field between men and machinery, war as a massive deciding event in a dispute in international affairs, such a war no longer exists' (ibid.) Today's wars are mostly internal conflicts, formerly termed civil wars. They are 'wars amongst the people', as Smith terms them. They are fought against insurgents and other non-state actors and aim not at victory, but at keeping a territory or a peace in the sense of making it possible for political actors to act. It is a thoroughly 'politicized' kind of war in the deepest sense of Clausewitz. The military tool is but one tool in the state's toolbox, deployed for limited and specific political ends. The military tool is used in integrated missions with other tools – police, diplomacy, democratisation programmes, humanitarian and other aid, and so forth. The soldiers are professionals, recruited on professional grounds. With the advent of the professional expeditionary military force, capital becomes the main constraint, not people. The masses are no longer mobilised.

If capital is the sole constraining factor in procuring the military tool, we will logically see a change away from the nation-state as the commander of this tool. There is also today a growing trend towards the privatisation of defence, caused partly by failed states and partly a logical corollary of neo-liberalism. Private actors of various kinds provide security to clients who can pay (Matlary and Østerud, 2007).

Taking the parameters of the Napoleonic paradigm as point of departure, *the changes that the paradigm shift imply are very important for any analysis of EU security policy.* Defence now not only includes defence of national borders, but defence of values such as democracy and human rights and whatever else seems to be threatened. The nation-state no longer has a monopoly on the ability to use force, and soldiers are bought in the private market, meaning that the states are no longer the only actors in the security field. For these reasons, *military force can no longer find legitimacy only in the concept of the nation*, but is tied both to ethics and to international law, that is, to internationally recognised norms and not to Westphalian state interests (Kennedy, 2006). Further, threats are diffuse and therefore blur the inside–outside dimension of the state's traditional monopoly on the use of force.

In short, defence has changed from primarily having a territorial, stationary function to having an international, even global scope, serving diffuse political interests. Such a defence concept is not necessarily tied to the nation-state as its political master. As we shall see, the paradigm shift in defence provides opportunities for an EU security policy and changes the role that the state plays in this policy field.

From nation-state to 'service-state' in Europe

The neo-liberal model of the state in Europe is developing rapidly today as a consequence of ideology and a new view of the state as a service provider to citizens that increasingly resemble 'clients' and 'customers'. There is ample evidence of a shift from nation-state to 'service-state' where the citizen becomes customer, comparing services rendered by the state to that of private actors. Schools, health care, and other formerly public sectors are subject to privatisation, out-sourcing, public–private partnering, and so forth. This trend also hits the defence sector, and effects in this sector are arguably multiplied by radically shrinking budgets, absence of former tasks, and the need for an altogether new basis of legitimacy (Matlary and Østerud, 2007). The citizen-soldier cannot serve in professional international operations unless he becomes professionally trained, and he will not serve as a citizen-soldier anyway. He can no longer accept the old legitimacy of service to the state which is irrelevant if the state is a service provider rather than a nation-state.

The relevance of this for the EU is that European political legitimacy in the security field changes. If states are no longer defined by their nation, but by the services they render to their citizens, a major obstacle to European integration in this area is overcome, namely the state-centred assumption.

Laffan et al. (2004) suggests that the EU as a political actor may be conceived in not only territorial terms but also *functional* terms. The function or 'services provided' today matter more than territorial state interests, she argues. If this is so, the intimate connection between territory and the military tool is weakened, and actors other than states can provide security. How the EU 'performs' as a security actor becomes essential to its success if function and not territory defines what defence is about. This allows for a defence policy role for the EU despite the fact that it is not a state.

On the 'service-state' model, the logical development is cost-effective procurement of military services when they are needed. Because of the specific nature of this sector, it cannot rely on the market alone. Logically, a state may hire a large range of services when it contributes to an international operation, and also at home in a public–private modality. There is much empirical evidence of the extent of public–private partnership, not only 'at home' but also in peace support operations. Undoubtedly market forces, as well as the pervasiveness of neo-liberal ideology, are strong drivers in the direction of making defence look like any other sector of modern society (Matlary and Østerud, 2005). To this comes another major factor: the strong demand for relevant and usable military capabilities in international operations. When the UN pleads for national contributions to international missions, the constant problem is a slow and inadequate response. Hiring private military companies (PMCs) for combat operations has been debated at the UN, but is so far kept at arm's length by politicians, despite possible advantages. Kofi Annan has remarked that the world is perhaps not yet ready for 'privatized peace'. But the driving forces are strong in combining 'peace time' ideology of neo-liberal New Public Management (NPM) and lower budgets.

A characteristic of the paradigm change after the cold war is that the military 'tool' becomes one of several tools at the disposal of the ruler, and that it is again used for foreign policy ends; as it was in the seventeenth century. The deployment of military force is for limited ends; the wars fought are no longer total wars, and they are not even state-to-state wars for the most part. Instead, the military tool is used in integrated missions with other tools – police, diplomacy, democratisation programmes and humanitarian and other aid, and so on. The soldiers are professionals, recruited on professional grounds. Diesen's typology retains the state as the font of this new military; yet it would seem necessary to go beyond the state as controlling actor. If capital is the only constraining factor in procuring the military tool, we will see – and already do see – *a change away from the nation-state as the commander of the military tool.*

Not only NATO and the UN, but also the EU plays a role. In a highly interesting paper, Krahmann points out that we are going from 'government' to 'governance', also in the security and defence field. This change implies a 'fragmentation of political authority among a diversity of public and private across levels of analysis' (Krahmann, 2003, p. 6). *The state is still the key actor in security, but no longer the only one.* This is a direct consequence of the paradigm shift away from the Napoleonic basis in the nation and territory of the state. When the military tool is but a tool, it can also be 'commanded' by non-state actors. There is a 'new medievalism' also in security policy, argues Krahmann. This provides a 'window of opportunity' for the EU in the security field. The role of international organisations as military masters is important in any discussion of the EU's role in deploying military force. In fact, even major states today prefer to deploy militarily through multilateral organisations. Around 1995, France started to seek formal multilateral support for all its missions, notes inter alia Treacher (2003), and the same holds for Britain. Legitimacy, as will be discussed later, is achieved today through multilateralism itself.

From existential, territorial threat to diffuse risk

The change in threat picture is the most important driver of change in all other parameters. A fixed, territorial threat is much easier to deal with than diffuse, partially non-territorial threats. In that sense, the cold war 'performed' well. Now, there is constant confusion about, disagreement over, and variable interpretation of the threat picture. The agreement one has in this area (NATO, UN, EU) is that instability and internal conflict remain a key threat as does terrorism. The possibility of non-state actors acquiring simpler weapons of mass destruction (WMDs) is perhaps the foremost risk today.[1] These two threats may merge in 'rogue' and/or 'failed' states that host such actors. The main geographical areas of instability in Europe's vicinity are the Balkans, South Caucasus, and the Middle East. But African conflicts also make their way onto Europe's agenda. NATO's former pre-occupation with 'out-of-area' has now given way to a clearly global role. NATO is engaged in the far-away country of Afghanistan in its major mission today, whereas the EU has conducted a sharp operation in DR Congo and prepares a mission to Chad – two most unlikely occurrences seen through an analyst's eye only a few years ago.

'Throughout the cold war, force was needed to deter the other side from doing bad things outside its borders; today, force is needed to compel the other side to do good things inside its borders', an analyst aptly summarises it (Prince in Hyde-Price, 2004, p. 338). The spectre of tasks known as 'crisis management' or peace support operations (PSOs) has a 'do-goodist' side which is of considerable political importance as well as a more traditional *Realpolitik* side which involves stark choices of national interest and deterrence against spill-over and terrorist activity. The public requires an elaborate explanation of both these threats in order to get acceptance for using military force, and the legitimacy for such is not a constant. The US defence secretary, Robert Gates, made the unprecedented move to address European publics directly in his intervention at the 2008 Munich security policy conference: 'I would like to ... speak *directly to the people* of Europe: The threat posed by violent extremism is real.'[2] [My emphasis]. Acceptance for deployments, once made, depends for its sustainability on developments in the field, and is thus hard to maintain. Governments take more risk now than before in their deployments, something which invites the safety of numbers in a multilateral setting.

Common to both humanitarian intervention and terrorist threats is that the military activity takes place inside another state. This means that offensive, expeditionary warfare, along the whole scale from high-intensity to 'imperial policing', is called for. In terms of military ability, European states can do much, but are also lacking in key capabilities, identified in the Prague Commitments and the EU European Capabilities Action Plan (ECAP). (See Chapter 2 for an outline of ECAP.) There is a very clear need for acquiring these capabilities in order to give substance to politics. The debate about which gaps to fill and whether to define a 'European way of warfare' or to emulate the United States is complex and detailed, and I will not enter that debate here. However, as the Venusberg report *An European Defence Strategy* underlines, 'what Europe needs is a force that can get anywhere, fight anywhere, eat anywhere, stay anywhere, be augmented and go back' (Lindley-French and Algieri, 2004, p. 26). However, viewpoints on 'gaps'; it is clear that a lot needs to happen in European militaries in terms of modernisation and interoperability.

The internal conflict or PSO has no proper place in the norms of war; the rules for ad *bellum* as well as in *bello* do not easily apply. The inside–outside classification of the international system and the concomitant basis this gives for international law is in flux. This is a considerable political problem. We now ask the unsettling questions such as, is this a war? – a military 'campaign'? – or something in between? Hyde-Price sums up, 'The range of military operations undertaken by NATO's armed forces in the 1990s ranges from classic high-intensity coalitional warfare to traditional peace-keeping. ... What is striking is that the bulk of new missions in the post-Cold war world would have fallen into the grey zone between peace and war' (Hyde-Price, 2004, p. 333).

Thus, the PSOs – this 'bastard' between peace and war – does not fit in with the laws on traditional state-to-state war. The rules for interventions are modified to fit accordingly, with a clear weakening of the intervention norm in the 1990s, from 'humanitarian' to 'democratic' intervention, mostly benign, but with the danger of giving pretexts for a new Brezhnev doctrine (Matlary, 2006). Added to this comes the renewed need to consider pre-emption and even prevention of terrorist actors. The threshold – both political and legal – against intervention is lowered; and this can create much more instability than before. Yet it also opens up for 'fixing' failed states; which is on the international agenda like never before.

This threat picture demands offensive strategic thinking and planning; with a degree of rapidity and flexibility in deployment that stands in immensely stark contrast to the static, defensive forces of the past. This places demands on decision-making. It cannot be long-drawn and too open. Reaction time is swift. The EU of 27 is unable to make swift decisions, yet swift decisions are needed in order to deploy rapidly. As we shall see, the nature of modern PSOs largely defines what kind of political dynamic the EU has to have in this area.

The large, mobilised armies of Europe face 'sudden death' after the cold war; they have to transform or perish. The use of force therefore has to be calibrated to new political demands. For instance, when Norwegian forces in Kosovo were attacked by mobs in Mitrovica in 2004, they could easily have used massive force to repress it, but chose not to. One Norwegian officer was wounded as a result. In addition to differing norms of force protection and force projection between the United States and Europe, Europeans and the EU must observe these new norms imposed by the politics of the PSO. According to Hyde-Price, strategic thinking in Europe today must take the following norms into account: *Coercion*, and not brute force, is necessary; force must be used *legitimately*, that is, in a multilateral manner and best of all, with a UN mandate; it must further have a motivation that is seen as *just*, force protection and *limited* collateral damage are further norms for the actual deployment (Hyde-Price, 2004, pp. 340–1). Finally, wars when they happen, must be short and hopefully happen early in an electoral cycle. As was seen in Blair's third re-election, the Iraq war proved to be the main drawback.

The new constraints on the operation itself are important to understand and to know how to cope with. Harvard law professor David Kennedy paraphrases Clausewitz, tongue-in-cheek, when he says that war today is the continuation of law with other means: 'Law is a strategic partner for military commanders when it increases the perception of outsiders that what the military is doing is legitimate' (Kennedy, 2006, p. 41). General Wesley Clark's *Modern War* (2003), based on his Kosovo experience, illustrates the new dilemmas well. The use of force was not only dictated by military but also by *political* rationale. NATO states' public opinion interfered with bombing targets and asked for justifications for military strategic choices: internal disagreement among states was founded on this new factor of public opinion. Milosevic capitulated at exactly the 'right' time. The truth is that NATO could not have gone on much longer – for purely political reasons.[3] And these reasons were not old-fashioned *raison d'état* deliberations, but the voices of churches, NGOs, the media, and so forth. These are the new players in security and defence policy today. European governments were immensely relieved when the pressure of internal dissolution of the alliance dissipated, thanks to the capitulation.

Thus, legitimacy is very important for the actual use of force in the post-national paradigm. The need for *human* and not *state* security relates to the new type of war that is on display in internal conflicts – with and against civilians, often without distinction between humanitarian and military actors, involving issues such as ethnic cleansing, human rights violation, and political corruption and abuse. These kinds of wars call for military force that is calibrated to the specific situation, often one involving low-level security tasks. Western deployment of force depends on legitimacy for deploying it as well as on acceptable ways of using it. 'Legitimacy is a force multiplier', it is often said. The deployment of the military tool is no longer in defence of existential survival, but in defence of values such as democracy, rule of law, and human rights. Legitimacy is tied both to ethics and to international law (Matlary, 2006), which is to internationally recognised norms and not to Westphalian state interests. Being a key security actor implies the 'right authority' to use military force, based on international norms.

Implications for non-state actors in security policy

In the European setting it is clear that security policy is both *de-territorialised* as well as de-nationalised. Regarding the former, most uses of military power take place far from national borders and do not involve territorial expansion, occupation, or conquest. Although holding and controlling territory is part of the mission in a peace-enforcement operation – at least to some extent – the main point is that territorial expansion or conquest is no longer the goal or reason for the use of military force. Herbst remarks that this development is entirely logical, since territory in our time is no longer the source of wealth and new income: 'States are no longer compelled to expand their territorial reach to get rich ... even states that can be easily conquered are no longer in danger because what they have is no longer worth fighting for' (Herbst, 2004, p. 305). For instance, there was no economic gain in occupying Kosovo. The peace operations where military force is used are limited in time and space, and they come about mainly for *human security* reasons, not for *territorial security* reasons.

Further, it is not the nation that is defended in these missions: on the contrary, it is 'the strangers' as Nicholas Wheeler (2000) so aptly calls them in his study of humanitarian intervention. Thus, nationals intervene militarily in other states in order to save non-nationals. This means that the old logic of calling on own nationals to defend the nation because they are 'our own blood' does not obtain any more, and likewise, the logic of defending the 'homeland' does not obtain for the most part. In fact, the emphasis on nationals is illogical also in another sense: one can only deploy professionals who are trained, recruited, and paid to fight for whatever state interest it is decided they fight for. The military tool has moved from being 'above politics', as the defence of *Land und Volk* with the compulsory risk of the ultimate sacrifice of the lives of male citizens to becoming a tool in the foreign policy toolbox of the state.

The state can now decide to use the military tool for security policy reasons but also for pure foreign policy reasons. The military professional does not question the political choices, but assesses the professional aspects of the mission: risk, cost, strategy, operations, and so forth. The fact that France sends their professional soldiers who are mostly French – apart from many in the Foreign Legion, and the fact that Britain sends British nationals – apart from the Ghurkas, *has less to do with the nationality of the soldiers than with the flag of the regiment.* Politically, what is important is that the contingent carries a French or a British standard. A Frenchman is no longer required because he defends the French nation or French territory; as it was in the period of the Napoleonic or nation-state paradigm. Today, one could think of a French-force contribution being made up of say, 50 per cent French and 50 per cent from other nationalities, but still fighting under the French standard. My point is the simple one that nationality matters less and less in a professional force. Like soccer teams that are national in name and banner, they are now made up of professionals.

We may thus see a gradual 'de-nationalisation' of states' force contributions, however hardly to the extent of the old mercenary armies of Europe – where, for example Gustavus II Adolphus's Swedish army contained 90 per cent non-Swedes. The current pragmatism is rather that nationals from various NATO and EU states serve in each other's militaries and there will be a natural internationalisation where multi-national units develop, both in procurement, deployment, maintenance, and support functions. This will make it easier to operate truly multinational units and for the EU to be a 'military master'. The role of private military companies (PMCs) in Europe is so far limited to supply and non-combat roles, although economic logic may suggest otherwise.

The line of reasoning that is important is that *the notion of nation is less and less relevant for the organisation, definition, and actual use of military force.* To defend own nationals naturally remains a key task for any European state, but increasingly 'the strangers' become almost as relevant for the actual deployment of force. Bosnia, Kosovo, and DR Congo were about 'saving strangers', not nationals. Saving nationals is a more likely task in anti-terror campaigns and crisis management in Europe after a terror attack. But note that this kind of saving nationals is also removed from the territorial dimension: Nation and territory are no longer like overlapping Venn diagrams (see Figure 1.1). Paradoxically, one may point out that strangers and territory are more connected today than nationals and territory, as stabilising and sometimes conquering territory is part of many peace-enforcement missions as was the case in both Bosnia and Kosovo.

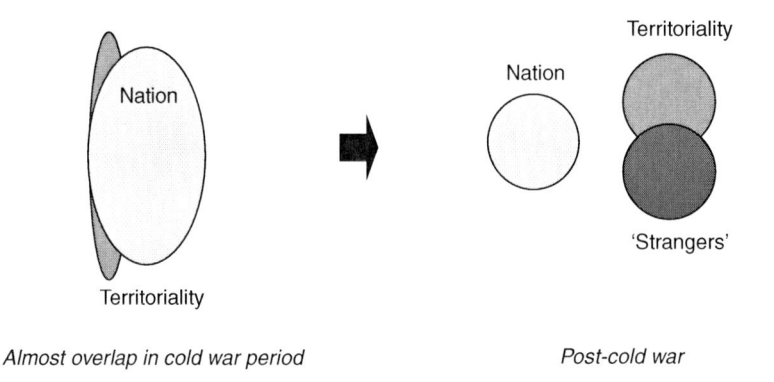

Figure 1.1 The de-territorialisation of security policy

If we posit one continuum where 'nationals' are at one end and 'strangers' at the other, we see that the use of military force today is employed in defending the personal security of both groups. To the extent that security policy is increasingly based on human rights and to a lesser extent on the old connection between nation and territory, the importance of nationals will decrease. An implication of this is that not only states can deploy force, but also other actors, such as international organisations (EU, NATO, UN, AU). Expressed differently, the more human security becomes the rationale for using force, the weaker the state's legitimate monopoly on the use of force.

Further, if we posit 'defending own territory' at one end of a continuum and 'expeditionary' on the other, we see that most use of force today is de-territorialised in the sense that holding territory is only a means to 'saving strangers' or to halting terrorism. A terrorist attack also has this de-territorialised character: it may hit own nationals anywhere – at home or abroad – and must also be averted anywhere, making borders increasingly less relevant.

The Norwegian Strategic Concept describes this new reality when it calls on national forces to become extremely flexible, ready to deal with a crisis anywhere.[4] Also the new Canadian policy document, *A Role of Pride and Influence in the World*, notes that although 'it is the first duty of government to protect its own citizens', there is both a 'responsibility to protect' in humanitarian terms and a 'responsibility to deny' in cases of terrorism: 'As the boundary between the domestic and the international continues to blur, Canada's defence and security policy must change'.[5]

The state may lose its monopoly on military force

When analysing what we here term internationalisation, it is easy to forget that our terms of analysis presuppose the current order of distinction between public and private, national and international. But these sets of categories are historically speaking quite recent. The establishment of the state's monopoly over the military tool was, not unexpectedly, a very gradual process. This commenced after 1648 but was only completed in 1856 with the international abolishment of privateering. David Kennedy (2006) analyses how multiple actors had legal rights to carry arms in the early days of international law. For Vattel, he recounts, there was no distinction between public and private, domestic or international, moral or legal. The doctrine of natural law was the common ethical framework of all law, and all rights-bearers, be they kings, popes, companies, or feudal lords, were embodied in this universal framework. Moreover, these rights-bearers moved about, carrying their military rights with them. The *right to use force* was not tied to territory but to the *actor*.

With the advent of the Westphalian norms of 1648 all this changed as some actors proclaimed themselves sovereign in a new, exclusive way, thereby excluding other actors. Law became something emanating from he who possessed a territory – a sovereign of that territory – and when military rights were gradually denied to all other actors but the sovereign, the law on using force came to rely on positivist notions about war and peace: war existed once a sovereign declared it, regardless of other factors. It is also useful to keep in mind that private military force was the rule rather than the exception prior to 1648 – both soldiers and officers were 'for hire' by rulers (Avant, 2005; Singer, 2003), and most merchant ships had letters of *marque* which enabled them to protect themselves as well as to act as privateers. During the Napoleonic wars privateering was encouraged by, for example, the Norwegian Chancellor, Prince Kristian of Schleswig-Holstein, who offered cannon and letters of marque to local seamen and traders in southern Norway in 1807 (Berge, 1914, p. 17).

The period in which *the state has enjoyed a monopoly on military force is therefore the exception* rather than the rule in European history. If we take Napoleon as the epitome of the ideological view that only the state is entitled to use force, we could shorten the effective period of this monopoly to about 200 years, from about 1800 to about 2000. The pervasiveness of this paradigm has been great, but it has not been around for very long historically.

Change in the practice of military force is therefore normal, if we judge by historical experience. Law appears to be a function of political practice. Kennedy (2006) recounts how international law on the use of force has changed to accommodate new military practice. As long as multiple actors were militarily active, not being bound to any particular territory, there was no distinction between public and private in the law on war because the sovereign was a person who acted on behalf of himself, not a specific nation or a specific territory. Rulers carried out their private wars with hired soldiers and officers. There was therefore no meaningful distinction between a private and a public war when politics was the personal activity of the ruler at his court. Likewise, there was no overlap between nationhood and this political activity. As stated, in Gustavus II Adolphus's army there were about 90 nationalities. The idea that a French officer or a Prussian soldier could not fight for a Swedish king made no sense at this time. The officer and the soldier were professionals, seeking professional employment. The distinction public–private likewise made no sense in this connection; they were not 'mercenaries' in the category of private as opposed to something public.

The point being made here is simply that our categories of analysis regarding 'privatisation' of military force or non-state command of force, such as when an international organisation commands it, reflect the logic of the state as monopolist for the use of force. The only *legitimate* arrangement in our modern paradigm is that the state enjoys such monopoly. We therefore tend to analyse the past with these very confining categories in mind. But there is no a *priori* reason why only states should enjoy the use of force other than the fact that states have become the cornerstones of the international system of sovereign territorial entities. There is no other ultimate authority, neither for law nor security, than states themselves. *We now see a weakening of the state monopoly paradigm*, and the EU or other international organisations – as well as private companies – may eventually come to command their own forces.

The changes we see to the Napoleonic paradigm in this regard today are relatively small in empirical terms, but may nonetheless portend systemic changes because *any* legitimation of military rights for non-state actors, however small, implies a principled shift away from the logic of monopoly because a monopoly cannot act as a continuum but remains a dichotomous variable: one either is a monopolist or one is not. The use of force is defined as the pre-eminent *political* tool; a definition that precludes other definitions such as 'security service' which can be provided by private as well as public actors. But if the military tool starts to be used – and as a 'security service' – is accepted by states, redefinition is already underway. There is thus an intimate relationship between legitimation and practice. If State X uses PMC for tasks that modern peace-enforcement troops undertake, the process of legitimation and redefinition is automatically under way. The amount of practice, which today actually makes up 100,000 hired hands in Iraq (Merk, 2006), demands that routines and rules be established, and finally that some kind of international regulation be developed since these personnel work in war zones that are not well covered by national legislation. At present, the process of legitimation of PMC actors are at the stage where the need for international rules is recognised by all parties. Like other service providers in the global economy, the business organises transnationally in lobbying efforts vis-à-vis the UN and international community, offering self-regulation unless international regulation is forthcoming. States are already facing an agenda set by the PMCs and have to find a way to deal with the former. The option of self-regulation for such an industry is obviously not very attractive.

The point here is to underline that it is *not the state alone* which decides whether to retain the monopoly on the use of force. The public willingness to fund ever-increasing defence needs is shrinking in peacetime while NPM is the hegemonic ideological model. Absent existential threats to the state and public acceptance of private service provision as a main rule, there is no reason but a very principled one that the state's monopoly on the use of force be retained as long as there exists a 'recall' mechanism for PMCs States undermine their own monopoly on the use of force through this piecemeal practice, by getting used to employing contractors in every international mission and in many tasks at home. *Legitimacy, and ultimately, law, follows pragmatic needs arising from practice.*

One should add that the state as such is not in a position to hinder PMC growth internationally, even if it wished to do so. PMCs are also hired by governments that are unable to govern, by non-state actors like guerrillas, by humanitarian organisations, and international business all over the globe.

The Weberian Western state is no longer as omnipotent as it once was. The larger picture in which the modern Western state finds itself is described well by Van Creveld:

> The likelihood grows that the state will lose its monopoly over those forms of organised violence which still remain viable ... *becoming*

one actor among many. Spreading from the bottom up, the conduct of that violence may revert to what it was as late as the first half of the 17th century: namely a capitalist enterprise little different from, and intimately linked with, so many others. Where princes and other military entrepreneurs used to contract with each other to make a profit – an Amsterdam capitalist Louis de Geer , once provided the Swedish government with a complete navy, sailors and commanders up to the vice-admiral included – in the future, various public, semi-public, and private corporations will do the same [my emphasis]. (1999, p. 407)

Driving forces of internationalisation

The Western use of military force is de-territorialised in the sense that force is no longer used to defend the territorial borders of the state, but often far away, even from Western territory. Further, wars are no longer won, says Coker, but security is enhanced. 'In the war on terror we seek more security, not victory' (Coker, 2007, p. 22). As threats are often not tied to national territory in a geopolitical, structural manner, the response to these threats comes in the form of multinational coercion/ deployments, and national military contributions are increasingly integrated with other states' militaries, as discussed by Ulriksen (2007). It is true that the 'old' NATO implied multinationality, but for the most part this was not a real issue. One's forces were kept at home, and only the major states were able to project force abroad. As Ulriksen points out, there was virtually no integration below the corps level, and no deployment beyond own borders (ibid.).

Now, these conditions of 'internationalisation' refer to *military* integration. They are far from clear, however, in terms of their *political* implications. It may be that national control of forces remains as tight as before, and that political decision-making remains entirely intergovernmental in both the EU and NATO, even under the internationalisation conditions mentioned above. The lack of political internationalisation may simply be dysfunctional, as generals Ralston and Naumann and Ralston (2005) argue. Political integration does not at all follow military integration and in fact hinders it. Frantzen (2005) finds that NATO has been hindered in its adaptation by national political interests that bear no relation to the new threat picture, and one senior officer points out that 'the greater the multi-nationality of an organisation, the less efficient it is militarily, but the more advantages it has politically.'⁶ This important point is echoed in the assessment of a symposion at the NATO Defence College:

> Multinational operations are paradoxical. ... Alliance members simply do not have the resources to engage in independent military action, and for political legitimacy, it has become essential even for the US to operate in coalitions ... (but) the dependence of states on these coalitions vitiates the very military effectiveness of the deployed forces. *The necessity of engaging in multilateral operations jeopardises the prospects of success.* (King, 2007, p. 251) [my emphasis]

The relationship between political integration and military integration is thus often a dysfunctional one, each sphere following its own logic. The experience of ISAF in Afghanistan shows that the hotter the warfighting, the more so-called national caveats pop up. It seems clear that no state wishes to lose national control over national military contributions or decision-making in this field, especially when risk increases. It is also vital for a state to 'show the flag', and this militates against political integration. Clearly there is no willed political process towards supranational military structures, neither in NATO, the EU, nor the UN. As one British diplomat remarked in a private conversation, 'There has to be national control when national lives are at risk if there is to be any meaning to democratic accountability'.

Yet there are structural drivers towards internationalisation and even integration. These include stagnant or shrinking budgets, needs for sharing cost and capabilities among states, the need to 'pool' risk in large-scale and long-term operations in non-existential wars and desires to increase political standing in international organisations, and to strengthen these. Together these drivers push towards increased military 'pooling', even integration, but the political mechanisms and decision-making processes remain largely intergovernmental, at least formally. This is increasingly dysfunctional, and therefore also invites private solutions.

How should one measure and assess the degree of military internationalisation at present? And how should one evaluate its political implications? The fact of deployments far away from home territory represents one type of internationalisation. Such interventions have increased manifold after the end of the cold war. Wulf (2005, p. 19) remarks that 'today, international military interventions have emerged as the primary task of armed forces'. The threat picture – be it terrorism, failed states, so-called humanitarian intervention, or all of these together – is sometimes global, sometimes regional, but no longer national. Coker remarks that war now is part of a comprehensive political effort to create more security, and this means that stabilisation and democratisation are as important as is traditional war-fighting (Coker, 2007). The Afghan case illustrates this well. Denial of room for the Taliban and creation of security on the ground is the precondition for civilian tools to be put to work, and it is these tools that will create sustainable security, if at all.

Moreover, great powers now act through international organisations in a multinational way. Even France and Britain prefer to carry out their security policy in a multinational manner. This places new demands on both political decision-making regarding the use of military force and how such force is governed in theatre. The internationalisation dimension thus concerns both political decisions on using force (*ad bellum*) as well as how to govern it in theatre (*in bello*), including how to govern capabilities that are militarily integrated in a multinational manner. For commanders, the task in the field is vastly difficult, as is well illustrated by the more than one hundred so-called national caveats for the use of forces in ISAF prior to the Riga NATO summit. Thus, governments are not interested in political integration of their powers in security policy, but find themselves nonetheless incurring new interdependencies as they become increasingly involved in multinational military missions that require real military integration. The 'Swiss' option of not participating is, however, not very appealing because modern international politics is about *presence, visibility,* and *participation* where the real action is.

Multilateral legitimacy

We have seen that legitimacy for the use of force in the Western world is of pre-eminent importance after the cold war. Post-national security and defence policy is based on a quite different rationale than was the state-to-state war. The key is no longer existential survival of the state but the various political interests of the state. These range from humanitarian intervention to the battle on terror. The scope for using military force has increased considerably after the cold war, precisely because the ends of such use no longer imply total war and perhaps total destruction. The mandates given by the UNSC have been 'stretched' in the sense that not only humanitarian tragedies and disasters now may qualify as a 'threat to international peace and security', but also 'regime change' in the form of democratisation (Matlary, 2006). After

9/11 the humanitarian intervention acquired a new footing – that of regime change. The 'responsibility to protect' became fused with anti-terror pre-emption as 'winning the peace' became a corollary of 'winning the war'. Thus NATO's European allies could legitimate ISAF and anti-terror became equated with state-building and 'reform' of failed states (Chesterman, 2004).

Legitimation, particularly by the UN, is a necessary but not sufficient condition for using force among Western states. Intervention practice has not led to any new rule for using force – neither for humanitarian intervention nor for preventive intervention against terrorists. Rather, the situation appears very unclear regarding the rules for using force. With the advent of global strategic terrorism, the need for regime change is no longer solely motivated by humanitarian 'value' concerns, but also and probably foremost by security policy concerns. This makes the rationale for using force an even more important issue: on the one hand, it is ethically acceptable to use for 'good', that is, to save others: on the other hand, can one risk own soldiers' lives for issues that are not relevant to one's own country's security and defence policy?

But when terrorism is presented as a military issue, many European states refuse to accept it as such. The rationale for risking own citizens' lives has to be concerned with serious threat to the sending state, but if governments do not see the battle on terror as such, this reason for using force also disappears. Indeed, the main division politically regarding ISAF is the lack of common threat perception across the Atlantic. At the Munich Security Conference in 2008, both the US defence secretary and NATO's secretary-general equated the terror threat with the cold war threat, but few European governments have spoken in such terms to their publics.

As stated, the deployment of the military tool is no longer in defence of existential survival, but in defence of values such as democracy, rule of law, and human rights. Few, if any, interventions take place for purely humanitarian/human rights reasons, but such factors clearly play an increasing role. This has to do with the salience of new self-styled actors in security policy (NGOs, churches, public, media) and with global communications. The key issue now is therefore not that the military tool must be deployed by the state, but rather that it is deployed with legitimacy. Such legitimacy has become proportionately more important in the post-cold war era, as the UNSC has become the key arena for bestowing legitimacy and state-to-state wars have receded in importance. The advent of a right (but not duty) to humanitarian intervention in the 1990s has put the emphasis on human security rather than on state security. This development is continuing with the emergence of 'integrated missions' in the UN context and is evident in the crisis-management policy of NATO and the especially the EU, which already has all but the most robust military tools in its 'toolbox'.

Being a key security actor in this era therefore implies two things: the first is 'right authority' to use military force – based on international norms; the other is military ability as well as other tools. The formal norms for using military force – the *ad bellum* norms – are enshrined in the UN Pact, Article 2 (4), which forbids both aggression and coercive diplomacy. Only the Security Council can grant a mandate to use force. However, throughout the cold war, states rarely resorted to the Security Council for a mandate: the informal rule for using force was that of 'spheres of interest'. The Soviets claimed their sphere and the Americans theirs, and the superpowers tolerated the use of force in these spheres. While protesting politically, they did nothing militarily to hinder the adversary. The wars fought by the superpowers were 'proxy' wars. Thus, in the cold war period the rules of the game, as it were, differed greatly from the norms of legal canon and there was seemingly no need for the legitimacy that the UNSC mandate provides. Legitimacy for using force was derived from the 'sphere of interest' logic.

In the post-cold war period, for the first time there has been a sustained and major emphasis on the role of the Security Council. Its legal norms are the same today as in the cold war period, but the Council plays a new and important role as the bestower of legitimacy for using force. States seek a mandate before they attack. However, the Council bestows mandates for interventions that never happen, such as in the case of Rwanda, and many conflicts – like the cold war period – never reach the Council's agenda because they are not allowed there by one or more veto powers. For example, China ensures that there is no mandate to intervene in Darfur. Despite this, a UNSC mandate is deemed necessary, even for the United States (Matlary, 2006).

Similar to the cold war period, states continue to invoke Article 51 for attacks on other states, but seek the UN approval for their interpretation, as in the case of Afghanistan. Using military force without the best available legitimacy – a mandate – is increasingly problematic. Using force therefore revolves around the UN and the UN Pact to an unprecedented degree. The rule for getting to the point of using force has changed: there is a need for a UN stamp of approval.

As stated, in the post-cold war period, the interpretation of this key concept has been widened extremely much, seconded by the work of key UN undertakings such as the International Commission on Intervention and State Sovereignty (ICISS) and the High-Level Panel's Report *A More Secure World* (2004). The new reading of the main norm, non-intervention, finally became a new political norm, the R2P – Responsibility to Protect. The role of the UN mandate in terms of political legitimation is very different in the United States and Europe. The US view is that the mandate is important but not vital, whereas the European view is that the mandate is the very key to legitimating the use of force (Matlary, 2006). There are differences between European governments here – neither the British nor the French government would want to depend on having a mandate, but as we saw in the Iraq case, it was Britain that needed an explicit mandate before the attack – one that was not forthcoming. But in states such as Germany and the Nordic ones, a UN mandate is seen to be almost a necessity. This implies that political legitimacy in Europe is tied to the UN mandate as the key 'ingredient', and that the UN as an organisation is important.

The formal aspect of multilateralism is the other important determinant of legitimacy in Europe. Whereas the US concept is that of 'effective multilateralism', that is the pragmatic point of departure of asking 'what works?', Europeans tend to look for formal rules and formal organisation as the defining aspect of multilateralism (McCormick, 2007). The use of force must therefore be launched by an international organisation, not by an *ad hoc* coalition of states. *The EU and NATO are therefore important in their formal roles.*

But legitimacy is also tied to the object of security policy. If it is no longer states and their survival, then it is the human being and his or her survival. Human rights and abuses of such were the key issues in the era of humanitarian intervention in the 1990s. This agenda fits very well with the European set of post-modern values and the EU's traditional role as a 'soft power' organisation. But to use force to combat terror is an altogether different issue. As we shall see, the basis for using force has become very contested. In the case of ISAF, European governments have emphasised the human development and democratisation aspect of the mandate and largely refused to speak against war-fighting in asymmetrical counter-insurgency situations. The referent object of security is what gives additional legitimacy in Europe. It is termed 'human security'.

In the emerging post-national security agenda, the point of reference is the *individual* person and his or her right to personal security.

The right to security is a human right enshrined in all relevant human rights documents. The term 'human security' was first used by the UN in its UNDP Human Development Index for 1994. In this document human security has no military implications and was, in fact, defined as a wholly civilian concept.[7] In it the concept was used for a plethora of situations, expanding the security concept so much that it seemed to comprise everything. However, the main contributions to the development of human security have come from the report of the *International Commission on Intervention and State Sovereignty* (ICISS) which finished its work in 2001. The ICISS report goes fairly far in indicating that an international responsibility exists to protect when a state fails to protect its own citizens. Adopting the definition of sovereignty that is conditional upon the respect for human rights, the report states that

> Sovereignty is more than just a functional principle of international relations.... The conditions under which sovereignty is exercised – and intervention is practised – have changed dramatically since 1945 ... it is acknowledged that sovereignty implies a dual responsibility: internally to respect the dignity and basic rights of all the people within the state. In international human rights covenants, in UN practice, and in state practice itself, sovereignty is now understood as embracing this. (ICISS, 2001, p. 8)

The commission proposes that 'where a population is suffering serious harm, as a result of internal war, insurgency, repression or state failure, and the state in question is unable or unwilling to halt or avert it, the principle of non-intervention yields to the international responsibility to protect' (ICISS, 2001, p. xi).

Summing up, the state-to-state war has largely been replaced by internal wars where Western states increasingly started to intervene when faced with major humanitarian crises. Peace-keeping became peace enforcement, and the so-called humanitarian intervention was born. In the 1990s, Western states intervened in Somalia, Bosnia, and Kosovo, and sent military missions to Macedonia and a number of African states. The lack of clear security interests made these interventions special. They seemed to signal that Western states were willing to use force to rectify gross violations of human rights and to stop genocide. However, in the case of Rwanda where the West simply stood by, and the case of Darfur, show that not even genocide suffices to prompt intervention. Further, the Bosnian intervention from the air mainly came about after, and not before, the genocide in Srebrenica. In the case of Kosovo, the driving force for the intervention was the lesson from Srebrenica, not one that was politically repeatable, it was deemed. *The novelty in the post-cold war period is the importance legitimacy plays.* It is no longer enough that major states condone intervention as previously. But neither is UN approval alone enough. There has to be a general consensus, also by the publics, for the use of force (Matlary, 2006).

The return of security interests: Doing good and fighting terrorism

After 9/11, the security situation has changed again, and we are back to threat assessments and existential interests also in Europe. However, there is no invasion threat of the old kind; territorial interests are a thing of the past for most European states. Now threats are diffuse and global in scope. Moreover, fighting terrorism involves stabilisation and development of so-called failed states where democratisation, broadly understood, is the only bulwark against resurgence of terrorism. Afghanistan is a case in point.

The fight against terrorism takes intervention to places that may harbour terrorists, and these places have by and large been identified as 'failed' states. Such states which could formerly hope for attention from those that advocate a 'responsibility to protect' (R2P) in order to restore or introduce human rights and democracy, suddenly find themselves potential targets for intervention because of the terrorist connection, real or alleged. According to B. Buzan and O. Wæver, failed states have become 'securitised.' (Buzan and Wæver, 2003). This moves the failed state to the forefront of security policy, indeed to the very top of a state's security threat hierarchy. It makes the failed state the number one candidate for intervention, but only if the failed state in question harbours terrorists.

The importance and relevance of the norm R2P here becomes clear: should a state wish to intervene in a failed state in order to haunt terrorists, it can invoke R2P as its basis for legitimacy. This is exactly what happened in the case of Afghanistan when a major NATO participation became desirable.

ISAF has a mandate of state building, not one of war-fighting against the Taliban, which remains the province of Operation Enduring Freedom (OEF). But developments on the ground obliterated the difference between the two operations from 2006 onwards as the Taliban returned to fight the international forces. The Bush administration embraced state building – the R2P agenda – only when it became clear that this was necessary in order to get the Europeans, including in particular their publics, on board.

In the case of Afghanistan we see, a growing 'mission creep' from intervention claimed as self-defence against terrorism to increasing 'nation-building'. At first President Bush proclaimed a 'lengthy campaign' involving 'far more than instant retaliation' (cited in Chesterman, 2004, p. 165). This was consistent with the insistence that 'nation-building' was no task of the US military, as was emphasised during the presidential campaign in 2000: 'we've got to be clear to our friends and allies about how we use our troops for nation-building exercises, which I have rebuffed as a kind of strategy for the military' (p. 167). However, as it became clear that military success was dependent on the wider effort to establish stable rule, and also that support from European states much depended on the willingness to assist in post-conflict work, the nation-building agenda was embraced. The need for more military contributions from Europe prompted the initial embrace of 'nation-building' on the part of the United States because it was the key to political legitimacy in many European publics.

I use this example because it illustrates *that Europeans need a value basis* – some kind of variation on the 'human security'-theme – in order to see the use of force as legitimate. Unless European governments were able to argue to their publics that ISAF was a good cause it would have been impossible to muster support for ISAF.

It is clear that the issue of *legitimacy is extremely important to the post-national use of military force*. This can be explained by several factors, all related to the paradigm change: non-existential wars, postmodern values in terms of war and human life, the normalisation of security policy and consequent strengthening of domestic actors in this area, and so forth. There is also a time-lag in the understanding of the *Realpolitik* character of the UN mandate – the great difference in how the UNSC is seen between the United States and Europe. The Europeans continue to attach considerable importance to the mandate as an institution, no matter how it has been arrived at. Yet the Kosovo case underlines that a mandate is not a sine qua non for using force, even in Europe. This is important, as the development we now see in Europe is one of even greater importance for domestic actors in this field. As the UN gives mandates for many cases where there is no subsequent intervention, and not in all cases where there is intervention, legitimacy may come to rest increasingly on *multilateral agreements* to undertake missions. Also, the more we see terrorism as a real cause in stabilisation operations, the more security needs will come into the foreground, and the 'luxury' of a UN mandate cannot be assumed if great powers have different interests. But the need to be multilateral in terms of being in a formal organisational setting will remain.

This chapter has provided a general overview of the paradigm shift that security and defence policy in Europe undergoes. Traditional interstate war is a thing of the past in Western Europe, and the conventional invasion scenario is highly unlikely. But Western states use military force much more than hitherto; they deploy in operations far from their own territory. They do so in a security interest, but it is no longer an existential one in the sense that their states and nations are at risk. They do not fight for their own survival as peoples. This monumental change in the threat scenario moves security and defence policy from 'above' politics to a status almost as 'normal' politics. This 'normalisation' in turn means that the political debate over security involves domestic actors, press, and the public in a new manner. There is major disagreement on where to deploy and why, and governments need legitimacy for their security policy in a new and different manner than previously.

Legitimacy for using force is achieved both internationally and at home. The best legitimacy is a UNSC mandate which provides legality to an operation and global political support (Matlary, 2006). This in turn provides legitimacy at home, to publics and parliaments alike. However, also other forms of multilateralism may provide legitimacy, with or without a UN mandate. Being in a coalition that is based on either NATO or the EU provides a degree of legitimacy that is explored later in this book. Going multilateral when one deploys has become, it seems, politically necessary even for great powers such as France and Britain. We can date this change to the mid-1990s in the case of both states.

Thus, security policy in the sense of international deployment implies a multilateral arrangement today. The advantage of multilateralism is also one of sharing the political risk at home for operations going badly, and for sharing the military risks in the theatre of operations. The infamous issue of 'national caveats' in ISAF in Afghanistan is a case in point. The NATO alliance may crumble under the collective impact of so many free riders, although it seems rational for each 'free rider' to leave the risk- and loss-taking to others. The incentives for multilateral security policy are thus many, and if we add that major states such as France and Britain are able to retain traditional security policy at national level, we see that this appears to be a 'win-win' situation. Both states are key players in both the EU and NATO, while retaining a nuclear deterrent and their permanent seats on the UNSC.

With regard to both the EU and NATO, we witness the same multinational logic: all states that participate gain the advantages of multilateralism outlined above. Small states gain international impact that they alone could never even envisage, whereas large states gain general influence in the organisation in question, often in lead military roles.

2
EU Security and Defence Policy: Legitimacy and Capability

This book investigates the political dynamics of the ESDP, which is a 'subset' of the Common Foreign and Security Policy (CFSP). The ESDP refers to security and defence policy only, whereas the CFSP refers to the entire foreign policy portfolio of the EU. As discussed in the preceding chapter, the main issue is the use of military force as part of the ESDP. An operation run by the EU usually consists of many civilian tools as well, and in fact the majority of EU operations to date are non-military, as detailed below. But the EU has ambitions to be a military actor to a much greater extent than hitherto, and this presents it with special challenges. As we have seen, a modern PSO concerns much more than military force, but the deployment of these tools of foreign policy is not particularly controversial. It is the use of force that is difficult, both for legitimacy as well as for capacity reasons.

The literature on the CFSP and its history is large. The ambition to develop a European foreign policy through the EU goes back to the very founding of the organisation. I will not include a discussion of this long and contested effort here. The gradual emergence of a common foreign policy was eventually confirmed in terms of treaty additions, first in 1970 when the European Political Cooperation (EPC) was codified as a common intergovernmental project inside the EU structure, and later when the concept of 'political union' was similarly injected in the Treaty on European Union (TEU) in 1992. The latter was a milestone in the history of the EU as it contained the proviso for crisis-management operations. As we shall see later, this concept has been developed to include so-called robust operations of combat as well.

The ESDP is about ten years old, and is the main theme of this book. The political dynamics of all foreign policy in the EU is formally intergovernmental, including the ESDP. But formal intergovernmentalism in no way precludes informal and even formal 'subsets' of decision-making rules that are the really decisive elements of the policy process. This is what interests us here.

The point of departure for our analysis is the paradigm shift and its political implications for using force in European states. The two variables that count are argued to be political legitimacy and military capacity. In this chapter we analyse what the EU and its members can provide with regard to both. We then proceed to an analysis of the ESDP in Chapter 3 where we also present our model of EU security dynamics.

EU legitimacy for the use of force

In post-national security policy, legitimacy is the key issue because the domestic public matters much more than previously in decision-making in this field. Before making an 'inventory' of the EU's military capacities, we first turn to this issue of whether the EU can provide a plausible legitimacy basis for a post-national security policy.[8]

On what basis is EU security policy built? It is one thing is to have the capacity to act; quite another the political will to do so. As discussed in the previous chapter, European states need value-based legitimacy to deploy and use military force. In addition to military capability, legitimacy is the most important variable in explaining why states participate in military missions. Legitimacy in most European states, we have argued, is now based on post-national security policy: humanitarian assistance and state-building. The latter is increasingly connected to the fight against terrorism, but in Europe the 'war on terror' is not regarded as an issue connected to the use of military power. Only Britain openly endorses the link between failed states and terrorism, but Britain nonetheless relies on having a UN mandate for most military missions. In the case of Iraq, although supporting the Bush policy of intervention, it was noteworthy that Britain insisted on the need for an explicit UN mandate (but failed to obtain it). Thus, the issue of legitimacy in some form of multilateral endorsement is the key for all European states, preferably given by the UN. France, the other military key power in Europe, insists on a UN mandate as a matter of course when the issue is an optional war.

The concept of *human security* is a candidate for the 'values' part of security policy that relates to humanitarian intervention, but not for the 'security' part that relates to the fight against terrorism. At the outset, it is clear that the EU does not purport to have a military security policy that relates to such questions. The use of force by the EU is limited to crisis management alone (Howorth and Menon, 1997). Bailes, who has written extensively on the ESDP, points out that the intention of the architects behind this policy was to create effective intervention capacity in Europe in the aftermath of the Balkan wars.

> As one who was directly involved in the genesis of the ESDP in 1999, this author can testify that no one talked much at the time about doing something for the 'good of the world'. Many people were thinking about the good of *Europe*: shocked by the events in Kosovo and the European lack of capacity to master that crisis, they sought new crisis management capacity. (Bailes, 2008, p. 115)

Bailes adds that the main point was to induce Europeans to modernise militarily and thereby to be able to shoulder the burden of taking care of European security. One motive was to make the Germans pay more for defence, another to make the United States more content with European efforts. We return to the analysis of the rationale for the ESDP in the following chapters, but point out at the outset that[9] there was no *'humanitarian' grand strategy* behind it.

Yet, as we have seen in the previous chapter, post-national security in Europe is evolving after the cold war, and the emphasis is very much on human rights and individual security. This legitimacy basis has become the only feasible one in states where there is no longer any perceived existential threat. As a consequence, European publics are no longer used to war-fighting, and are extremely reluctant to use military force. This claim is substantiated in Chapter 5.

Here, it is important to point to this factor as the *point of departure* when we move to consider the EU and its ability to provide a legitimacy basis for using military force. It is clear that human rights and not state interests form the formal basis of the EU policies, and as argued in Chapter 1, such a value basis for security policy is becoming increasingly relevant in post-national European politics, at least on the rhetorical level of justification for using force. Human rights were included in the Maastricht Treaty in 1992 and developed in the Amsterdam Treaty which stipulated that 'the Union is founded on the principles of liberty, democracy, respect for human rights and fundamental freedoms, and the rule of law' (Art. 6). In the Amsterdam Treaty there was added a sanction possibility inserted in a new Article 7 stating that the Council, meeting in the capacity of heads of state or government, and with the consent of the European Parliament (EP) 'may determine the existence of a serious or persistent breach of the principles mentioned above'.

This article was further extended in the Nice Treaty of December 2000. The EU also has explicit policy tools for promoting human rights and democracy. In extreme cases of human rights abuse inside an EU state it can revoke the voting rights of such state.

In the Amsterdam Treaty it is noteworthy that human rights, democracy, and the rule of law also figure prominently in the definition of foreign policy: 'The Union shall define and implement a common foreign and security policy covering all areas of foreign and security policy, the objectives of which shall be ... to develop and consolidate democracy and the rule of law, and respect for human rights and fundamental freedoms' (Art. 11, TEU). However, most 'stick and carrot' tools are far more subtle and process-oriented, emphasising the 'carrot'. The tools of the Commission and the European Council contain the suspension clause mentioned above, but this is a tool of last resort. Usually, results will be achieved by positive measures. The EU as a whole has stipulated the conditions that must be met by new member states when they accede to the Union.

The so-called Copenhagen Criteria are specific and straightforward, placing the emphasis on the duty of the applicant state to comply *prior* to being admitted. These criteria, adopted in 1993, stipulate that candidate states must have stable institutions guaranteeing democracy, the rule of law, and human rights as well as respect for the protection of minorities; a functioning market economy together with the capacity to cope with the competitive pressures and market forces within the EU; and the ability to adopt the EU's *acquis*.

How does this human rights basis for policy relate to the ESDP? How will the EU react to the development of humanitarian and democratic intervention? This is where the 'human security' thinking enters with relevance. The human rights and democracy basis of the EU as an actor would also seem to require a security policy based on these values, logically speaking. If human rights are gradually mainstreamed into all EU foreign policy, what about security and defence?[10]

In the ESS, which is the only strategy document of the EU, the main response to security challenges is to 'build an international order based on "effective multilateralism"' (ESS, 2003, p. 9) – a term also used by Washington. In the EU context it has another definition: this order has to be 'rule-based' as

> we are committed to upholding and developing international law …. The fundamental framework for international relations is the UN Charter. Here we note that multilateralism is defined as a formal

order, based on explicit rules and embedded in an organisation. The UNSC has the primary responsibility for the maintenance of international peace and security. Strengthening the UN, equipping it to fulfil its responsibilities and to act effectively, is an European priority. (ibid.)

The European Security Strategy (ESS) does not explicitly discuss the importance of the UN mandate, nor does it explicitly require such mandate in order to deploy military force. A reasonable interpretation is that a mandate is not a requirement but that it is highly desirable. The backdrop to the ESS was the American security strategy of 2002 which was a response to the terrorist attacks just before 2001 and which emphasised the possible need for pre-emption and even prevention. The ESS adopts a very similar threat assessment to the American strategy, but deviates from it in its call for UN mandate and formal multilateralism. Yet the context is important in order to understand why the Europeans did not put more emphasis on the UNSC mandate. Moreover, the ESS was largely penned in Whitehall (Hill, 2004), in close cooperation with Paris, and drafted by the former Blair advisor, now Solana advisor, Robert Cooper. It was therefore calibrated to meet American demands for realistic security planning while being acceptable to all EU states.

The ESS led to further studies. Solana commissioned a study on the concept of human security, the so-called Barcelona Report, formally entitled 'Human Security Doctrine for Europe'.[11] It represents the first coherent attempt to develop a policy for intervention based on individual rights to security, not only in terms of policy and legal principles – as is the case of the ICISS report– but also in terms of the needs of civilian–military integration. The reports suggest that the ESDP should be based on seven principles: 'The primacy of human rights, clear political authority, multilateralism, a bottom-up approach, regional focus, the use of legal instruments, and the appropriate use of force' (Barcelona Report, 2004: Executive Summary). The report suggests that an EU military force should be created and referred to as 'the Human Security Response Force', totalling 15,000 persons.

The authors of the report, led by Professor Mary Kaldor, make a link between legitimacy and the use of inadequate types of force: 'Human rights have become much more prominent, and an intervention that uses traditional war-fighting means, such as bombardment from the air, may be unacceptable when viewed through the lens of human rights' (ibid., p. 9). The first NATO actions in Bosnia and the Kosovo intervention come to mind. Thus, interventions will increasingly be judged not only in terms of military and other results, but also in terms of military methods, even beyond the existing regulations on weapons and their use.

The criteria for using force are formally based on international law, but in reality public support matters most. The report goes far in the direction of replacing existing rules on state actors with human rights based rules: 'Unlike classic wars where only states bore responsibility, armed forces have to act within a legal framework that applies to individuals' (ibid., p. 19). There should be a legal framework with local responsibility, the authors argue, and clear links between the military actors and local population without, however, detailing how this may work out.

Interestingly, the Barcelona Report remarks that the EU is 'hindered by the absence of a single and coherent body of international law governing foreign deployments' (ibid., p. 24). They note that this body of law relates to states as actors, not to individuals. The suggestions in this report are however quite unrealistic. To change international law in the direction away from state sovereignty towards human security is exceedingly difficult as states that are wary of intervention zealously guard their status. But also in terms of military capacity, the proposals are unrealistic.

In a comprehensive analysis of the concept, aptly entitled *A human security agenda for the EU: Would it make a difference?*, Kotsopoulos (2007) concludes that

> the concept of human security can have both internal and external benefits for the EU. From improved coherence within the policy-making realm, to an improved presence abroad, a human security agenda can indeed provide added-value to the EU. It can also facilitate the ESS goal of 'effective multilateralism' since it opens doors to cooperation, with the UN in particular. (Kotsopoulos, 2007, p. 230).

But what happens when human security meets political reality? When Kaldor et al. touch the topic of war, the normative prejudices against military power become apparent. The description of modern stabilisation and reconstruction operations is very ideological:

> Human security ... is not about war-fighting, it is about protection of individuals and communities ... in a human security operation, the job of the military is to protect and preserve the (humanitarian) space rather than to fight an enemy. Thus human security is about ... an entirely new way of functioning in crises (ibid., p. 280).

These claims are unfounded in political and military reality. An operation like ISAF, which would fit the criteria of a human-security operation, has to undertake offensive war-fighting in many cases. Modern wars amongst the people, as Sir Rupert Smith has put it, share certain characteristics that involve robust military power when needed, but the aim is development and reconstruction. They are human-security operations, but military force is very rarely deployed for purely humanitarian purposes.

The contribution made by the concept of human security is to give a name to a security paradigm based on the human rights of the individual. It is useful at the rhetorical level in the EU for this reason. As we have seen, *the EU has a political basis for using force in the current mode of post-national security thinking in Europe*. It has no territorial interests to defend, but a treaty and policy basis which consists of the values that underlie the 'human-security' paradigm.

We have argued that the two main requirements for using the military tool in Europe are political ability and military ability. The political ability is first and foremost determined by the question of legitimacy in domestic publics, as we shall see in greater detail later in this book. But without military capability, no amount of political will matters. Military capability is naturally the necessary but not sufficient condition for using force. We now turn to the EU's assets in this regard.

EU military capabilities

To date, the EU has launched only one sharp operation, the Artemis in DR Congo in 2003. But it has also fielded about 7,000 troops in Bosnia and some 600 in Macedonia, in addition to many operations of a 'law-and-order' nature.

If we look at the EU's crisis-management portfolio – to be discussed in greater detail later in this chapter – this mainly consists of missions taken over from NATO (*Concordia* and *Althea*), and missions without much military content. The exception is the quick reaction force in operation *Artemis*, which was at the sharp end of war-fighting. All EU operations have been, and are concerned with human security – *Artemis* in the most direct sense: a sharp operation in order to stop genocide. The reality of the high end of the spectrum war to stop the dramatic human-security drama of genocide emphasises that human security may require just as tough use of military force as traditional state-security operations. Human security is therefore not at all 'softer' or less 'war-like' than state security. The problem is not that human security is not a good idea, but that interventions rarely happen for human-security reasons alone. To 'talk the talk' and not 'walk the walk' therefore becomes especially problematic from an ethical standpoint. The EU may benefit from calling all its security policy 'human security', but when rhetoric promises more than what policy can deliver this has a serious ethical dimension. Willingness and ability to contribute with risk and money to operations to 'save strangers' remain the hard questions, for NATO as well as for the EU.

However, with a basis in human security in its treaties the EU can launch a post-national security policy more easily than a state with its traditional security interests. The human-security paradigm therefore fits very well with the crisis-management focus of the ESDP. It is an intellectually and logically coherent ideological paradigm but, as argued, without concrete implementation it will lose political stature quickly. In the remainder of this book we will *inter alia* analyse the extent to which EU security policy actually materialises itself as the new 'human security'. So far, we can conclude that a post-national security policy paradigm has been developed in the 1990s, and that it is well established in the UN system. The R2P norm is a political and not (yet) a legal norm, but one that has now become established (Matlary, 2006). The political coherence of this post-national paradigm is a fact, but the lack of coherence in value-based intervention is evident.

The EU has become a security and defence actor of importance after the cold war. This is particularly the case after 1998, and the famous St. Malo declaration between France and Britain. While the EU is now rapidly developing a military capability (battlegroups, intervention force, decision-making in security and defence with only three or more states), acquiring military and crisis-management experience (from sharp missions like *Artemis* to major undertakings like *Althea*), and building capacity on the military-strategic side in its own organisation (military staff, planning, Armaments Agency, etc.), it is also developing a *global* strategy (see European Security Strategy, December 2003). The major developments in this field are *rapid*, and the St. Malo declaration was a turning point, thus completing the EU crisis-management portfolio. As Bailes concludes, there has been a major development in EU security policy over the last ten years (Bailes, 2007).

In the EU, there is thus a post-national legitimacy basis for a security policy based on values like human rights and security for the individual. But as we shall argue, EU security policy does not follow from a blue print or strategy which is worked out by the organisation. On the contrary, EU security policy is made *ad hoc*, driven by the interests of the major players, in this case France and Britain.

Before we discuss whether EU security policy is a new type of postnational policy, let us look at what makes up this policy in practise. What are the capacities, deployments, and actions undertaken? What do they amount to? Only when we have knowledge of these realities will it be possible to assess EU security policy and its political dynamics.

In military security policy, there are certain basics that have to be met. As discussed in Chapter 1, there is no escape from military modernisation. The so-called revolution in military affairs (RMA) implies that deployable forces must be able to inter-operate and to take on war-fighting at the high end of operations in addition to being able to do reconstruction work in theatres far away from home. As stated, European forces were extremely unprepared for the changes away from stationary defence based on mobilisation to expeditionary, war-fighting units. The changes were costly in terms of money and caused much political resistance. France and Britain are the only two major military forces in Europe with an expeditionary focus. This is so because of their size and their former colonies. For the rest, the situation is completely different. According to the EU's own Security Policy Institute, only 5 per cent of European forces are deployable anywhere on the globe as opposed to 50 per cent of US forces![12]

Undoubtedly, military modernisation occurs in the EU (e.g. ECAP, EDA, cf. below). This is a necessary development which is urgent; key capacities are missing in Europe. The EU is, however, still in its infancy in terms of military capacity, planning, and institutional factors. The main military transformation process occurs in NATO. Its transformation needs were defined in Prague in 2002 (PCC) and identified as the Defence Capability Initiative (DCI) as well as in the response force (RRF) which consists of 25,000 men on a six-month rotational basis with a deployment time of five days. This force will sustain up to 30 days of high-intensity combat. In NATO, the new command structure, Allied Command Transformation (ACT) assists in both transformation and force generation.

In the EU, 16 battlegroups have been determined, each with 1,500 men and a deployment time of six days. They are multinational and will operate on a rotational basis that will be coordinated with the NATO force. In addition, the EU works on a much larger force that can be deployed for less-intensive crisis management on a longer basis, referred to as the Helsinki Headline Goals 2010. Further, the EU has its own modernisation plan, but perhaps the most interesting decision was the establishment of the EDA in 2004.

The battlegroup initiative was taken in late 2003 and aimed at making European troops more deployable (Cornish and Edwards, 2005, p. 804). The battlegroups have proved to be the key vehicle for co-training, integration, and military modernisation so far in the EU:

> A Battlegroup consists of highly trained, battalion – size formation – including all combat and service support as well as deployability and sustainability assets. These should be available within 15 days notice and sustainable for at least 30 days (extendable to 120 days by rotation). They should be flexible enough to promptly undertake operations in distant crises areas (i.e. failing states), under, but not exclusively, a UN mandate, and to conduct combat missions in an extremely hostile environment (mountains, desert, jungle, etc.). As such, they should prepare the ground for larger, more traditional peacekeeping forces, ideally provided by the UN or the member states. They should also be compatible with the NATO Response Force (NRF). (Cameron and Quille, 2004, p. 14)

In April 2004, it was planned that the EU should have nine battlegroups available for deployment by 2007. From 2005 to 2007, at least one 'coherent battlegroup package' would be able to undertake an operational deployment. The full operating capability, due in 2007, would enable two concurrent, single-battlegroup, rapid response operations, launched 'nearly simultaneously'. The timetable seemed achievable particularly when, at the November 2004 Capabilities Commitments Conference, EU defence ministers made commitments sufficient for 13 battlegroups (Cornish and Edwards, 2005, p. 804–5).

European Capabilities Action Plan (ECAP)

At the Laeken European Summit in December 2001, the European Council decided to launch the European Capabilities Action Plan (ECAP) to address shortfalls in the development of EU rapid reaction capabilities which had begun at the Helsinki European Council in December 1999 .The ECAP process has been guided by four core principles. The first is 'the improvement of the effectiveness and efficiency of European defence efforts, enhancing cooperation between Member States or groups of Member States'; second, 'a "bottom up" approach to European defence cooperation, relying on voluntary national commitments'; third, 'Coordination between EU Member States as well as coordination with NATO'; fourth, the process is guided by 'Public support through ECAP's transparency and visibility' (Schmitt, 2005).

Nineteen panels of national experts have been working on possible solutions to the capabilities shortfall. The panels met independently and were composed of at least one 'lead nation', active participants, and observers. The work of the panels was coordinated by the 'Headline Goal Task Force' (HTF) which drew upon the support of the EU Military Staff (EUMS) and reported to the EU Military Committee (EUMC) (ibid.).

ECAP is generally considered to be a promising approach to tackle capability shortfalls, but has a number of weak points. One is that it remains voluntary and lacks credibility as long as commitments are not underpinned with the necessary funding. Further, it has lacked leadership and the working method of regular meetings of national experts has been hardly innovative. Finally, it has been a pure *ad hoc* exercise, limited in time and scope since it only focuses on the current shortfalls in commitments to the Helsinki Headline Goal (ibid.).

Headline goal 2010

The Thessaloníki European Council acknowledged that the EU operational capability was limited and constrained by shortfalls. In June 2004, the Council adopted the new Headline Goal 2010, reflecting the ESS, the evolution of the strategic environment and of technology. It contains the main parameters in the development of EU military capacities with 2010 as the time horizon, and includes a definition of the ambition level of the Rapid Reaction Force (RRF).

The new goals clearly state that the new security tasks require both military and civilian tools, and include a Headline Goal Catalogue, a Headline Force Catalogue, and a Headline Progress Catalogue. The initial Helsinki goals led to deficiencies in several areas but a 'surplus' in other areas, such as troops, combat aircraft, and ships. Now the EU plans to rectify its deficiencies in areas such as lift capacity in sea, land, and air; precision-guided missiles (PGM), logistics, and communications and surveillance (Cameron and Quille, 2004).

NATO had already initiated a similar process called the DCI, narrowed down to eight priorities in 2003. Both 'wish-lists' suffer from lack of states' political (and economic) will, but the pressure towards further commitment is clearly increasing. The ESS cannot be realised without it. The new Headline Goals therefore specify the time limit for the various military developments that must take place. These goals for military improvement will, of course, depend on political will, but they are sufficiently clear to make states commit much more decisively than the original headline goals.

Most importantly, the EU's main actors in terms of military capacity, France and Britain, are behind these proposals and have promoted them with strength. For instance, they have 'endorsed the commitment to acquire aircraft with its associated air wing and escort by 2008' (ibid., p. 13).

In May 2005, a third Capability Improvement Chart was published. This revealed that while projects and initiatives abound, progress on the stated objectives was still slow, though advances have been made on the programmatic side. The Headline Goal 2010 was discussed at the council meeting in November 2005. The Council approved the Requirements Catalogue 2005 which identified the military capabilities and force requirements needed. This represented an important step in the capability development process of the Headline Goal 2010. It put renewed emphasis on rapidly deployable, highly interoperable armed forces that can be sustained as necessary over long periods on operations through rotation of forces and provision of the required enabling, support, and logistic elements (European Council, 2005, p. 11).

In light of a Single Progress Report on military capabilities, the Council recognised 'that there has been further progress in capability development since the Helsinki Progress Catalogue 03, but stressed the urgent need for further progress to be made in the development of military capabilities to remedy the current shortfalls and to address the largely qualitative limitations and constraints stemming from them' (ibid., p. 12). The key role of French–British cooperation in the capability modernisation is noticeable here.

EDA

At the Thessaloníki European Council in June 2003, it was agreed to establish a European Armaments, Research and Military Capabilities Agency which was to be created immediately. The reasons behind this were the relative failure of previous attempts to coordinate procurement and armaments cooperation and the acceleration reality of the ESDP agenda as well as the perceived need to link capabilities to armaments production (Howorth, 2005, p. 198). Hence, in the first half year after the ESS, an important accomplishment of the Council was to set up the EDA. The Agency was established by the Council on 12 July 2004, and is designed 'to support the Council and the Member States in their effort to improve European defence capabilities in the field of crisis management and to sustain the ESDP as it stands now and develops in the future' (EDA, 2006).[13]

The EDA ascribes five functions which are related to defence capabilities development, armaments cooperation, the European defence technological and industrial base, and defence equipment market, and also to research and technology. The Agency's tasks are to work for a more comprehensive and systematic approach to defining and meeting the capability needs of ESDP, to promote equipment collaboration, to contribute to defence capabilities and act as catalysts for further restructuring of the European defence industry, and to promote European defence-relevant research and technology (R&T) as vital both to a healthy defence technological and industrial base, and to defining and satisfying future capability requirements. This will involve pursuing collaborative use of national defence R&T funds in the context of a European policy which identifies priorities (ibid.). According to Howorth, the EDA offers the first real opportunity for the EU to bring its defence planning, military capability objectives, and armaments coordination in line with the urgent tasks it is facing on the ground (ibid., p. 199).

All the Member States of the EU, except Denmark which has a national caveat with regard to the ESDP, participate in the EDA. The first head of the Agency was British, Nick Whitney. The High Representative, Javier Solana of the CFSP, is chairman of the Steering Board, which acts under the Council's authority and within the framework of guidelines issued by the Council.

In its first years, the Agency has focused on specific 'flagships' in their four areas of activity. On 21 November, the Steering Board decided to take a careful first step towards opening up the European defence equipment market within Europe. A voluntary, non-binding, intergovernmental regime based on a Code of Conduct on Defence Procurement was proposed. The purpose of the code is to inject transparency and competition into defence procurement, an area where a majority of defence contracts are currently exempt from cross-border competition. The new regime covers contracts worth more than one million Euros and took effect from 1 July 2006 (EDA).[14]

Another important decision was reached on 13 October when eleven Member States agreed to work together in an EDA-supported *ad hoc* group to monitor current developments and consider possible new approaches to filling the air-tanking capability gap.[15] Regarding unmanned air vehicles and armoured fighting vehicles, the EDA has primarily focused on identifying 'communities of interest' among participating Member States, with a view to consolidation of demand and joint investment. With regard to command, control, and communication, a number of important strands to pursue has been defined, with proposals now emerging for effective collaboration on Satellite Communications and Software Defined Radio in particular.[16] Also in this case France and Britain were the key actors.[17]

The civilian headline goals for 2008

In December 2004 goals for civilian tools in crisis-management or peace support operations (PSOs) were adopted. These set out a number of ambitions for the development of the ESDP. They include commitment to being able to act in six different areas and reiterate the EU's strategic ambition to 'be able to act before a crisis occurs through preventive activities'. They call for the development of capacities to enable the EU to deploy integrated civilian crisis-management packages, conduct concurrent civilian missions at different levels of engagement, deploy at short notice, work with the military, promote coherence of EU action and a smooth transition from ESDP operations to follow-on long-term EC programmes, and to respond to requests from other international organisations. Currently, the Commission estimates that approximately 13,000 civilian persons are available in the various categories. The process of developing the civilian headline goals is the first attempt to use military methodology to systematically identify which civilian capacities the EU needs to develop in order to be effectively operational as envisaged in the ESS.

Gendarmerie force

In 2004, the initiative of an European Gendarmerie Force (EGF) was launched through an agreement between five members of the European Union which have such forces (France, Italy, Spain, Portugal, and the Netherlands). More countries will be allowed to join in the future. The purpose was the creation of a European intervention force which would have military police (*gendarmerie*) functions, and be specialised in crisis management. The EGF will be based in north-eastern Italy and will have a core of between 800 and 900 members ready to deploy within 30 days. This will include elements from the French Gendarmerie, the Italian Carabinieri, and their equivalents from the other three nations. A pool of 2,300 reinforcements will be on stand-by. The force was proposed by the former French Defence Minister, Alliot-Marie, in September 2003, and the agreement was signed in September 2004 by the defence ministers of the five countries. British police are unarmed, and for this reason Britain cannot participate in such a force.

In sum, the EU has acquired a rapid reaction mechanism and has started to tackle the problem of capacities through the EDA. As the report from the EU Security Institute shows, the way ahead is long and winding. In Europe, there are some 89 national procurement projects in the area of tanks, armoured vehicles, fighter airplanes, and so forth. There are 16 projects to build armoured vehicles and 7 different fighter aircraft, all within a military budget that taken together is smaller than the US defence budget. In comparison, in the United States there are only 29 projects.[18] In addition, in Europe there are now two organisations that undertake to help in military modernisation, the EU and NATO. Thus, on the capacity side, very much still needs to be done. We discuss this further in Chapter 6.

However, if we assume for a moment that the EU will have the necessary military capacity at its disposal, does it have the *political* capacity to act?

Institutional capacity building

The EU has developed capacity in the security and defence field over a few years, both in the Commission and in the Council Secretariat. Through 'learning-by-doing' when exposed to external shocks, a set of policy processes has been set in motion. These processes often overlap, but over time has led to an impressive array of bureaucratic capacities that deal with both civilian and military aspects of crises. There is early warning capacity, humanitarian aid capacity, a pool of police officers (European Gendarmerie Force, led by France), and a pool of other experts (Civilian Response Teams).

The Commission has established a *'Rapid Reaction Mechanism'*, a financial facility that provides for fast financing and payment of civil crisis-management missions and which uses conflict indicators to identify risk factors in each partner country and to systematise the information that already exists within the Commission and its delegations. It performs Country Conflict Assessments for more than 120 countries and keeps an EU 'match-list' of the most critical countries or regions (Boin, Ekengren and Rhinard, 2005, p. 10).

The Commission also has a *Crisis Room* that facilitates initial reaction to a variety of threatening events including terrorism incidents, acts of war, and natural emergencies. It produces open source intelligence by using a web-based information resource system that offers internal capacity for early warning analysis in the security field. In crisis situations, this Crisis Room is the only entry point for information flows between the Commission and the 'situation centre' (SITCEN) in the Council (ibid., pp. 10–11).

The EU has thus developed capacities for both civilian and military crises and for the integration of both elements, inter alia under Civilian Headline Goals 2008 adopted in 2004, while military capacity has been institutionalised through both rapid reaction force (battlegroups), follow-on forces, and institutional capacity such as the PSC (Political and Security Committee), the EUMC, and the EUMS.

Planning Cell instead of headquarter

There is also a 'Civil-Military Cell' in the EUMS. This was a compromise and created following a proposal by Britain, France, and Germany. The tasks, functions, and organisation of the Civil-Military Cell were approved by the Council on 13 December, 2004 and by the European Council 16–17 December, 2004. The Civil-Military Cell contains civilian elements. It is responsible for building capacity to plan and implement independent EU military operations, and for maintaining the capacity (within EUMS) to rapid establishment of an operations centre for a given operation, especially when there is the need for a common civil–military effort, and when a national headquarters is not chosen. The Cell falls far short of a military headquarter (HQ), which was the French wish. The strong opposition from Britain led to this Cell as a compromise.

The Cell has four main functions. First, it can provide an autonomous planning capacity for ESDP operations that do not make use of Berlin Plus arrangements with NATO. Second, it is to function as a kind of think-tank and strategic planning cell, to conduct advance planning, and to assist in crisis-response planning in support of both DG VIII on defence aspects, and DG IX on civilian crisis management. Strategic planning on a specific topic is initiated upon request by the High Representative/Secretary-General or the PSC. The Civil-Military Cell was not given a remit to produce any concepts at its own initiative, as the Member States want to retain control over its activities (Hansen, 2006). Third, the Cell can function as an operations centre when an operation is ongoing. Finally, it can take the lead in civil–military coordination. There has been some confusion whether the Cell is only to be used for military operations and for civil purposes in addition. In Aceh and Sudan, it was used for missions which were both civil and military operations. While a military component is not a prerequisite for activating the Cell, civil-civil missions are not the primary target for the Cell (ibid.).

The Cell totals approximately 25 staff members, which is about the same as the mission support and planning capacity that is handling all ongoing operations. The Member States have high expectations of the Cell – the importance of the civil–military interface is particularly being promoted by Britain – and expect the Cell to be involved in a wide range of planning processes. The Civil-Military Cell will work in close cooperation with the existing national joint headquarters.

In relation to the Commission, the Cell can potentially take on the role that the Crisis Response Coordination Team was intended to play in those cases where the Cell engages in specific operational planning. Two out of approximately 20 staff members in the Cell are from the Commission. The Cell is one of the few permanent bodies in which both the Council and the Commission are represented. The Commission is, of course, represented in the PSC, but that is at a strategic rather than an operational level.

Outside the EU institutions, initiatives are taken to cooperate on defence issues. In November 2005, a Spanish–French Defence Council was established. The council, consisting of the French president and the Spanish prime minister, with the participation of foreign and defence ministers, will meet annually. France has similar arrangements with Germany and Britain.

The EUMC consists of the chiefs of defence of Member States, and the EUMS of seconded officers that undertake politico-strategic planning. Along with the Cell, they are in the same building as the other military bodies, a separate and secure building called the Kortenberg. *There is thus an embryonic military HQ at the EU, but the calls for a real HQ, introduced by France, have been met by resistance from Britain.* The compromise has been the small 'planning cell', and as the number of officers in the EUMS is only about 200, it is clear that the EU cannot plan and execute a military operation. In order to do this it has to rely on a national HQ provided by a Member State or by NATO. After much foot-dragging, an agreement between NATO and the EU was signed in 2006. This agreement allows the EU to use Supreme Headquarters Allied Powers Europe (SHAPE) (the NATO military command in Mons) as the command and control centre for its operations. To date, two EU operations have relied on SHAPE and two on national HQs.

EU operations

The EU missions so far include the following: the EUPM (European Union Police Mission) in Bosnia, which is to be continued for another two years comprising 500 police staff. There is also now the EUFOR ALTHEA in Bosnia, a military force of 7,000 which replaced SFOR, NATO's force from the Dayton agreement in 1995. In Macedonia, there was operation *Concordia* with 400 military personnel, using NATO assets and Berlin Plus arrangements. The sharp operation *Artemis* took place in the Bunia province in DR Congo from June to September 2003 and consisted of 1,300 military personnel. Then there is a police operation, EUPOL Proxima, which is a follow-on mission for Concordia, consisting of 200 police officers. It is still ongoing.

EUJUST THEMIS in far-away Georgia is a rule of law mission with ten lawyers, which commenced in 2004 and is ongoing. It makes use of NATO assets under the Berlin Plus agreement. Another police mission was EUPOL in Kinshasa, DR Congo, in 2005, which consisted of 30 police staff. There was also the EUJUST LEX for Iraq, made up of training courses held in EU Member States in 2005 and 2006 as well as the EUSEC DR Congo, a military mission to reform armed forces which started in 2005 and to end in 2008. Further, there is the EU Support AMIS II in Darfur, consisting of both military and police support elements, from 2005 to the present, and the AMM (Aceh Monitoring Mission) which has demobilisation tasks and consists of 230 personnel, mainly officers. From 2005 to 2006 the EU launched COPPS (EUPOL Coordination Office for Palestinian Police Support) in the Palestine, and the EU BAM RAFAH, EU Border Assistance Mission Rafah which has 70 police and military personnel.

A mission recently launched is the EUFOR Tchad/RCA adopted by the Council on 15 October 2007 and which is planning to deploy 4,000 troops for one year. This mission has been surrounded by uncertainty as there was an attempted coup against President Idriss Deby in February 2008. The French troops already in the country helped avert this event, which was organised by rebels aided by Khartoum. The EU mission has been delayed because of this, and fears of a 'French interest' in the latter have been voiced.[19]

Then there was the EUPT Kosovo/ESDP Mission Kosovo, 2006–7, mandated to ensure a smooth transition of authority from UNMIK to the Kosovo authorities; a EUSR Border support Team in Georgia from 2007 to 2008; another EU Border Assistance Mission (EUBAM) to Moldova/Ukraine from 2005 until 2009 where the personnel counted more than 200; an EU support team for the African Union Mission in Somalia (AMISOM) from 2007 to the present, comprising financial and military support. Further, the EU Police Mission (EUPOL) to Afghanistan, 2007 to present (with a duration of at least three years) where personnel amounts to 195, including police, law enforcement, and justice experts. In 2008, the EU sent a 'law-and-order' mission of approximately 2,000 police and law enforcement officers to the newly created state of Kosovo.

Of these operations not all are military, and not all military operations imply war-fighting or the risk of such. *Artemis* is the only EU mission that is of this nature. Yet as we see, the EU deploys in risky places, mostly in Africa and in the Balkans. It is also important that the pace of EU deployments has been very brisk: all this activity has happened in the span of less than ten years.

In conclusion, it is clear that political capacities are being developed in the EU for all aspects of crisis management. The Commission commands a wide variety of political and civilian tools, and there is a set of plans and policies for EU crisis management. There is also a growing portfolio of experience in the field through current and past missions. Decisions about deployment, which means where and under which circumstances to participate, are, however, beyond these fora in the EU and which take their point of departure in already-determined participation. The EU today can offer a template of tools and capacities for crisis-management missions. The decision on the use of EU capacities remains intergovernmental, but as we shall see later in this book, this is often simply a formal procedure.

So far we have seen that the EU is able to conduct smaller military missions and has a certain capacity for so doing. We have also seen that there is a process of military modernisation in the EU. How does this compare to the situation in NATO, and what is the relationship between these organisations?

NATO's role

The new missions NATO takes on require forces that can reach further and faster and can stay in the field longer than what was needed previously. NATO has devised a detailed programme of political and military transformation. The November 2002 summit in Prague was presented as NATO's 'transformation summit' (Cornish, 2005, p. 64). Three key military transformation initiatives were launched, all essential in adapting NATO's military capabilities.

The first initiative is the *Prague Capabilities Commitment* (PCC) which intends to replace the complex and largely ineffectual Defence Capabilities initiative of 1999. The member countries had undertaken a commitment to improve capabilities in more than four hundred areas covering chemical, biological, radiological, and nuclear defence; intelligence, surveillance, and target acquisition; air-to-ground surveillance; command, control, and communications; combat effectiveness, including precision-guided munitions and suppression of enemy air defences; strategic air and sea lift; air-to-air refuelling and deployable combat support, and combat service support units.

The second initiative concerns the NATO *Response Force* (NRF), which is a permanently available multinational joint force at very high state of readiness, consisting of land, air, and sea components and various specialist functions. At the NATO summit in Riga in November 2006, the NRF was declared to be at full operational capability with up to 25,000 troops. The force is able to start to deploy after five days' notice and sustain itself for operations lasting 30 days or longer if re-supplied. It is capable of performing missions worldwide across the whole spectrum of operations including evacuations, disaster management, counterterrorism, and acting as 'an initial entry force' for larger forces to follow. The force is the driving engine of the military transformation of NATO. The NRF can be given authorisation on a case-by-case basis by the North Atlantic Council (NAC), and will be the result of a consensual decision which is usually the case for NATO decisions.

The third initiative regards the *military command structure*. The restructuring is based on the agreed minimum military requirements document for the Alliance's command arrangements. The result is a significant reduction in headquarters and Combined Air Operations Centres. This radical simplification of the Alliance's vast headquarters structure is part of a move away from an organisation still geared essentially to territorial defence to one designed to carry out expeditionary operations by 'joint' forces. The number of high-level headquarters (strategic and operational) is being reduced from 20 to 12, with the Alliance's Atlantic Command, based in Norfolk, Virginia, becoming Allied Command Transformation, designed to be the 'forcing agent' for the re-invention of the Alliance (ibid., pp. 64–5).

The Prague summit also adopted a Military Concept for Defence against Terrorism and initiated a new Missile Defence Feasibility Study. 'The alliance has also discussed the broadening of its functional remit to include counterterrorism, counter-proliferation of weapons of mass destruction and expeditionary combat operations. There have been suggestions that NATO should branch out into "soft power" activities such as post-conflict nation-building' (ibid., p. 64).

Relations between NATO and the EU

'NATO and the European Union are working together to prevent and resolve crises and armed conflicts in Europe and beyond .... They share common strategic interests and cooperate in a spirit of complementarity and partnership' according to the official version of this difficult relationship.[20] The decision to cooperate on security issues goes back to 24 January 2001, when the NATO Secretary-General and the EU Presidency exchanged letters defining the scope of cooperation and the modalities of consultation between the two organisations. Cooperation accelerated with the signing of the landmark 'NATO–EU Declaration on ESDP' which paved the way for the 'Berlin Plus' arrangements. The Berlin Plus arrangements were agreed between NATO and the EU in March 2003, and is a short title for a comprehensive package of agreements. The arrangements cover three main elements that are directly connected to operations and which can be combined: EU access to NATO planning, NATO European command options, and use of NATO assets and capabilities. It grants EU access to NATO equipment and planning assets and promises to yield the long-awaited settlement of the complex debate about Europe's security institutions (ibid., p. 64). The '"Berlin Plus" package has been in effect since 17 March 2003, and serves as the foundation for practical work between the EU and NATO ... These possibilities were used for the first time in March 2003 when NATO's Operation Allied Harmony in Macedonia was taken over by the EU and renamed Operation Concordia' (ibid., p. 74). Berlin Plus also provided the framework when EU took over NATO's military operation in Bosnia (SFOR) in 2004.

Cooperation between NATO and the EU also takes place with regard to capability development. Concerted planning of capabilities development and mutual reinforcement between NATO's PCC and the EU European Capabilities Action Plan (ECAP) have also become part of the NATO–EU agenda. These issues are being addressed in the NATO–EU Capability Group established in May 2003.

Several arenas exist for cooperation between the organisations. 'NATO and EU officials meet on a regular basis at different levels at foreign ministers' level twice a year; at ambassadors' level (the North Atlantic Council with the EU's PSC) a minimum of three times per semester; at the level of the Military Committee twice every semester;

at the committee level on a regular basis; and at staff level on a routine basis. The establishment of permanent military liaison arrangements is being considered to facilitate cooperation at the operational level. Proposals include establishing an EU cell at SHAPE (NATO's strategic command for operations in Mons, Belgium), and NATO liaison arrangements at the EU Military Staff'.

EU and NATO foreign ministers have reaffirmed their willingness to develop closer cooperation to combat terrorism and the proliferation of weapons of mass destruction. The institutions have already exchanged information on their activities in the field of protection of civilian populations against chemical, biological, radiological, and nuclear attacks. NATO and the EU also consult on other issues of common interest such as the situation in Moldova and Afghanistan. But it is nonetheless true that cooperation is severely hindered by a diplomatic problem. Turkey is a member of NATO but not of the EU, and Cyprus is a member of the EU but not of NATO. The lack of diplomatic recognition of Cyprus on the part of Turkey stops EU–NATO collaboration on all aspects of security and defence apart from ongoing operations where the EU uses SHAPE. This is a considerable problem that comes in addition to sensitivities stemming from uncertainty about which role the EU will play in this field. Unfortunately the contact between NATO and the EU remains quite poor, and there is clearly duplication in rapid reaction forces. But the EU has developed institutional capacity for more efficient procurement in the defence agency, EDA, and trumps NATO in terms of civilian capacities. As long duration with several state-building capacities is essential to the success of missions, the EU has great potential as an important actor.

How are decisions made in the EU?

In sum, the EU has developed a number of military capacities and gained experience through several operations. Crisis management spans all military as well as civilian capacities, and the EU is now able to deploy both rapidly and for a longer period of time. However, it is clear that it depends heavily on NATO or larger Member States for headquarters (HQ), and that it is not comparable to NATO in terms of military capacity. The EU undertakes follow-on missions rather than the sharper end of military intervention, and cannot plan military missions beyond the very general level of the political strategy. The only sharp mission to date is Operation *Artemis* which was led and largely executed by France.

The EU has developed its security policy role over the last ten years, and at a brisk pace. The capacities for planning and commanding operations is minuscule compared to NATO, but the EU nonetheless has a rudimentary planning capacity at the polico-strategic level in the military staff of about 200 officers. It also has a growing experience in running operations, and commands a host of civilian tools that NATO lacks. These tools are of increasing relevance in modern wars that concern stabilisation and democratisation as the main security strategy.

Decision-making for using force – *ad bellum* – is potentially also a matter for the EU, although as such, the EU has never made a decision on its own. It has always acted on UN mandates. However, in the ESS, which is the EU strategic plan, there is no explicit condition for such a mandate. In a given situation, the EU can decide to use force autonomously, as NATO did in the Kosovo case. The EU has launched four peacekeeping and peace-enforcement operations, two using the command and control assets of NATO ('Berlin Plus'), two using national HQs. All of these have had UN mandates. Regarding *in bello* decision-making, the EU has an intergovernmental decision-making structure in security and defence policy which is limited to robust peace enforcement. However, in practice the system is one of differentiated integration whereby some lead states decide on deployment after a formal request from the UN. Such a request is only forthcoming when there is a real will to respond favourably, as we will see in the case of Operation *Artemis* in the Bunia province of DR Congo. Thus, the real decision-making on *in bello* is made by the contributing states.

The formal decision-making procedure proposed in the text of the constitutional treaty which later changed its name to the Lisbon Treaty, is named 'permanent structured cooperation' (Art. III 213) which allows for 'avant-garde' groups in this area, to be discussed in detail in Chapter 4. It should be noted that the EU battlegroups were adopted under this rule, initially by France and Britain, and with the inclusion of Germany as the third state when the modalities were already decided by these two states. This is important to note because the possibility of avant-gardism can be the result of an agreement between only two states to go forward. It is then up to the others to associate themselves with these proposals, and although the possibility of the veto exists under the formal intergovernmental scheme, it is rarely if ever used. This is in line with the general foreign policy logic of the EU whereby some states suggest policy, and those that resist, usually abstain.

Collective decision-making remains subject to the national veto, but at the same time there is a preference for constructive abstention in which governments do nothing to undermine a collective policy if it is agreed by a majority of EU states (Forster, 2006, p. 141). However, there is no strategic consensus among EU states on which missions to undertake or how to develop in the security and defence area. Whereas France and Britain are able to conduct coercive diplomacy with global power projection, smaller and medium-sized states prefer non-military EU foreign policy, particularly the formerly neutral states. This concern revolves around the risk of being involved in war-fighting at the high end of the spectrum, and when the battlegroups were agreed in 2004, the possibility of an opt-out for states was important in reaching an agreement. The question is whether the possibility of avant-gardism will be impeded by these states or not. The French model of an independent EU security policy is pitted against the British model of NATO–EU complementarity, as we will analyse in Chapter 4. However, the willingness on the part of other EU states to develop coercive diplomacy is dubious. This means that in the areas where there may be British–French agreement to launch a mission, the support of the remaining Member States is not automatic.

With the deployment of the new EU battlegroups, the decision-making will be more critical, as these groups are in a formal system of rotation and involve military contributions from many EU states. For the EU Member States, it will no longer be a question of accepting a British or French operation with high risk (the concept of the battlegroup is rapid intervention in an ongoing crisis), but of deploying one's own forces. We can safely assume that the EU Member States contributing to the battlegroups in rotation will take a close interest in their deployment. Research on the relationship between political vulnerability and own casualties shows that vulnerability increases inversely with the political interest in the mission: *the less existential the threat, the more vulnerable a government becomes* (Arreguin-Toft, 2005). This is not unexpected, and provides a good prediction about EU missions, which are all non-existential in character. They will tend to be deployed for less dangerous operations. This also fits with the traditional main thrust of EU foreign policy which is 'civilian' (Duchene, 1972). The admonition that the EU must be willing to engage in coercive diplomacy when moving beyond its borders (Cooper, 2004) is factually right, but not likely to play the role it ought to.

Among the Nordic states in the EU, Sweden has been an eager participant in EU missions. Denmark has a national caveat which prohibits such participation due to the national compromise over the Treaty of Political Union dating from 1993, and Finland has few forces for international deployment. The case of Sweden illustrates the strategic possibility for a medium-sized state in gaining international power and standing in this issue – area. It volunteered to play an active role in EU security policy from the very beginning of its membership in the organisation using the logic that participation equals influence. Moreover, one wanted to show that Sweden not only took an interest in Northern Europe where it is likely to have national interests, but also in areas that are important to the EU as a whole. To be a 'constructive EU citizen' is extremely important within an organisation that calls itself 'a union' and which relies on a high degree of commonality. To pursue one's own national interests too often and too openly is scorned upon in this political culture. Instead, the key to legitimacy and trust is to be in the 'inner core' of the EU, and the way to such status is through general commitment to EU goals. Based on this logic, Sweden and Finland have both consistently pursued policies aimed at landing them in this 'inner core', with Finland picking some areas where they excel in common expertise and problem-solving ability, such as Russian affairs. For its part, Sweden is active in the Euromed-strategy and peace enforcement in Africa, such as in the D R Congo in 2003 and 2006. This is both geographically and functionally far beyond the traditional area of Swedish national interests (Eriksson, 2006).

Both Finnish and Swedish elites have worked hard to ensure that something akin to an 'Article 5' does not develop in the EU. This would make them into 'second class' – members in the organisation because they are (still) formally neutral states. On the definition of the security policy of the EU, these two states therefore made a major, common effort (Bailes, 2007, p. 12) .They also both sought to redefine 'neutrality' through making it compatible with all EU security policy. The impact of the EU on domestic Swedish and Finnish security policy is very well documented in recent scholarship (Eriksson, 2006; Rieker, 2006). As for Norway, it remains wholly on the outside of *ad bellum* decisions in the EU, but has ensured that Sweden will keep it informed of all details on this with a gloss of decision-making power, as Sweden will consult with Norway on all aspects of battlegroup decision-making in the EU and ensure that also Norway agrees to decisions about deployment (Andersson, 2006). However, the Norwegian say in the matter is bound to be illusory as one 'defection' from an actual deployment means that Norway will not be trusted in the future. Credibility is a major asset in defence policy.

However, when we look at the impact of EU policy on defence modernisation, there is little evidence of any influence from EU institutions themselves, apart from the recent policy proposals from the EDA on R&D, procurement, and common projects. The potential of the EDA to direct military integration is a major one, but it is too early to tell whether states will opt for pooling in this field. So far, the EDA meets considerable British scepticism about common projects[21] and there seems to be a fear that it is designed on a French model of supranational EU security policy.

The ESDP has come a long way in a short time, but suffers from two weaknesses: one is a lack of military capacity; the other is the precariousness of using military force in post-national societies like the European. The first problem is rooted in the dramatic lack of relevant military capacity in Europe. Only some few states can provide modern, interoperable intervention forces and HQs. Shrinking defence budgets imply that pooling capacities is increasingly important. Yet the EU and NATO 'compete' in this field. They both have newly re-established rapid reaction forces but are unable to field much beyond these. In fact, the NATO RRF has been put 'on hold' until the ISAF mission in Afghanistan is over due to lack of capacity. The shortage of such for ISAF is a well-known fact. Thus, NATO and the EU face the same problems of too few military input factors to meet the demand from the missions undertaken by these organisations. If we add the demand from UN missions, the problem of shortage is even clearer: out of about 100,000 soldiers deployed as blue helmets, only some 7,000 come from Western states. The many UN missions in Africa are beset with the same capability difficulty as the EU and NATO: a shortage of airlift, sealift, intelligence and reconnaissance ability (ISTAR), unmanned aerial vehicles (UAVs), interoperable communications, battle and transport helicopters, and so forth.

The other problem the EU faces is that of political will. This is what we can term the problem of legitimacy. Under which circumstances can military force be used? Throughout the cold war period this problem was seldom discussed as the UN played no role in questions of war and peace. In the decade after the end of the cold war, from 1990 to 2001, the issue was defined as one of humanitarian intervention. The UNSC played the key role, and European states equated legitimacy with legality in the form of a UN mandate. After the attacks on the Twin Towers all this changed. No one talked about humanitarian intervention, but about combating terrorism with all available means – as in the US 'war on terror' or in the form of 'doing good' in terms of state-building as in the case of Europe. ISAF in Afghanistan is the best example of the difference in political frameworks needed for the United States and Europe respectively. The Europeans could not achieve political support for their use of military support in Afghanistan if this was presented as war on terrorists. The state-building and humanitarian framework was needed for public opinion to condone the mission. The UN mandate for ISAF was undoubtedly the most important part of this, but the fact that a multilateral organisation undertook the mission played a key role as well. Multilateralism provides legitimacy.

But *ad bellum* legitimacy is only the start. A mission cannot be sustained without continuous support from the public. Here we enter a delicate new 'problem' for the post-national society in Europe. Publics will be engaged in modern wars in a normalised political mood, not in a traditional political manner where unity against an outer enemy is called for. On the contrary, European publics will disagree as much over the deployment of military force somewhere as they will disagree over taxes or any other policy area. This in turn means that own losses, cost, and setbacks in the mission may lead to rapid withdrawals, or at least major criticism of governments. As argued at the outset of this book, the political dynamics of modern post-national wars are very difficult to manage for any government. True, the stronger the FPP (foreign policy prerogative), the more insulated the government is from domestic pressures. But wars have a tendency to effect heavy political blows on any government when going badly as they concern the drama of life and death. Even the British government, traditionally left alone to pursue expeditionary warfare anywhere in the world, has felt the impact of the Iraq war very heavily as the fighting gave scant results. PM Blair was a very popular politician on account of his foreign policy, but lost greatly over the Iraq war participation.

Thus, in Europe's post-national security policy we face a double challenge: military capacity and political will. The first is a *sine qua non* for the second, but the second is the most difficult issue. The new role that publics play in 'normalised' security policy is what poses the problem for governments that want to participate in modern wars. How can they satisfy a divided public that is risk-averse because the wars fought are not existential? How can they persist for years in conflicts that cannot bring results quickly enough to win the next election? And how can governments justify the losses of their own nationals in such wars?

The constraints that these political dynamics place upon governments are formidable. Governments have to participate in order to act on security threats that are real, such as terrorism in the form of the Taliban, for example, and in order to keep the United States interested in maintaining NATO. But such arguments do no fly well with post-national European publics who by now are quite foreign to the concept of war. Instead, they need a cause to fight for that is ethically 'good' in a humanitarian sense, and they expect that there will not be many, if any, losses. Governments realise that they must be in a mission for a long time, as foreign policy goals are long term. But publics are not used to dealing with foreign and security policy. Yet, in the 'normalised' security policy situation of today they have become the main actors. Governments have no other choice than to 'insulate' themselves as much as possible from the impact of their publics. They do so by playing two-level games.

The issue of creating political will enough to sustain expeditionary warfare is therefore very important. Through multilateralism in security policy, European governments are able to solve their two problems of military capacity and political legitimacy. Through a pooling of sovereignty they can manage to deploy in several operations at the same time, and through playing two-level games they can manage to sustain the missions politically. When pressures to withdraw mount at home they can argue that this would undermine NATO or the EU if they withdrew, or at least undermine their own state's standing in these organisations. When there are own losses and/or new costs, they can point to the losses incurred by other states and call for solidarity. The claims governments make are often true and real. The point here is simply that the political dynamics of two-level games are very useful for governments in post-national societies that need to be at war.

Thus, we can expect the EU to serve national governments much in the same manner as NATO and the UN in security policy – as arenas for political collusion and capacity 'pooling'. Again, it should be underlined that there is nothing ethically negative implied in this concept. There are, after all, some good reasons why security and defence policy ought to remain a prerogative of governments. Only they can take the responsibility of losses and plan for the long term. The essence of statesmanship is leadership. Yet today, governments and their PMs rarely seem able to call for sacrifices from their publics. This has a lot to do with the remoteness of war in Europe today – 60 years after the Second World War – but in terms that are more concrete, it is a consequence of the political dynamics of post-national politics.

3
EU Security Dynamics: The New National Interests

What can we assume about the EU's future role in security and defence policy? Not much. The scenarios seem wide open and undetermined. One predicts that the EU will become the key actor in European security because the modern use of military power is one of integrated peace-building and democratisation. Hence the military tool is simply becoming integrated with the EU's other tools. The optimist is often a European who favours soft power on principle, and who admits to military power only as a benign addition to other, nicer tools of statecraft. He or she will often have a rather teleological view of the EU as an alternative to the crass realism of US foreign policy, and will, as William Wallace remarks, be convinced of the moral superiority of the EU (Wallace, 2005).

Another scenario is the unreflected realist one. Here states are states and remain states; they are vested with static national interests in security policy, and will never yield an inch to integration of their sacred sovereignty. This view is equally normative and unappealing in intellectual terms. Here the United States is seen to play states against each other in a *divide et impera* strategy, and the EU remains wimpish. From Robert Kagan to European realists, proponents of this view hold that security policy is far too important to be left to the EU. But they cannot explain why the EU in fact undertakes fighting and develops battlegroups as well as a European Defence Agency (EDA); nor why the EU security policy has speeded up developments since the St. Malo declaration in 1998 between those two most unlikely states, Britain and France.

These two unsatisfactory scenarios are reflections of a larger and equally unsatisfactory state of affairs in EU integration research itself. For too long the study of the EU has been marked by normative assumptions and a hope of integration or the opposite on the part of researchers in international politics. From the time of neo-functionalism until the *revanche* of realism undertaken by Stanley Hoffmann (1972) and beyond. The academic study of the EU has had to contend with much normative hopefulness one way or the other. One should therefore be forewarned about the difficulty of finding sober and objective analyses of integration.

However, present-day analysts situate the EU firmly in the context of international politics and theory. But with regard to security and defence policy, there seems to be a tendency of either underestimating or overestimating the role of the EU. Given this, what can we reasonably assume at the outset, and what can we expect?

In this book we argue that the main dynamic in the ESDP is a bilateral one, with an addition of *directoire* elements in the form of German inclusion in the process of decision-making. As we shall see, all the major decisions of the ESDP were taken by the French–British duo in bilateral cooperation.

First, although the EU is a multi-level system of governance, it is the states that determine EU security policy, especially in its military aspects. Among the states it is France and Britain that are the key actors. They make sure to include Germany in order to ensure support from the third major state. When we look for clues to further developments of the EU in this field, we should first and foremost concentrate *on these two states*.

Second, we should pay attention to the reality of differentiated integration. Although the new text on 'permanent structured cooperation' in the Constitutional Treaty was in political limbo for a long time, it is a fact that this paragraph was agreed following much work to get Britain on board, and also that it was retrained in the revised Lisbon treaty. It only applies to practical military cooperation, but is clearly the way out of the intergovernmental mode of decision-making that otherwise governs the EU in Pillar Two. As we will see, it was used as the basis for the decision-making on the battlegroups, and it can be used again, notwithstanding the status of the treaty. If France and Britain, possibly plus other states, decide to intensify military cooperation, they are free to suggest concrete proposals. It is clear that only some few states in the EU are capable militarily and take an interest in this field, and that many will remain outside such cooperation. There is no alternative to some kind of 'reinforced cooperation' or *'coalitions of the willing and able' inside the EU*.

Further, there is no action for crisis management without capacities, both military, political, and bureaucratic. The EU has built up much capacity, both military and political, over the last few years. This involves civil–military cooperation as well as planning, but no HQ. For the latter, it relies on national HQs or NATO. The history of the EU has shown time and again that capacities that are built up – in the budget and routinised in the policy process – create their own agenda and their own tasks. With regard to launching an operation, initial intervention forces, and/or follow-on forces and civilian elements, only actors with relevant capacity come into question. *The EU's capacity building is therefore a necessary, but not sufficient, basis for becoming a strategic actor in security policy.* In this process it positions itself to be the preferred organisation for crisis management in the future because it has all the relevant tools in the 'toolbox'.

The future of the EU in security policy will also depend on the role of NATO. NATO as well as the EU suffers from a 'political deficit' these days: neither organisation is highly preferred as *the* security organisation for Europe. In NATO, France and some other states prefer the EU to rise to this occasion, and they deal with NATO accordingly. In the EU, the British are first among those that hold a 'NATO first' policy and make sure that EU integration does not go too far or assume too autonomous a role. Thus, to predict the future of the EU in security policy requires us to make predictions about the role of NATO as well.

Finally, two other factors are pertinent in a realistic prediction. The first is the driving force constituted by *military integration* in Europe. This factor is only now becoming visible, but it will grow in importance. The EDA may come to play a key role here as states are forced to realise that they need some kind of top-down direction for military research, procurement, training, maintenance, and operations. So far we see many bi and multilateral cooperation schemes, but little is truly supranational. The need for a rational, functional direction of the military integration process is however now becoming clearer, and this could take place in either the EU or in NATO, through the transformation command. I predict that the economic necessities of rational integration will become a strong driver for EU security policy simply because the EU is a mature political system that commands a number of civilian elements that will also become more central to peace support operations. In NATO, the transatlantic differences are quite big, and are not likely to go away any time soon.

The other important factor is that despite drivers of military integration, capacity building, and civil–military integration. The EU *is not likely to become a strategic actor.* This is despite the fact that governments will have incentives to integrate on the logic of two-level games – 'the EU made me do it' – to hedge against overly activist and 'difficult' publics. Yet there remains a major obstacle to the EU as a strategic actor, which means a unitary actor capable of coercive diplomacy – of threatening the use of force and of actually using military force as a political tool. The EU is not likely to become a unitary actor in security policy – it is not now a unitary actor in sensitive foreign policy areas, and security is the most sensitive of all. Further, the 'strategic culture' of Europe is such that a 'warrior ethic' is almost non-existent. It still exists in the major military traditions in France and the United Kingdom, but nowhere else. As we shall see, the use of force in Europe is likely to remain concentrated on crisis management *after the fact of the crisis*.

In the following pages I substantiate the various arguments introduced so far. I started with an analysis of the paradigm shift in security policy in Europe which implies that European governments do not *have to* fight wars anymore. They have a degree of freedom in whether to develop and deploy the military tool, and in choosing where to deploy it. This means that legitimacy has become much more important than before, when wars were not optional. Further, the limited use of force in most PSOs means that we do not speak about high-intensity warfare most of the time. The military tool has become 'normalised'. This means that it is on the one hand, easier to justify to publics, yet on the other hand, more difficult to justify because it is no longer about existential survival.

The consequences of the paradigm shift are new parameters for security policy and the use of force in Europe. As stated, this book argues that the main driving force for EU security policy are great powers and their old, but particularly, their *new* type of national interests. The 'old' national interests centre on power balance and great power status: both Britain and France maintain a national security policy in their nuclear power status and in retaining their national veto in the United Nations Security Council (UNSC). Britain puts major emphasis on its relationship with the United States, the so-called special relationship. They are thus not abandoning their national security and defence policy in pursuit of an EU-level one.

The security policy of the EU is not a substitute for national defence policy. Britain has recently decided to renew its Trident nuclear missile capacity and France retains its *force de frappe*, while both states refuse any discussion of their veto power as P-5 states in the UNSC. EU security policy is therefore an addition for these states as well as for most others that are NATO members and which therefore enjoy a collective defence guarantee.

But this does not mean that EU security policy is weak or unimportant. It serves useful purposes in crisis-response situations but is also a vehicle for shaping the international security and defence architecture. Both France and Britain seek to shape the ESDP in ways that benefit their grand political strategy. France seeks an *'Europe puissance'* that will have real military power and which therefore can balance the United States and undertake autonomous military missions whereas Britain seeks an ESDP that will complement NATO and let NATO take military precedence. Since around 1995, both these states have been particularly active in developing policy in a practical sense. The invention of 'permanent structured cooperation' allows two or more states to take practical measures in military capacity building. France and Britain have developed the battlegroups, the European Defence Agency, and been partners in robust crisis response in DR Congo under this paragraph. Germany has usually been invited to join these proposals, and also other states have done so. There is clear evidence of a 'core logic' in the EU in this policy field.

Thus, at the outset we have an ESDP that is driven by the major European military powers and which serves their political interests. There is nothing wrong in this from an ethical perspective; great powers are after all the traditional actors in international politics. It is clear that the actual military and civilian contributions to an operation depend very much on some few states: regarding military contributions, very much on the great powers mentioned. No small or medium-sized EU state can field a military HQ, to mention an important fact. Only France and Britain have military reach in a truly global manner. Thus, the ESDP, however defined in political rhetoric and political documents, is dependent on specific input factors that are mostly owned by the great powers.

The EU and NATO are both multilateral organisations which undertake crisis operations, but the EU's security policy does not entail high-intensity war-fighting. It is limited to stabilisation and reconstruction, and there exists a tacit division of labour between the two organisations. Only NATO can undertake warfare; only the EU can undertake missions that require all the tools of statecraft: economic, political, and military. The EU is in the process of adding the military tool as a complement to the rest of its toolbox, but this is not intended to be a full-scale military set of instruments.

EU and NATO capabilities meet in the battlegroups and their intended use. There is an overlap in the EU and NATO capabilities in respect of the battlegroups to the extent they are in competition. The question is whether NATO and the EU will complement or compete with each other in stabilisation and reconstruction missions. This is a question of national interests and not one that is determined by institutional dynamics, I argue in this book. The security dynamics of both the EU and NATO – and of the UN for that matter – are driven by states and their interests. This is hardly news. However, the novelty consists of the *new* type of national interests in the field of security in Europe.

The *new* national interests in security policy

There is a clear shift in both French and British security policy in the mid-1990s towards multinational participation. The argument here is that even great powers now need to pursue their security policy in a multilateral setting where they share risk, cost, blame, and incur legitimacy. The EU and NATO are the two Western arenas in this policy field.

Small and weak states need multilateral organisations much more than great powers. This is a truism. The small state is not militarily able to do anything alone, even more so as defence budgets decrease. Military integration, or at least military cooperation, is the only way out of this. But France and Britain are not in this category. Integration needs cannot therefore explain the shift in their security policy as it can in the case of smaller states.

However, the argument we explore here is that these states need the multilateral arena – in this study the EU – in order to influence the security architecture of the transatlantic relationship. This is what we term 'the great power game'. NATO's future role depends on how the EU will develop, and vice versa. The long-standing French strategy is to develop an autonomous European military capacity, and this is now pursued in the EU. The adverse model of Britain is to ensure that the EU is a complement to NATO, not its rival. But Britain and France share the interest in developing more capable military forces in Europe.

In addition to the 'great game', states play 'small games' in multilateral settings in accordance with their domestic policy needs and ability to influence at home. They use the international organisation in question as a scapegoat at home when things go wrong, arguing that their hands are tied and that they therefore must be accommodated when they are at the international level, and they can hide behind the international organisation's multilateral decision-making process when they are criticised by other states or domestic actors. Since government elites usually enjoy gate-keeping privileges between these two levels – as there are few journalists and NGOs that have access to the inner workings of policy at the international level – they can maximise their power through shifting agendas in domestic struggles and escape accountability and criticism both at home and in the international organisation.

As mentioned in the introduction, Robert Putnam (1988) has devised a rational choice-model of 'win-sets' for negotiations between domestic and international settings which will be drawn upon in this study. More precisely, we argue that all states – also the great powers – have some new security interests after the cold war. These include – mainly in a multilateral setting – the need to acquire legitimacy for the use of force, the need to share blame and risk, and the need to share cost.

These 'new' national interests in security policy are not equally distributed across the states studied here. For France, domestic public opinion plays little role with regard to troop deployments or the fatalities, and the president still enjoys the traditional foreign policy privilege (FPP). In the case of Britain, this has traditionally also obtained, and still does formally, but with participation in the Iraq war the public has become much more seized on security matters, and much opposition to the war has developed. We observe that security policy is becoming increasingly politicised, and a major debate erupted over the mandate of British troops in Afghanistan.

This study has a third state – Germany. France and Britain are the dominant actors in EU security policy, but they need German support in order to succeed. In the German case there is also a national interest in playing the 'great power' game, and this lies between the French and British positions. But there is much more of an interest in the 'small powers' game: German security policy is in many ways a function of EU and NATO security policy. In order to deploy abroad, German government elites need major international backing in order to ensure legitimacy, and the strong pasificist elements of domestic policy can only be met by arguing that Germany must honour international commitments. As we shall see, German interests are centred on acquiring legitimacy, sharing risk, and sharing blame.

Thus, the three great powers in Europe – the leading actors of the EU and the leading security actors on the continent – all seem to have various national interests in developing an EU security and defence policy. These interests are traditional in the 'great game', and 'new' in the 'smaller game'. What does this imply for the concept of national interest? What does it imply for the EU – is it but an arena for national interest promotion?

Domestic support for an EU security and defence policy is strong in all Member States as reflected in Euro barometer polls. Between 1992 and 2005, support was consistently at 70 per cent, and when broken down, there is about the same level of support for all aspects of such a policy, including military peace enforcement. New Member States show the same level of support as do old. When data is broken down according to country, we find that Britain and the Nordic states are the most sceptical, with Germany and Spain the most supportive. Ekman finds that populations in pro-EU states are supportive of ESDP, which is not surprising. On the overall level, domestic audiences therefore support the development of the ESDP. But there are differences between publics that impinge on how governments may play their two-level games: an EU-friendly public may make matters much easier for its government. There are two variables that are central to the freedom of action that a government enjoys in this field: its decision-making capacity in security policy *and the general* standing of its EU policy in the public.

The French and the British publics are more sceptical towards the EU in general than is the German public. This works in the direction of less general support for what these governments do in the EU. But in Germany the government is heavily circumscribed in security policy, whereas the French and the British governments enjoy a very independent status in that respect. In Britain, the opposition Tory party has acquired a reputation for being extremely anti-EU, to the point of being rude in Brussels. This works to the advantage of the party in terms of election prospects at home, and forces PM Brown to keep a very critical posture vis-à-vis the EU. In other words, two-level games are also played by domestic actors versus their government. When Brown excused himself from signing the Lisbon treaty at the official ceremony, this was probably necessary in order to avoid being portrayed as pro-EU at home. But after some time he had to come to Brussels 'on a charm offensive' to make up for the diplomatic and political damage done. Thus, when a government is weak on either the 'EU variable' or the 'military variable', it may have to engage in two-level game playing in order to manage politics at home. Britain and France both have a very strong position for their governments in terms of the FPP, but Britain's Blair governments have been particularly weak in terms of domestic backing for their pro-EU stance.

French political strategy has been based on de Gaulle's vision of Europe, which is not one that included Britain traditionally. He stated that only a united Europe could play the key role he wanted, and where

France would play a constitutive role. France could only be France as a great power: la *France ne peut être la France sans la grandeur*. Chirac continued on this basis, trying to create an EU where states would play the key role, 'une federation d'Etats-nations'.

In Britain, the historical stance has been Atlantic rather than European. Churchill famously defined Britain outside of Europe: 'With Europe, but not of Europe', and Thatcher attacked the EU for creating only problems for the British: 'In my lifetime all our problems have come from mainland Europe and all the solutions have come from the English-speaking nations across the world' (Haugevik, 2006, p. 489). But as we shall see, there is major change in traditional interests today. A key analytical concept of this analysis is that of 'national interests'. If national interests change, why and how do they change?

The scholarly debate about interests falls in two broad camps: that which takes interests as given, as a point of departure for analysis – inspired by realism, and the one which looks for dynamics of interest change. In the latter group, there are again subdivisions that are very important. The central debate today in international relations is between the liberal camp which uses rationalist premises of methodological individualism and strategic interest pursuit, and the constructivist camp, which argues that identity leads to interests, and that interests are rarely explicit and pursued strategically.

Liberal intergovernmentalism assumes that interests are exogenously given when we negotiate in the EU. The most famous statement of this position is that of Moravcsik, who posits an *interest struggle at the domestic level* before a mandate is determined and the international negotiation gets under way.[22] He thereby assumes that governments simply represents the aggregated national interest or preference when they arrive at the negotiation table of the EU. But governments act according to their own preferences as well if they have the power to do so, seeking to shape domestic agendas. However, Moravcsik's model lacks the international level as one that can empower a government vis-a-vis its domestic opponents.

The mainstream political science literature on interests and international organisations is characterised by either realist or rationalist assumptions about interests. The realist tradition has dominated security studies, often combined with some version of rationalist negotiation theory. Most studies of the EU share some such intergovernmentalist and rationalist assumption.

Here, I argue that neither neo-realist balance of power theory nor institutionalist theory can explain great power support for the ESDP.

However, let us examine alternative explanations of this in some detail. These fall into two categories – the thesis that the EU balances or at least tries to balance US power, derived from a realist model, and the thesis that the ESDP follows from integration in EU in general, and even from identity changes, which is the constructivist version.

Realist models of the ESDP

In the balancing argument, realism is the basis for the prediction that states will seek to meet a hegemon's power through cooperation in a bloc like the EU. Important contributions to this literature include Guay (2005), Jones (2007), and Posen (2003). American scholars especially seem to adapt this analytical framework. The most comprehensive and recent analysis of the ESDP in this tradition is provided by Seth G Jones in his book *The Rise of European Security Cooperation* (2007).

In this very well researched and well argued book, Jones advances the thesis that the ESDP was created because European powers feared that the United States would no longer provide security to the continent: 'security cooperation through the EU has been inversely correlated with American power in Europe: the lower the American military presence and commitment to the continent, the greater the incentive for cooperation through the EU to ameliorate the potential security dilemma' (p. 92). He continues 'it has also been correlated with German power: the greater the power of Germany, the greater the impetus for cooperation' (ibid.). The fear of Germany as a great power thus induced France and Britain to cooperate in creating the ESDP as a way to 'tie in' the emerging great Germany. There is thus a 'double balancing' involved: against the United States and against Germany.

This thesis is, however, basically not borne out by the facts. There is little evidence that France and Britain have sought to contain Germany through a binding strategy in the EU, and Germany has not sought great power status in military terms. As we shall see in Chapter 5, Germany has become increasingly more 'pacifist' in its political choices. Further, European states have not sought to rival the United States, neither in NATO nor in the EU. On the contrary, they have sought to develop some level of complementarity through hard-attained military modernisation.

It is remarkably foreign to a European to hear assertions like this: 'The reunification of Germany created a potentially unstable regional situation, and British and French leaders were deeply concerned that a Germany which opted out of Europe would destabilise the region'

(Jones, 2007, p. 11). It is true that President Mitterrand and PM Thatcher were concerned about German power at the time, and also that Mitterrand would have preferred a Europe with a strong USSR and with privileged access. But this is far from explaining EU developments. The German government realised that unless it could 'bind' itself in a common EU foreign policy, it could not have its own foreign policy. The effect of becoming a great power again as a united state was in fact the very opposite of the realist expectation. German power, in order to be legitimate, must be multilateral. This was especially true for its security and defence power. Unilateralism, the traditional way of powerful states, was therefore no option for Germany. Jones is mistaken when he asserts that 'binding Germany ensured peace because German leaders renounced unilateralism and agreed to a number of limitations' (ibid.). The very German desire has been such a binding in the EU for as long as the organisation has existed because multilateral legitimacy was and remains the condition for Germany's external role. The burden of the past is such that a new great power Germany would immediately raise objection, suspicion, and evoke reaction. The main political dynamics is therefore not the realist one, but one where domestic public opinion must be satisfied through international self-binding in a multilateral setting – the EU, NATO, or the UN. The same political dynamics applies to Germany's international setting: it cannot act alone without reactions that act on reflexes from the past. One may object that this is irrational, but I am not suggesting that self-image is what explains political action. The point is not a constructivist one, but a rationalist one: governments must manoeuvre between publics which share common understandings of foreign policy and political culture, and international audiences that do the same. My argument is that national interests reflect history and the art of the possible. In the German case, security and defence policy will remain sensitive for as long as there is living memory of the two world wars, and German governments therefore quite rationally seek embeddedness in multilateral organisations because this provides the legitimacy essential to being able to act.

A similar lack of evidence exists with regard to the argument that European states seek to balance the United States in the creation of the ESDP. Jones makes the argument that the end of the cold war and subsequent American unilateralism 'caused European states to cooperate in the security realm for two reasons: to increase Europe's ability to project power abroad, and to decrease reliance on the US' (ibid., p. 222). In other words, says Jones, 'the changing structure of the international system explains the creation and deployment of European Union forces' (p. 182). However, apart from the habitual French political rhetoric about independence from the United States there is little to suggest that the above thesis holds. Even the French know that military cooperation with the United States is necessary and desirable if there is going to be enough intervention strength, and the ESDP is as much an attempt to create more such capacity as it is a 'competing' pole of military power. In fact, the British interest in an ESDP is motivated by the belief that more funding for capacity building can be had through an EU than through NATO policy – European finance ministers have heard to clarion call of NATO far too often to heed it, but EU policy proposals may carry more weight, as a British diplomat suggested in an interview (MOD, London, April 2007).

The realist thesis of power balancing appears to be very far from political realities in Europe, and perhaps no European scholar therefore seems to entertain it. The assumption that the state can act on a united national interest in isolation from domestic policy in this area is very remote. As we shall demonstrate, it is primarily domestic factors that matter. Jones writes these off: 'The historical evidence demonstrates that domestic actors had remarkably little impact and influence on European states' (Jones, 2007, p. 225). But as we shall see, domestic variables play the key roles in security and defence policy today.

Constructivist and institutionalist approaches

As stated, the realist thesis, so common in American political science, has few European proponents. European studies of the ESDP are very much focused on institutional processes in the EU itself. Some argue from a constructivist premise, maintaining that political interaction in the EU leads to changes in security identities, and therefore in interests (Aggestam, 2004; Haugevik, 2005; Rieker, 2004 and 2006; Sjursen, 2007; Smith, 2004).

Haugevik (2005, p. 83) concludes that Britain has become more European in its understanding of security policy as 'The British security discourse has come to focus more on European security, values, and interests than before ... Britain's European partners have become an increasingly important part of Britain's identity'. This conclusion is reached through the analysis of official speeches and political statements. However, unless one subscribes to the view that statements equal interests, such a method of analysis cannot yield conclusions, especially not in the sensitive and secretive area of security and defence policy. What seems more likely is that Blair speaks about real British motivations when he says that 'we willingly pay the price of pooled sovereignty in defence, for the greater prize of collective security through NATO. We should be ready to pay a similar price in the European Union. We must equip Europe with better machinery' (cited in Haugevik, 2005, p. 40). This motivation is consistent with British security interests, marked by pragmatic concerns about modernisation, interoperability with US forces and sufficient capacity. There is no indication that a constructivitist explanation will do here. Why should a so-called identity play any role in calculating interests in the first place? And why have recourse to constructivism in order to explain how interests *change*?

The proponents of this approach argue that only constructivism allows for changes in national security interests, but this is a misconstruction of other theories. Only neo-realism posits *exogenously given* security interests, whereas liberal intergovernmentalism does not. Strategic interests do not change in the basic sense of retaining independence and sovereignty, gaining influence, and so forth, but these goals on the part of the state are so general that they are largely uninteresting in an analytical sense. What matters is whether security interests now are common, that is shared, and therefore can be pursued multilaterally.

The constructivists seek interest change in a postulated identity change. For instance, in her dissertation, Rieker (2003, p. 271) concludes that 'community norms influence nation-state identities and interests' in the case of Nordic security policy adaptation. However, such changes may very well be the result of clever two-level game playing where government elites use EU arguments in order to forge change at the domestic level. Rieker argues that foreign policy has become institutionalised in the EU and that interests change as a result of learning and socialisation (Rieker, 2006). She and other constructivists maintain that learning changes identity and that identity is the basis of interests. This remains an epistemological position, but one that is not sustained by empirical evidence. For instance, in a study of French strategic thinking in security policy she concludes that 'the content of this strategic vision seems to have been somewhat modified by influence from the EU. ... French ambitions for a European defence seem to have been oriented away from a more military and offensive approach' (ibid., p. 525). This conclusion does not, however, seem to be borne out by the facts. Rieker argues that the evidence is constituted by the fact that 'civilian and military instruments are increasingly seen as a whole, and that the EU as a postmodern security actor focusing on comprehensive security is also supported by France' (ibid.). But as we have pointed out, civil–military integration is what modern stabilisation operations is about and this has nothing to do with a changed security identity. The traditional interest in the French strategic model of a multipolar kind where the EU is an autonomous military actor is perfectly compatible with French support for ESDP crisis management. In fact, the ESDP exists alongside the more traditional French defence policy of nuclear power status and a UNSC veto. As Rieker rightly queries 'is this change in discourse merely the result of an instrumental adaptation to a changed environment, with the French ambition of an independent European defence policy remaining the ultimate goal?' (ibid.). It would seem so. First, why should we assume that changes in discourse leads to changes in policy? Further, why should interests be related to the hazy and much more general concept of identity?

Thus, the literature on the 'Europeanisation' of national interests is not very convincing in its insistence that interests are changed through learning and socialisation. The causal chain from an identity arrived at through analysis of political statements and rhetoric to interests is nowhere shown empirically. Nonetheless it remains a pervasive assumption.

Such an analysis is used as a way to detect interest change, and this is a major problem from the epistemological point of view. Then there is the assumption that interests are changed because national actors learn in the EU setting. This is a very unlikely assumption. Professional diplomats are used to interacting without becoming influenced by 'going native'. The profession consists of finding out whether a tactical change will improve the national interest, that is the strategic goal. Studies of diplomatic interaction in the institutions of the Council Secretariat of the EU do not show that national interests change through this process but that the *EU context is highly relevant* for the formulation of such national positions because the interests and powers of other actors will determine the possibility of success of one's own position (Kassim et al., 2001). Kassim et al. conducted a broad, comparative study of how capitals interact with the EU and concluded that

> the intergovernmentalist view that national preferences are fixed in a first domestic game, then defended in 'hard bargaining' by national officials in Council negotiations in a second game at

the European level is strongly contested by the findings of the country studies ... the idea that the position advanced by national delegations in Brussels is the product of a process that is strictly domestic, is hard to sustain .... However, all country studies report that Member States relay European-level considerations to national policy-makers. (ibid.)

Thus, the evidence is against the Moravcsik model which assumes that interests are transmitted to the EU and bargained from the domestic to the EU level only. National interests are formed in an interaction between domestic and international constraints where governments are gate-keepers and where they themselves shape interests: 'Officials based in Brussels make a vital contribution to shaping national policy'(ibid.). National interests, as Sandholz (1992) found, are forged in an interactive process.

In summary, despite its fashionable status in parts of international relations, I find that constructivist interpretations of the states–EU relationship rarely provide empirical evidence of the causes of interest change. Rieker is also very modest in her conclusions, using terms like 'seems to have been modified' and inferring the *post hoc propter hoc* without any other reason than chronology: 'Since the shift in the security approach has taken place shortly after some important changes in the EU, it may therefore be interpreted as a result of a process of adaptation and learning within the EU' (Rieker, 2006). But is this in any way more likely than tactical adaptation to a moving bargaining game in the EU?

The current EU scholarship on foreign policy largely evolves around this set of ideas and propositions. There is more often than not a confusion of the empirical and the normative. Thus, Manners (2008) laments what he calls a 'militarization' of the CFSP thereby assuming that the use of military force contradicts normative power – in the sense of following the norms of international law, or for that matter, following ethical norms. Many authors postulate that the EU's foreign policy has a 'mission civilicatrice', but as one may recall, this term was coined in and for France, a great power. There is no reason why great powers should have less of a civilising mission than the EU.

In a somewhat related manner, Michael Smith argues that states change their foreign policy identity through EU participation: 'My examination ... shows that it is possible to discern some persistent features of the EU's external identity from the way it behaves in world politics, and to see evidence of changes in the domestic politics of EU

Member States resulting from EU foreign policy cooperation ... ' (Smith, 2004, p. 8). Smith argues that the ESDP is a result of gradual integration and institutional processes in the EU, but offers very scant empirical evidence for this conclusion. He postulates that elite socialisation, learning, and processes of increasing cooperation have led to increasing common foreign policy in the EU: 'A number of observers have pointed to the importance of elite socialization in the development of the EPC/CFSP, and I have confirmed this argument throughout this study'. He continues 'I have shown that EU membership has far more pervasive effects on EU states than one might otherwise expect from the obligations set out in the treaties' (ibid., p. 5).

Smith concludes that the political dynamics at work in the ESDP are not driven by intergovernmentalism but that three different logics play a role: 'A functional logic, a logic of normative appropriateness, and a logic of socialization' (ibid., p. 240). He argues that interest bargaining between major players does not explain the ESDP, but that the general integrative logic postulated by neo-functionalism does. This model of the EU rests on the historical analysis of policy development in many issue areas, right from the inception of the EU. The empirical result is often an increased supranationalisation of the EU. But this logic does not hold in the case of the ESDP, we argue, although there are some signs of 'communitarisation' of foreign policy in the CFSP. Yet here also there are clear limits to this process. One indication of this is that there is no plan to give up national diplomacy for a common EU diplomacy.

Smith's argument also suffers from a lack of specification of which dynamics is the most important. If we look at the CFSP as a whole and not just at the ESDP, there is not much empirical indication of such a gradual development towards a common foreign policy. The TEU was a compromise between France and Germany over the Economic and Monetary Union (EMU) and political union in its time. The ESDP became important only after the St. Malo compromise between France and Britain in 1998. Smith operates with a five-phase model which starts with an intergovernmental logic but which continues with a logic of information sharing and the creation of common norms, something which in turn leads to common institutions and a common system of governance. But the ESDP is rather characterised by the lack of common institutions that can undertake independent actor roles, as we shall see. As noted in Chapter 2, the ESDP has many facilitators of action, but these serve Member States, mostly as part of the Council Secretariat.

The EU: Soft power – therefore ethical power?

The argument of gradual institutionalisation is echoed by H. Sjursen and L. Aggestam, and is logically correlated with the claim that the EU is a *qualitatively different kind of power* compared to the traditional nation-state. It is a 'normative' power (Sjursen, 2007). In asking whether the EU is a 'civilian or military power?', a false dichotomy is introduced, associating normatively acceptable or good power with civilian power, and the opposite with military power (ibid.). Much of the debate about the ESDP and the general foreign policy of the EU is cast in terms of this dichotomy, confusing the empirical and ethical meaning of the terms civilian and military power.

Bailes criticises this on two counts: first, the often implicit assumption that 'soft' power equals 'goodness', and second, the lack of robust intervention capacity and will in cases where a humanitarian intervention seems called for (Bailes, 2008). She makes the important point that the EU now has a 'strategic weight of its own and an external impact that can be experienced in many places as oppressive and challenging' (p. 119), while being an actor that is characterised by 'a continuing evasion of strategic responsibility' (ibid.). This is a point overlooked in most analyses, as few seem to think that it is unethical not to play the role that a major player implicitly plays as it is powerful enough to count.

A number of scholars, mostly American, argue that the EU is simply a weak foreign policy actor, lacking an ability and a culture for using military force (see for example Kagan, 2003). Another school, European and constructivist, argues that the EU is a civilian or normative power, influenced by legal norms, international law, sometimes used synonymously with ethical norms, and that this is somehow morally superior to traditional nation-states, not any sign of weakness or lack, and in fact the emerging type of post-national foreign policy actor. Ian Manners postulates that the EU 'has been and always will be a normative power in world politics' (Manners, 2008, p. 45) and that this means that it promotes gender equality, sustainable peace, social freedom, consensual democracy, human rights, social solidarity, rule of law, inclusive equality, good governance, and solidarity (pp. 47–52). All these good things are presumably achieved without interests and power, in a manner which is post-national.

This kind of scholarship is in itself highly normative; it is not the EU's power which is normative. The problem is elementary: one mistakes the political rhetoric for political results. Yet many scholars persist in analysing the EU empirically in these normative and rhetorical terms: Barbe and Johansson (2008) argue that the EU is 'a force for good', and Mayer that its 'rhetorical action' is politically important to such an extent that all which is needed in global politics is that the EU develops a 'new narrative' for its role in the world. 'What is needed is a revised, galvanising story' (Barbe and Johansson, 2008, p. 77). These approaches are clearly constructivist in the stress on rhetoric, seemingly making assumptions about political impact from the way the EU speaks about itself. Implicit in this type of analysis is not only the problem of facts versus talk, a distinction constructivists do not make, but also the pervasive idea that non-military forms of power are more benign than military ones.

Another such argument is made by McCormick (2007) in his book *The European Superpower*. He presents the EU as a new 'super-power', but the arguments remain but conjecture: why should we believe that normative power has an impact? Or rather is belief any good in political science? The evidence is lacking that the EU is as powerful as a traditional superpower. One does not become powerful through wishful thinking. His assertion that 'the most conspicuous change of the modern era has been the declining value of military power' (p. 13) remains but a conjecture and is truly paradoxical in a Europe where the very lack of relevant military capacity is the main problem both in NATO and the EU. McCormick becomes even more explicitly normative when he asserts that 'the merits of military power are still championed by many American policy makers – particularly those realists who see the world full of threats – but Europeans have tired of violence and conflict, and have chosen instead to emphasize the economic, political, technological and moral dimensions of power ... ' (p. 14). In this statement the empirical and the normative is confused, and the normative criticism of military power is clear: it is seen to be an unethical and undesirable form of power.

Much of the EU literature on 'soft power' follows the argument that soft power is normatively championed as ethically better than hard power. But as Kagan points out, here soft power is often in fact weak power. Those that promote the notion that soft power is good are eager to show that the EU is a 'different' power than a normal, traditional state, and that the EU's power is as powerful as is, say, the United States with its strong military power. This normative agenda often takes precedence over an empirical assessment of power.

In this book we argue that the immaterial power of legitimacy is a key type of power which either stops or allows the deployment of military power. There is, thus, major political importance in immaterial power types, but this is a different argument from the one that confuses normative and empirical factors.

Indirect power: The shaping of institutions

Why does Britain participate so intensely in the development of an EU policy in the security and defence field? Why not stick to NATO and the 'special relationship'? Likewise, why do the French re-enter NATO at a time when the alliance is no longer existentially needed? Why not continue to let others maintain the security backup and remain a great power with unilateral deployments in Africa, France's special area of interest? The fact is that both states became actively involved in the EU and NATO respectively from about 1995. They are militarily able to, but almost never deploy military force alone any more. They integrate more and more with each other and with others. Why?

As discussed in Chapter 1, the territorial dimension of power is not the most relevant today. This is also true for military power in the European/EU region. Power is related to innovation, education, and global attractiveness. It is more and more a matter of effective public diplomacy and of being, in the words of Chayes and Chayes (1995) a constructive international citizen. One's standing within various international regimes and organisations is what matters.

Small states in particular seem to seek power within international organisations as they do not have the great power option. The typology of power suggested by Barnett and Duvall (2005) is useful in this regard. Power can be direct: A makes B do something B would not otherwise do; but it can also be indirect, in the form of institutional rule-making. When A cannot compel B to do something, he can create conditions for B's freedom of action that sets the agenda or precludes certain types of decisions. Thus, *building international regimes, institutions, and law are not power-neutral activities, but are as much a result of strategic thinking as is coercive diplomacy.*

Barnett and Duvall (2005, p. 9) criticise much of the liberal institutionalist literature on the score that it ignores power and presents international cooperation and the concept of governance as benign arrangements for solving 'cooperation problems'. But institutional power they point out, 'can operate ... in underlying social structures and systems of knowledge that advantage some and disadvantage others'. Thus, states that are powerful enough to use coercive power can choose to do so; but smaller and medium-sized states are confined to relying on indirect power, often through international organisations.

This perspective on power allows for the analysis of strategic action on the part of states *inside* international organisations. When ad bellum is to be decided, it is usually via a UNSC mandate or Article 51 of the UN Charter by one or several states. When in *bello* is governed, it is almost always inside an international organisation, the UN, the EU, or NATO, and states have power as a function of their military contribution. Not contributing militarily does not provide power, as Japan has realised in its effort to become powerful through being the world's biggest aid donor. 'Checkbook diplomacy ... has been judged a failure. Japan spent 13 billion dollars to help pay for the first Gulf War in 1990. But when Kuwait published a roll-call of countries, the great bankroller was not mentioned.'[23] The Japanese MFA has evaluated the effect of its policy, and concluded that the power effect of it does not justify such a choice of tool. The problem for a country like Japan is similar to that of Germany: one is restrained from opting for risky military contributions. Yet the general point made here is clear and of general validity. When military force is called for, one cannot substitute it with money.

The actorness of the state may be no less inside the international organisation than outside it in the case of a direct power relationship to another actor. Realism is a poor theory for understanding why great powers chose to work inside international organisations in order to shape them, because realism is concentrated on direct power relations between states. But today, only the United States has power enough to act unilaterally, and when it does, it experiences how damaging this can be in terms of losing legitimacy. In fact, the second Bush administration puts major emphasis on changing the unilateralist image for this very reason. Public diplomacy is again fashionable in Washington.

The key point here is that legitimacy matters increasingly for the use of military force, as discussed in Chapter 1. There, we also pointed out that most European states lack enough military capacities, thereby impelling them to cooperate. If we take these two factors as the parameters of departure we see that European states need a multilateral organisation when they want to use force. But these states not only want to 'play safe' in the individual deployment, they also want to shape the EU and promote their other interests in the EU. Thus, the strength of the individual government is the key variable in this political dynamic.

The importance of military force exists at two interrelated levels, the structural level and the agency level. The structural level conditions and even determines what can be done at the agency level: Unless a state is embedded in a security structure, it can only do as much by way of deterrence and/or defence as its own military resources allow for. For great powers, the structural level is less important than the agency level as they themselves make up the structure. This is particularly true in the US case. However, for all small and medium-sized states, the structural level of defence remains the most important. For the Nordic countries, this is either NATO and/or the EU. The EU offers an implicit security guarantee, as a 'security community' (Adler and Barnett, 1998; Buzan and Wæver, 2003; Cooper, 2004), and NATO remains the pre-eminent military alliance in the world.

National defence resources are a precondition for NATO membership, and are increasingly integrated with such. Only if a state provides relevant military resources to the NATO or to the EU can it expect to be included in the decisive inner group of states regarding decision-making. In NATO there are four such groups where the United States is in a class by itself, followed by Britain and France, and beyond these states such as Canada, the Netherlands, Poland, Spain, and Italy and sometimes medium-sized and even small states if they can contribute relevant capabilities. In the EU, the inner core in security policy is made up of the contributing states to any one mission, but led by France and Britain with Germany as the third partner in many cases.

Small states must therefore maintain relevant national military resources in order to contribute to the international operations of the organisation in question, and in the case of NATO, to maintain a threshold level of defence at home. There is no choice between national and international contributions – states that are not willing to contribute internationally do not count in either organisation. The reason for this 'new sovereignty' are globalised threats and demand for 'humanitarian intervention': being a constructive international citizen is now much more important than remaining inside national borders with a passive foreign policy, and the activity of NATO or the EU will not primarily be 'in area'. As the threat picture has changed to de-territorialised threats, be they terrorist or genocide policies must meet them where they are.

This shift in security policy thus implies that states are willing and able to contribute internationally, even globally. By so doing they maintain and strengthen their security through the important structural level. NATO and/or the EU are reinforced the more if these organisations are able to act with relevance in meeting security threats. The 'old' cold war structure only demanded that states take care of their national defence. Today, international contributions are a sine qua non.

The way to analyse current national security policy is therefore very different from the old territorial defence scheme. Now as before small states must concentrate on the structural level much more than great powers, but *solidifying the structure today implies active and constant international activity and deployments.* Norway or Denmark are part of the NATO structure in a much more direct manner than during the cold war because this very structure is upheld by successful international deployments. For the present, such success is indicated by success in ISAF. Should ISAF fail, NATO fails, and the structure on which Norway and Denmark is dependent is weakened. Likewise, Sweden and Finland contribute to EU missions in order to gain influence in EU security policy.

Thus, being passive, keeping one's military tool statically deployed behind own borders is unimportant and counterproductive in both the NATO and the EU setting. The importance of being active within international organisations in order to increase one's standing in them is what counts.[24] For the post-modern European state, 'national control' is therefore only interesting as an analytical category when we speak about relative national importance within an international setting, be it in the organisation or in the field.

The arena for states is thus the multinational one, and they exercise power in this arena. As Barnett and *Duvall* (2005) point out, there are few studies of how this kind of internationalisation/globalisation is tied to power. Which states are powerful inside international organisations? How do these states shape these organisations to their advantage? This is what we now proceed to investigate, using the ESDP case.

Exercising power in the ESDP

We have argued that the power of legitimacy is of key importance in post-national European security policy. The transparent policy process of all foreign affairs today, including security policy, demands that governments be able to muster public support at all times. This is particularly difficult when military force is used. The choice of multilateral settings for security policy allows states to diffuse the pressures from domestic publics and to gain 'safety in numbers'. The reasons for opting for multilateralism are several, as argued, and they add up to what we call the 'new' national interests.

The need for legitimacy is equally important for great powers. France and Britain would not be acceptable today if they used military power alone or in a bilateral fashion. In fact, coalitions of the willing without a formal organisation as its 'seat' is not seen to be acceptable in Europe (Matlary, 2006). In the case of OEF, such a coalition was launched. It consisted of 36 states and had the backing of international law and the UNSC. But most European states preferred to work through NATO in forming ISAF. Thus, in Europe, the more formal the multilateral setting, the greater the legitimacy.

This is one reason why also great military powers opt for formal multilateralism, but there are others. The great power cannot put direct pressure on other states, especially not with regard to coercive diplomacy. Britain and France could not decide to threaten other states as a duo. They would need a formal multilateral setting. Thus, the agency of coercive diplomacy, and also much non-coercive diplomacy, must be played out in the multilateral setting. In the EU, almost all major diplomatic initiatives are multilateral. In this situation, which is most pronounced in Europe, we need to study how power is exercised in international institutions.

The literature on power in international governance is poor in terms of understanding indirect power through institutional design (Gruber, 2005). There is little attention to the strategies of the main players because one often assumes that what goes on in international cooperation concerns solving cooperation problems. As Barnett and Duvall (2005) point out, such theories often assume that actors do not pursue power and their own interests, but only seek solutions to common problems. Much of the literature on institutionalism as well as negotiation has *no theory of power*. Power is defined away as one looks for Pareto-optimal solutions or institutional trajectories. There is a pressing need to return to studies of how power works in multilateral settings, these authors argue.

Power is, as stated, indirect or direct. Realism's main point is direct, coercive power where state A makes state B comply. But coercive power is very crude power. It is much less powerful than the power of persuasion, where new views are internalised. Yet such power is rare in an anarchic system. Realism has little to say about power in institutional settings. But this also holds for liberal theories of cooperation. They assume rational interests and look at the various game solutions that exist, given preferences and numbers of actors. But rational choice theories cannot say anything about the relative power of actors, or about institutional settings where power remains embedded.

The power literature from the 1960s and 1970s is relevant to any discussion of power. From Dahl's (1957) definition of direct power to Bachrach and Baratz's (1962) criticism that he omits the key issue of 'non-power', that is, when an issue is not put on the agenda. Agenda-setting and non-agenda-setting are key concepts when we try to understand how power works in multilateral settings. Gruber points out that there are clear similarities, and quotes Bachrach and Baratz: ' ... Power is also exercised when A devotes his energies to creating and reinforcing social and political values and institutional practises that limit the scope of the political process' (cited in Gruber, 2005, p. 104). In such cases, A sets the agenda and thereby limits the 'menu' of what can be decided. This is what France and Britain have done in the ESDP. By making their own imprint on the ESDP in the form of a key decision-rule, they are able to structure the ESFP in a way that defines the main political dynamic as a bilateral one, possibly as a *directoire*.

Power is exercised at the agency or the structural level. The typology offered by Barnett and Duvall (2005) is useful here. We have agency power exercised in institutions, and agency power leads to structural power in terms *of shaping institutions*. In our case the 'enactors', France and Britain, exercise agency power when they create battlegroups, the EDA, and so forth. But over time these acts lead to structural power. The ESDP as an institution is shaped by these decisions.

The relationship between agency in individual decisions and structure is illustrated by the decision-rule 'permanent structured cooperation' which resulted from the 'experiment' of the battlegroup. France and Britain, as we shall see in Chapter 4, first decided to create the battlegroup. This was such a successful move that they could agree on a new decision-rule for similar cases.

Thus, we see that indirect power through multilateral institutions is a logical choice for security policy at a time where legitimacy is important. Gruber makes the point that exercising indirect power is preferable in terms of legitimacy: 'Efforts to exercise direct leverage in the Barnett-Duvall sense of "compulsory power" typically impose high costs on the compeller and compellee alike and are thus riddled with credibility problems, and A that wants to alter the behaviour of B is far more likely to engage in indirect methods' (Gruber, 2005, p. 105). The main gain in terms of legitimacy is that A thereby leaves the policy response to B, a choice which remains voluntary in formal terms, but which is heavily circumscribed. Thus, states that want to participate in ESDP military missions can do so and acquire influence in the EU and over the mission, or they can let others contribute and place themselves on the sidelines of the ESDP. States that remain passive and opt not to contribute, remain outside the EU core. There is a 'free' choice, but the parameters are set by France and Britain. Gruber concludes 'As the agenda-control literature reminds us, there are other, less transparent (than compulsion) but potentially no less effective, means of exercising power' (p. 106). He also reminds us that international institutions usually benefit 'powerful states far more than weaker states' (p. 125).

Post-national security policy, as most policy, is still firmly vested in a national structure of democratic accountability and national power plays. Nothing can 'back fire' as quickly as deployment of one's own forces. What was heroic and acclaimed one day is often the object of devastating criticism the next. From the Iraq and Afghan wars there are reports of US and Canadian politicians who try to cover against media coverage of own losses, and fierce debates about dangerous deployments.[25] One's own losses are increasingly hard to accept for politicians seeking re-election. Both President Bush and former PM Blair experienced tremendous domestic problems over Iraq, to the extent that they staged a 'mea culpa' press conference in Washington, DC in mid-May 2006 where errors were openly admitted. Kosovo was almost unbearably difficult for NATO governments because their publics demanded changes and recalls, detailed information on military choices and strategies, and so forth. (Clark, 2003).

Further, both NATO, the EU, and the UN ask for more troops and there is a constant problem of procuring what is necessary for all three international organisations. As we have seen, governments want to participate more in order to keep NATO going, build the EU, and strengthen the UN – and they want to gain international power and prestige. The military tool is one which gives much status and influence, especially as the risks involved are such that many states shy away from commitment. Cimbala and Forster's (2004) study of NATO burden-sharing shows that all Member States are keen to participate and willing to take risks despite the danger of national losses and domestic unpopularity. 'Checkbook' diplomacy is not accepted as a substitute, they point out.

What can a government do about this dilemma? It has to 'deliver' on two arenas, at home and internationally, where the demands are conflicting, even in opposition to each other. The reality of this dilemma is increasingly evident in European politics. Many states have withdrawn forces from Iraq after domestic opposition – Norway, Spain, Hungary, Italy – to mention some, and the debate about ongoing deployments in Iraq is very strong in Denmark. Former PM Berlusconi's statement that 'I am against the war' to the Italian newspaper *la Repubblica* on 31 October 2005 underlined the absurdity of the 'two-level' game elites may play in this regard. To become re-elected in 2006 and to appease a critical public opinion, Berlusconi was suddenly turning against the war, but to please Washington, Italian forces were still present in Iraq with more than 2,500 troops as of April 2006. Most state leaders cannot get away with this type of inconsistency. They have to make painful choices. The BBC reported from Kabul that both the British and the Dutch force increases for the extended ISAF would be smaller than promised at NATO ministerial meetings.

On the model of 'two-level' games, governments want maximum autonomy not only abroad, but also vis-à-vis their publics. Participation and even integration in international organisations tend to increase governments' power over domestic actors, and they may find the trade off between domestic and international power in favour of strengthening their national hand through 'self-binding' or collusive delegation. It follows from this that a government that is weak domestically in an issue area will seek international 'self-binding'. Such 'tying of hands' may make the government able to change domestic agendas and marginalise various actors in pointing out that international obligations narrow or even determine national freedom of choice. The need to transform domestically as a result of binding agreements within NATO and/or the EU is one example of such an international argument used in the Norwegian domestic debate where politicians use the NATO-argument extensively (Heier, 2006).

There is an important change from the national to the post-national or post-modern setting in Europe: The 'Swiss' option is not available to states that seek to influence the security architecture. As Howorth puts it 'There is a paradox in the France–British security relationship. The two sides cannot manage a European security policy without one another, yet they have enormous difficulty, where transatlantic policy is concerned, in working with one another'(Howorth, 2005, p. 39). There is an interdependence between France and Britain despite their different strategic interests. Even strong governments thus have a need for the second, international level, in this case that of the EU. This illustrates the importance of multilateralism that is underlined in this study: the International organisation (IO) level is necessary in a post-national setting where neither legitimacy nor political efficiency can be had in old-fashioned bilateral diplomacy. France and Britain could not agree to develop common military operations bilaterally and undertake such – they would have lacked legitimacy for any such action today. But in traditional diplomacy, the great powers agreed between themselves, many times bilaterally, about when and where to intervene.

The concept of national interest advanced here is therefore one that is arrived at in the continuous negotiation between the government, its domestic constituents, and the international regime in question and its players. The government has its own preference hierarchy in this dynamics, but meets increasing resistance at the domestic level because even security and defence policy today is so hotly contested. Likewise, at the international level the government advances its own interests, but sometimes it colludes with other states in order to trump domestic resistance. This is a tactic that weak governments are especially apt to adopt.

Part II
EU Security Dynamics: Pursuing National Interests

4
Playing the Great Game: France, Britain, and Germany

The 'great game' analysed in this chapter refers to the activity by the main states in shaping the ESDP. This process has direct implications for the EU relationship to NATO and the United States. In other words, this concerns the question about the overarching security structure of the West.

To recapitulate the arguments made earlier in this book, the modern European state is too small in military terms to undertake major interventions alone, although France and Britain are able to project force globally. Yet both prefer to deploy in a multinational setting only. The time of unilateral intervention and deployment seems to be over for good. This is because few wars today are existential for the state, while nonetheless entailing risk and cost. Moreover, after the cold war, national publics engage in security policy and 'interfere' with ongoing operations to an unprecedented degree. Governments therefore need to have a 'second level' for political risk and burden sharing, a venue to blame when things go wrong and allies that share cost and risk. Further, as operations are no longer existential wars for the state's survival, one may argue that it is not the wars themselves that matter as much as the state's stakes in the international organisation at hand, in this case the EU. The implication of this is that Sweden, for example, deploys in Africa, not primarily in order to solve a crisis there, but to enhance its standing in the EU (Eriksson, 2006; Wegge, 2003). Likewise, Norway is the active NATO contributor because it strengthens NATO and Norway's position in the organisation (Matlary, 2005).

If we maintain that France and Britain are the indispensable actors in all ESDP policies and operations that involve military resources, these two states are also those which can assume lead nation roles in actual missions. A sharp EU operation without either state is highly unlikely.

The national interests of these two states are therefore the key to any scenario about EU developments. In addition, Germany is the third state of high political importance in this field: France traditionally works with Germany in the EU, and the reluctance of former chancellor, Gerhard Schröder, in terms of military commitment to international operations, has been replaced by a different policy under Merkel where Germany clearly desires to play a lead role in the EU and NATO alike. However, the fact remains that the United Kingdom spends 2.6 per cent of GDP on defence, France 2.4 per cent, but Germany only 1.4 per cent, similar to most other European states. France and Britain therefore stand out, but when compared to the 4.3 per cent of the United States or even higher levels for China and Russia, all European nations are located at the lower range of the spectrum (Guay, 2005).

Since the three states we concentrate on in this book are key to any decision to deploy in an operation, the EU will only be asked for such deployment once there is a political will on the part of one of them to contribute. Here, a German decision will not be enough. Germany does not take on leadership functions easily, and hesitates to play such roles. In reality, a French and/or British decision to lead is essential to any EU operation. This fact gives these two states a unique role. The point here is simply that the decision to deploy, which is unanimous in the EU, is rather artificial: the only decisions to be made in this regard are those where a coalition of the willing has already been established informally. This in turn means that the real decision is the only one made at this informal stage by those states which are willing and able. The states in this category are the three mentioned plus a number of smaller states eager to play a role in the EU in this field such as Poland, Sweden, and the Netherlands. But yet again, no operation is launched without the participation of at least one of the three main states analysed in this chapter. These three states, especially France and Britain, are therefore 'veto powers' in this field of EU policy-making.

So far we have argued that one or more of these three states determines whether the EU will deploy military force or not, and that the Union's unanimous decision to deploy is more a formality than a real decision. This in turn justifies the choice to study these three states only. However, the central question in this chapter does not only concern internal EU decision-making. Rather, the issue is why these states desire EU-level cooperation in this field in the first place. The explanations for this are to be sought in the two types of strategy we have indicated. The two-level game is the most important strategy for states with a weak role in the policy area of security and defence, as we will see in

Chapter 5. But for states that do not need the second level in order to manipulate domestic policy, it is nonetheless important to participate in the ESDP. France and Britain need each other in order to develop a more effective European military capacity, but they also need to block each other from shaping the EU according to each state's strategic interest. This is the grand strategic 'game' analysed in this chapter:

Grand strategy in Europe

As discussed in Chapter 2, it is a well-known fact that the EU–NATO relationship is very poor (Yost, 2007). There are formal as well as structural reasons for this. The formal problems belong to classical diplomacy and are constituted by the Turkey–Cyprus impasse. There are no meetings between NATO and the EU beyond 'Berlin Plus' operations because Turkey vetoes NATO, and Cyprus vetoes the EU. This reduces the formal meetings to discussions about 'Althea' in Bosnia. However, various informal meetings take place in the form of lunches or dinners, but the overall assessment is that the general relationship between the two organisations is extremely poor.[26] The scarce resources for European crisis management are therefore not utilised in an optimal manner – there is duplication in having two rapid reaction forces, to mention but one example. Equally important is the lack of strategic discussions concerning where Western forces should be deployed. In addition comes the very normal institutional rivalry that always dominates international diplomacy. As Simon Lunn, secretary-general of the NATO parliamentary assembly observes: 'Whenever a fresh crisis arises, there is always a strong sense of rivalry and competition' (Yost, p. 81). Such rivalry was evident in the question concerning assistance to Darfur, for example.

In this situation, the major military actors in Europe – France and Britain – seek to promote their strategic interests. These include a divergent view of how NATO should relate to the EU. France wants the EU to be an autonomous military actor with global reach – a power pole in the international system that can balance as well as cooperate with the United States. Britain desires an EU that can complement NATO but which allows NATO to remain the main security and defence organisation of the two. NATO should decide when the EU should be engaged.

But beyond this familiar and traditional difference of strategic vision, there are new national interests as argued in Chapter 3. These concern the transatlantic relationship with the United States: Britain's special relationship is now more relaxed on the part of the British than during

Blair's tenure (Dunne, 2004). Blair's support for the Iraq war has come at a steep price in British public opinion and international standing. Britain's support seems to have been unilateral, with few returns. Tony Blair was criticised on the score of giving support but not gaining much in return. As the war has unfolded, it became a major burden for both PM Blair, and now for PM Brown. The time of exit has been set for a large number of troops, and the war is largely deemed a failure, one which has led to more, not less, terrorism. The use of the military tool is always extremely risky, and this war was started without a UN mandate and on faulty intelligence. Tony Blair, having been one of the most popular PMs in Britain, lost almost all credibility and popularity due to this war.

The feeling that Britain lost most in the bilateral US–Britain relationship is also related to the Kosovo experience where the United States dominated completely in military terms, and also in political terms. Both France and Britain decided that European forces must modernise much more, and much more rapidly after the Bosnian and Kosovo experiences. Without military relevance, no European influence. Both France and Britain developed such relevance in their own forces, but needed to spur general modernisation throughout Europe. In NATO, the Americans have always called for greater European spending on defence, but mostly to no avail. European militaries have adopted a NATO policy of spending 2 per cent of Gross Domestic Product (GDP) on defence, but few do so. One of the main British motivations for inserting security and defence in the EU was the thesis that it would be easier to get finance ministers to contribute more if this policy area was developed in the EU. There was a practical and logical interest behind this, one that was shared with Paris. The *common interest in 'beefing up' European military capacity* is a very important one because almost all political influence in this policy area is based on the ability to contribute to international operations. A story from a NATO meeting illustrates this. An ambassador from a NATO state that contributes little repeatedly took the floor in the NAC and opined on this or that matter. The British ambassador at the time bent over to his American counterpart and said; 'so what do they contribute?'[27]

The evaluation of the importance of contributions is unanimous. Those with experience from the military field and international operations agree that what counts is what materialises on the ground. Heier's doctoral thesis shows this. Norwegian special forces brought influence in Washington when deployed to Afghanistan. When they were withdrawn, the influence subsided (Heier, 2006). And it is equally clear that not any military contribution will matter: it has to be modern in terms of interoperable, networked, and expeditionary as well as willing to take risks. The demands are as close to state-of-the-art as possible, and the United States remains in the lead setting the standard followed by Britain and France. Following these states are the Dutch, the Germans, the Nordics, Spain, and Italy.

In his extensive work on this issue, Howorth underlines the central importance of relevant military capacity:

> The EU is in a new historical situation in which it is called upon to perform. Both France and Britain care deeply about quality of the EU's military capacity. Both intend the EU to intervene regularly, possibly even concurrently, in fighting regional and possibly even global bush fires. Both recognize that the ability to fight alongside the US is a sine qua non for the retention of their own strategic status. (Howorth, 2005, p. 51)

Thus, the argument of this book enters very much on 'nuts and bolts', that is on the demands on modern military capability that the so-called Revolution in Military Affairs (RMA) and general technological developments incur. Having an outdated mobilisation force is equal to having no force at all in post-national wars. The issue of 'critical mass' enters here: only larger states can afford a balanced set of military capabilities today, and such states are therefore necessarily the leading states. But even they need each other, and others. The political dynamics that dominate security and defence policy are therefore very different from those of other policy areas in this one respect. In other respects there is less and less difference – an analytical point not only made by me but also by Hill (2004) and Eriksson (2006) in their studies of the ESDP.

France

French security policy is guided by a specific model of the EU where the main objective is an autonomous and militarily strong Europe (Rieker, 2004; Treacher, 2003). In his intervention at the Munich security policy conference in 2008, French Defence Minister Herve Morin called for *L'Europe de la Défense*, pointing to the *Realpolitik* needs of Europe:[28] 'The EU cannot rest content to be the civil agency of NATO.'[i] He further underlined that Europe must get out of its military 'infancy' and 'grow

---

[i] *'L'Europe (EU) ne peut se contenter d'être l'agence civile de l'OTAN'.*

up' to assume the responsibility of an actor with a global role. Without proper military backing, Europe cannot play any role at all globally, he continued. The first priority in Europe is military capability, he continued: 'I am convinced that the difficulties were experience in force generation, in Afghanistan as well as Chad, is nothing but the expression of political resignation' (p. 13)[ii]. The lack of preparedness to modernise the military is a reflection of the lack of strategic ambition in Europe which continues to complain about its dependence on the United States. He adds that the United States sees this as a problem, yet has a rather 'schizophrenic' view of whether Europe should have independent military capability or not (ibid.)

In his intervention, Morin underlined that without military capacity, there will be no global power role for Europe. He pointed out that he was in full accord with both the British and the Americans on this. He also added that the EU record, ten years after St. Malo, was impressive and that Africa remains the key area where Europe is destined to play a role. 'France is determined to use all the possibilities offered us under the terms of the Lisbon Treaty to reinforce the ESDP in a concrete manner, and to engage with the Member States to produce common crisis management capacities' (p. 17).[iii] The reason for this is not only to be able to intervene abroad, but also to defend Europe: 'When one has common interests, one also needs to defend them in common' (ibid.).[iv] There is thus a full recognition that Europe must not only be able to play a global role, but actually stop depending upon 'importing' American security. The theme of European security of its 'homeland' is one that is usually only raised by American congress members who are concerned that Europeans pay too little for their defence.

The same message was evident in an article[29] by French Foreign Minister Bernard Kouchner in March 2008 where he points out that 'Les Europeens devaient avoir les moyens militaires pour leurs ambitions politiques' and that for this reason, France has worked on the development of the ESDP since 1990. In this article, Kouchner speaks the same language as would a Briton: there is a need for pragmatism in

---

[ii] *'Je suis convaincu que les difficultés que nous éprouvons dans la génération de forces, en Afghanistan comme au Tchad, ne sont rien d'autre que l'expression de la résignation politique européenne'*

[iii] *'La France est décidée a saisir toutes les opportunes et les instruments qui nous sont offerts par le traite de Lisbonne pour renforces concrètement la PESD et engager avec les Etats-membres la production de capacités de gestion de crise sous une forme mutualisée.'*

[iv] *'Quand on a des interets commun. on a besoin de les defendre en commun.'*

the development of this policy area, as there is a need for pragmatism in the relationship between the EU and NATO. The two are complementary, he underlines, and France has no other interest than the close complementarity of the two organisations. 'Our new approach to NATO is not that we fall into line, but a reinforced European dynamic [akin to the French interest]' (ibid).[v]

In this highly interesting article we see the current French strategic thinking in all its implications: a Europe without military capacity to defend itself and intervene globally cannot have a global foreign policy. This is in the interest not only of France, but also of Britain and the United States. Moreover, this must be achieved in a pragmatic manner, a way of speaking of foreign policy that is uncommon to the French. Finally, the relationship between NATO and the EU must be complementary, another key term for the United States and Britain, and Kouchner stresses that France wants to be a full member of all NATO structures. Gone is the talk about 'autonomous EU military capacity' which used to be emphasised in French politics.

What do these rhetorical changes mean? The key is to understand the changed transatlantic political landscape after 9/11. The common interest in improving European military capacity is transatlantic, and the fact that the EU already has a foreign policy makes it impossible to ignore the situation whereby the EU will develop, also in the security field. The United States has to accept that the EU will develop a corresponding military capacity. This provides the French with a political platform for their vision, *L'Europe de défense*, and makes it imperative that with the support of Washington, the British will participate in this development to ensure the NATO complementarity. The close French–British cooperation is sealed also with common terminology, such as pragmatism, complementarity, etc. The French stand to gain much by these developments, as *'L'Europe de défense'* is going to mean enhanced military capacity for the EU and therefore increased political importance in the world for this actor.

There is, in my view, no change in French strategic thinking in this development, only a continuation with tactical adaptations. There is also a coincidence between French strategic interests and the needs of the EU at present.

---

[v] *'Notre nouvelle approche de l'OTAN n'est pas un alignement, mais une dynamique européenne renforcée.'*

The evolution of French strategic thinking

In France, General de Gaulle formulated the French security strategy which seeks to secure a place for France as a global great power. In the immediate aftermath of Second World War, the fear of German domination shaped French political tactics in building the EU and trying to adopt a supranational defence community, albeit one dominated by France. As the intentions of Stalin became clearer, NATO became the preferred security organisation, and the two superpowers maintained a systemic level 'order' that allowed France to utilise the famous exceptionalism (Treacher, 2003).

But this tactic could not work after the cold war, and France has to consider how great power status could be secured in an entirely new environment. The new active role of NATO made it clear that French forces in international operations would not only be commanded by Americans, but be subject to the political decision-making of states in Europe when France was not at the table. A return to the NATO military structure was suddenly imperative. This tactical shift was made by French leaders in the early 1990s because 'France of the 1990s was suffering from not being at the West's principal security decision-making table ... the habitual rhetoric denouncing calls for reintegration had served to diminish French influence in the European security debate' (ibid., p. 85). Bosnia was a formative experience in this regard. 'French perceptions had undergone something of a transformation' (p. 94) and another commentator adds: 'NATO is changing, and France cannot let herself be on the margin of an indispensible military force needed to manage crises where France is involved.'[vi] (Beyleu, quoted in Treacher, 2003).

The impressive tradition of French strategic thinking was again at work: How could the strategy of *rang et grandeur* be promoted in the post-cold war setting? The ensuing strategy was three-fold. First, use the status as one of the five permanent members of the UN Security Council to the greatest extent by being willing to contribute maximally to UN operations; second, insert oneself as much as possible into NATO, accompanied by the same willingness to contribute troops; third, seek to shape the European and thereby the Atlantic security structure through the EU, again accompanied by troop contributions. If one looks at the elite debate about the new tactic, one is struck by the ability to formulate

---

[vi] *'L' OTAN est en pleine evolution, et la France ne peut se permettre de demeurer trop en marge d'une militaire indispensable a la gestion des crises ou elle est impliquee.'*

tactical responses to this new situation, and also by the clear embrace of the same strategy that de Gaulle made: France will be a global player in security and defence, but the way to achieve this will have to adjust to circumstance (Blunden, 2000).

But France also desires general political influence through relevant military participation. Ulriksen (1996) has shown that French and British military participation in multilateral missions is motivated by a general desire for influence in NATO as well as the EU. It thus seems safe to assume that both states will choose to continue their active role in these organisations, employing the military tool. The question here, however, is whether they wish to pursue political integration in this field, especially in the form of a 'pooling of sovereignty' that creates interdependencies.

The tactics after the cold war entail a new element with regard to multilateral cooperation: it is no longer desirable or possible to undertake major military missions alone. Great powers have ceased to act in this way for reasons of military limitations as well as legitimacy and risk. We see this clearly in French military behaviour in Africa. Having intervened at will, often semi-clandestinely and for decades, after 1990 France has had to seek partners for interventions even when it is not necessary in military terms. The role in Africa is also scaled down considerably, from some 8,200 troops stationed on the continent in 1997, to about 5,500 in 2000. In 2008, a decision was made by the newly elected President Sarkozy to re-negotiate all agreements for military cooperation with former colonies: 'The French military presence in Africa is still grounded in agreements reached just after the end of colonialism. We find ourselves in a situation in which our political, military, and economic engagement alongside Africa is seen by many as ... neo-colonial interference'.[30]

The French 'soul-searching' on Africa has come full circle. What was formerly a secretive policy carried out by a mere handful of officials is today presented as a candidate for transparent and multilateral policy. No doubt the issue of legitimacy is important here, as is the burden-sharing issue.

The need for multilateralism also has to do with cost in a down-scaled military. Treacher concludes that the conservative and sometimes scandal-ridden French policy in Africa has to fail, but that fewer military resources also made multilateralism imperative. Not least have the political parameters of great power politics on the African continent changed after the cold war, so that 'multilateral endeavours have become *l'ordre du jour*' (Treacher, 2003, p. 141).

But multilateralism, be it in the field or at the political table, implies some decision-sharing: 'Chirac made a simple calculation: France had to sacrifice a measure of ... national sovereignty for the reality of continued influence' (p. 91). Here we see the concept of pooling of sovereignty and not integration, but acknowledgement of a certain degree of mutual interdependence which is military (resources are scarcer after the cold war, national defence budgets have decreased by about 30 per cent in each state), political (great powers cannot realise their security policy alone any longer), and also useful as a mechanism whereby states can share risk, blame, and cost, even to the point of blaming the international organisation.

'Europe has to achieve the goals that France can no longer attain for itself', was the conclusion in Paris (ibid., p. 153). Whereas the strategy of de Gaulle remains; the new tactic of necessity includes the pooling of sovereignty: 'The pursuit of rank and grandeur remains the principal security quest for the French. ... The emphasis is now on actively working and cooperating in organisations like the EU and NATO in order to boost European cooperation' (ibid.) because 'Europe is required to function as a multiplier for French power' (ibid.). This implies the willingness to be deeply inserted into multilateral decision-making while attempting to shape the latter in the direction of French strategic goals: 'Gone is the sentiment that the French should distance themself from all international initiatives they cannot control' (p. 154). However, 'the quest for rang and grandeur remain as fervent as ever' (ibid.).

As of 2008, France wants to return to NATO in full capacity. Sarkozy's first major foreign policy speech stated that NATO was no rival for the ESDP. In 1996, the result was only a partial integration of some 120 officers into the military structure, and participation in missions and exercises. France is absent from other NATO fora, something which Defence Minister Morin claims 'left France punching below its weight'. He added: 'We are not getting the full benefit, notably in terms of influence and command posts.' Prior to the NATO summit in Bucharest in April 2008, President Sarkozy signalled a full return of France to NATO.[31]

If we look at French security interests in the EU, we find a similar emphasis on national sovereignty as in the British case. However, France has a strategic plan for the EU to become an autonomous power in this field, as Europe puissance (Balme and Voll, 2005, p. 97). The sovereignty conceptions of de Gaulle are gone, and France now has a pragmatic and close military cooperation with both the United States, in NATO missions, and in the EU (Rieker, 2004). The major difference lies in the general French view of the international system which favours a multipolar system and opposes a unilateral one.

The change in French security strategy dates from about 1980 when Paris abandoned the policy of grandeur and sought an integrated defence structure in the EU instead. This has resulted in 'an almost frenetic activism' (Howorth, 1997, p. 43), which implies active contributions to multinational operations in NATO, the EU, and the UN. But among these international organisations the EU is the most important, as 'France is intensely committed to the creation of an integrated European defence structure and to a common foreign and security policy' (ibid.).

Thus, both Britain and France share interests in creating a viable security policy in the EU – as in NATO; and they both share the interest in being first among equals in this process. The British retain the 'special relationship' and a high politico-military profile in the EU while France retains its preference for 'EU first' while also being very active in NATO and in bilateral military cooperation with the United States.

There is no contradiction in any of this. What it means for the purpose of this analysis is that both states, *albeit strong in domestic terms, have advantages in the pooling of sovereignty in the EU in this area.* None of these states have to 'import' EU demands in this field, but they can take advantage of issue linkages, risk diversification, and balance of power possibilities in their relationship with each other inside the EU as well as towards the United States.

Is France a strong state in security and defence? The answer is a clear yes. Venneson finds that there is a strikingly high level of support for the military today, even among intellectual elites: 'In France, the overall legitimacy of the armed forces has never been as high'.[32] Steadily rising, the support for the military is above 80 per cent.

France wanted to build its power on Europe, including even the idea of a European nuclear power as Mitterrand suggested in 1992.[33] France had always wanted a new balance within NATO, not a rejection of it. In 1994, the White Paper on defence, *Le loi de programmation militaire*, pointed out that France could only reach its goals through multilateralism: 'It cannot be excluded as European states approach each other in the long term, that French interests will coincide with European common interests' (pp. 24–25).[vii] A little later, the Intergovernmental Conference (IGC) for the Amsterdam

---

[vii] *'Il ne peut être exclu en effet, a long-terme, qu'à mesure que se rapprocheront les intérêts des nations européennes, la conception qu'a la France de ses intérêts vitaux n'en vienne a coïncider avec celle de ses voisins.'*

treaty started where Chirac envisaged a common defence for the EU including a nuclear policy.[34] 'I have indicated that the French nuclear arsenal ... may be an element.'[viii] The ambition for the EU security and defence policy was thus far more than crisis management on their part of France.

The Amsterdam summit, however, led to the inclusion of the Petersberg tasks only. Instead of a French triumph, there was the compromise proposal by the Finns and Swedes, both non-aligned states. This limited the ESDP to robust crisis management. But for the French, this was a step towards more EU policy in the security and defence area. They decided to make the most of what was possible by contributing to robustness and to missions. In the *Loi de la programmation* of 2002, there is renewed emphasis on Europe and modernisation, and the point is made that French and European goals are identical. In an interview cited by Rieker, the defence minister argues in fact that *French influence will be enhanced the more embedded* it is in the crisis management of EU:[35] 'This allows France to increase its political and military weight in Europe.'[ix] The new *Loi* points out that pre-emption may be necessary in a world of terrorism, just as the US national security strategy, and that French modernisation of its military will contribute to making it an engine in the ESDP.

The French political discourse in 2003 and 2004 continues to emphasise the ESDP and its progress. The ESDP figures prominently in key speeches. The stress is on comprehensive approach, that is the integration of military and civilian tools. Whereas France refuses such a CA – Comprehensive Approach – in NATO, where is it especially favoured by the United States, Britain, and the Nordic members, it promotes them in the EU. By trying to keep NATO as a traditional military alliance, it also keeps NATO outside of the main tasks that require military force today, namely crisis management. Rieker interprets these changes as a 'result of adaptation and learning within the EU' (ibid, p. 19). My analysis disagrees. It rather suggests that the only possible compromise on the ESDP was made, and that France decided to make the most of it.

The French cooperation with the United States was very good throughout this time. In the period after 9/11, the disagreement over Iraq was largely one of principles, that is of not accepting to go without a UN mandate. The military cooperation with the United States continued, including intelligence cooperation. This has been reinforced and

---

[viii] *'J'ai indique que la force nucleaire francaise...pouvait etre un element.'*
[ix] *'Il permettra a la France de renforcer ses poids politique et militaire en Europe.'*

remains in an excellent state after 9/11, various sources affirm remained 'better than ever', a veteran CIA person stated (ibid.), and this was confirmed by the US ambassador to Paris. The head of DST (*Direction de la surveillance de la Territoire*) agreed, stating daily contact between the security services of the two states. Intelligence on counterterrorism from France has been of great importance to the United States, also prior to 9/11 (Rieker, 2004). French–American military cooperation also continued throughout the period of chill over Iraq.

In the 'Priorités PESD et affaires stratégiques', the plans for the French presidency of the EU in 2008, we see the strategic 'game' presented in full. France will ensure that the ESS receives a proper strategic implementation, making sure that the paragraphs on reinforced military cooperation 'fondées sur les critères des engagements capacitaires' are inserted in the Lisbon treaty, develop common training of European officers, develop military cooperation with third countries, develop a military dialogue between the EU and the United States, renew military planning in the EU, implement the EU-Africa strategy, and develop the EU's role in non-proliferation. The development of *'l'Europe de défense'* is one of the major priorities of the French presidency',[x] it is stated.

Summing up, we see that French strategic thinking remains constant: the objective is to create a military capacity in Europe that matches its political weight and global ambitions. This should occur in the EU and not in NATO in the interest of multipolarity, but this 'great game' aspect of strategy is not mentioned much any more. Behind this thinking is the plausible realist insight that without military power there can be no credible coercive diplomacy in places where this matters, mostly outside Europe. But the French also intend Europe to be able to take care of its own security and not depend on the United States. Also this seems rather obvious, but as we have seen in Chapter 3, there is an idea which is pervasive in political as well as scholarly circles that presents Europe as the region of 'soft power'. French thinking is very foreign to this. As Morin emphasised in his speech in Munich, diplomacy without the possibility of military backing does not amount to much in global settings.

French tactical moves are, however, changing with circumstances. Legitimacy requires multilateralism, and it is quite clear that unilateral French deployments or initiatives are a thing of the past. Further, in order to influence, the French want to participate as much as possible in both

---

[x] '... les grandes priorités de la présidence de la France.'

NATO and the EU. The current relationship with NATO is recognised to imply lack of such influence, and may therefore change soon.

In the EU, the French have changed the main partnership mode in recent years: The 'motor' of the EU, the French–German relationship, no longer holds. This close bilateral cooperation, which has been some kind of 'core' for almost 50 years, shows severe signs of change. Top level meetings have been cancelled, something which is unprecedented. When President Sarkozy started a unilateral approach to an 'EU–Mediterranean Union' in 2007, Merkel was irritated. There were also disagreements over security policy as Germany refused to join the EU force in Darfur. 'The talk in both capitals is of a serious rift in the single most important national partnership in Europe.'[36] Instead of the French–German 'core' in the EU, there is close British–French collaboration, as we shall see. The view of sovereignty and integration differs more between France and Germany than between France and Britain. The latter two states want an intergovernmental EU with a strong military arm. Germany wants an integrated EU without much emphasis on military capability.

France has changed its tactical interests in security and defence policy towards maximum participation in multilateral fora. This is primarily because *'l'Europe de défense'* cannot be had alone, and because the use of the military tool today requires a new type of popular legitimacy. The return of France to NATO's military command structure seems very likely, coupled with an announcement of a major French contribution to the South of Afghanistan. This allows France to demand important returns in terms of high-level positions in NATO, for instance a new appointment will be made for the post of secretary-general in 2009. In this year, the sixtieth anniversary of NATO, there will also be the decision on a new strategic concept. Thus, for a state that wants to influence, full participation in NATO as well as the EU is essential.

Britain

Turning to the other great military power of Europe, Britain, we see a similar pattern. Britain's strategic goal has never been to develop any EU security policy or strategy, but a turning point nevertheless came in 1998 when France and Britain presented the bilateral St. Malo declaration. This document underlined the willingness to develop an 'autonomous military capacity' in the EU, and simultaneously marked a tactical shift in British policy.

Prior to this, there had been a reappraisal of British security and defence policy in the defence review of 2002 where the lack of European military ability in the Kosovo operation was an important factor. Prime Minister Blair clearly wanted a more able and modernised European military. But there were also other reasons for the shift from sovereignty hedging to sovereignty pooling. These included the need to influence the EU, not least for use in Washington, the realisation that Britain would not join EMU and therefore not achieve influence in monetary policy, making the CFSP an alternative venue for British EU policy; and the factor that it makes sense to be influential in several quarters simultaneously so as not to be dependent on Washington only.

The academic literature on Britain's tactical shift expresses this: 'The British government has used EU structures to multilateralise British policy and to provide leadership ... [it has] used the EU as a multiplier to deliver financial benefit in pursuit of national policy' (Forster, 2000, p. 53). Moreover, such leadership is best when it is bilateral, according to British thinking, hence the French–British St. Malo cooperation (p. 56). Thus, both Britain and France continue to pursue great power politics as much as they can, but this now happens in a concerted cooperation between the two of them initially, and then within the multilateral organisation of the EU. It is instructive in this regard that the battlegroups was a concept wholly developed by these two states before Germany was invited as a third partner.

British EU policy remains pragmatic. If the objective is to enhance EU military capacity, it can only cooperate with France. As Chuter (1997, p. 119) notes, 'The British will be happy to engage in ad hoc cooperation where it is in their interest to do so. Effective cooperation in Europe really requires co-operation with the French'. He continues: 'There has been no change in the underlying British strategy in recent years and only a modest change in tactics' (ibid.). Now, these words were written in 1997, immediately prior to the St. Malo agreement. But the assessment is valid. St. Malo was a change of tactics, not of strategy.

From a strategic perspective, Britain's 'special relationship' with the United States remains the key partnership, but a strong EU role is also desired by the United States as long as it does not challenge the preeminence of NATO (Dumbrell, 2006; Forster and Blair, 2002; George, 1994). As for Britain, it is only strong vis-à-vis the United States when it is strong in Brussels. Then it can bring balancing power to the negotiation table and retain a 'special relationship' because it is a key player in the EU. It becomes a 'bridge-builder' between the EU and Washington. Thus, the rationale for this kind of balancing behaviour is clear: the stronger Britain is in the ESDP, the more interesting it is to the United States, and the more power it can bring to the table in its interactions with the United States.

There are two elements here. First, in order to advance the US and British views of the ESDP as a complement to NATO, Britain must maximise its power in the ESDP. Second, in order to have leverage against the superpower, Britain must embed itself in the EU and 'import' EU multilateral power. A third element that favours a strong British role in Brussels should also be mentioned – the difficult British public with regard to European integration. The hostility of this public is matched only by Sweden and Denmark, and although the British public does not oppose international military engagements, the key here is that the British government needs a strong role in general in Brussels for the reasons discussed above.

Further, for Britain, a major motive behind embarking on the St. Malo process was the lack of influence in the EMU, where Britain is not a member. Since Britain is a key military actor, it could bring power to bear in the EU. 'St. Malo was planned by a small group of top diplomats from the Ministries of Defence in London and Paris. Tony Blair wanted it, and it is an area where Britain is strong, the opposite of the EMU, so to speak', said a source at the British MOD.[37] He added that the French–British relationship is pragmatic, and that there was a need to use multilateral structures in a new way, and stated that there is no risk of integration in this policy field. The main trigger for this cooperation was the urgent need to get Europeans to spend more on defence, and that it was easier to get Europeans to do this in the EU than in NATO where calls for more spending had been made for decades.

The EU allows issue linkages because of the permanent nature of membership – weakness in one area is compensated by strength in another. Also, the British-lead role in the CFSP ensured that the French could not dominate and fashion ESDP as an alternative or competitor to NATO. Thus, the EU 'offers' not only security and defence policy, but also the possibility of issue linkages in the sense that a state with a weak EU role in one policy area may seek a strong role in another as compensation. This explains part of the British interest in developing the ESDP.

We can therefore argue that the British government will be keen to pool sovereignty, albeit not to integrate, in the security and defence field. The shift in national position on the ESDP came when Blair was elected. Instead of the typical Euro-scepticism, he wanted a general *rapprochement* with the EU. In his study of the special relationship, Dumbrell concludes that 'an ESDP was not credible without a strong British commitment. In its early incarnation, however, the Blair government continued the traditional British suspicion of ESDP. By the end of 1998, the position has shifted' (Dumbrell, 2007, p. 235). Here the ability for transatlantic bridge-building also played a role, according to Dumbrell.

The realisation that influence is had through participation seems to underlie this: 'The agenda of New Labour revolved around the concepts of globalisation, interdependence, and the network economy. A particular emphasis was placed upon the end of sovereignty ... with an emphasis instead being upon cooperation with European and other partners, and a relaxed attitude to issues of independence'. One major aspect of this was a moral obligation to intervene in humanitarian crises, an obligation that later included anti-terror and failed states. Blair developed his own version of the New World Order, dubbed 'the doctrine of the international community', where sovereignty was made conditional upon the respect for human rights and democracy. 'Nine-eleven' included security on the value agenda, and the traditional concept of sovereignty and national interests gave way to an interconnected, Western value agenda that fitted well with the EU's human-security concept. In fact, the concept of values or 'an ethical foreign policy', Britain as a 'force for good in the world', and so forth, became central to New Labour's foreign policy and resonated very well with the EU. 'One element common to the thinking of Cook, Straw, and Blair has been their assumption that Britain must be a major international player, legitimized as much through the notion of a "force for good" as through the traditional assertion of "the national interest."' (p. 134).

In terms of the ESDP, the Iraq crisis did not create permanent damage to the French–British relationship. The strong disagreement between the two leaders did not stop their officials from the respective ministries of defence. The importance of this decade-long close cooperation is confirmed both through interviews,[38] and by Howorth (2007) as well as by Hill and Oliver, who describe this continuity thus

> Indeed, Britain, France, and Germany were still working together in developing a trilateral relationship ... While Blair and Chirac has clashed bitterly over Iraq, their officials nevertheless continued to discuss the creation of a common European armaments agency

and cooperation on proposed new aircraft carriers. The EU's draft 'Security Strategy ... also reflected some joint working among the three (ibid., p. 125).

Hill (2003) reports that the main input to the drafting of the ESS came from London.

The new pro-European stance as a response to power under globalisation caused considerable stir domestically. The Iraq war has led to major loss of credibility for Blair, who was portrayed as a 'defiant warmonger to the last' by the *Daily Telegraph* when he left office.[39] He was criticised for being an ally of Bush over Iraq and also for being too pro-EU. The press saw the importance of the ESDP. The *Financial Times* had an editorial entitled 'The Case for an adult, outward-looking EU'[40] where the 'more muscular defence capability must go hand in hand with a more coherent foreign policy' (ibid., p. 10).

The major change both in the 'moral' and the interventionist directions is widely recognised to have come with the Kosovo war. Blair was personally convinced that it was imperative to intervene, and that this had to be done with military ability. The Bosnian war was not regarded as a threat to national interests, and the old version of national interest prevailed in British foreign policy circles then. Sir Malcolm Rifkind (2007, p. 107) wrote that the only military deployment envisaged was security for humanitarian convoys, which was the mandate UNPROFOR was granted. Even this very limited deployment met massive resistance in the British cabinet, 'which did not want Britain to be militarily involved at all'. There was no security interest involved, according to traditional realist logic.

The special relationship with Washington sanctioned cooperation with the French as long as the result was more military capacity and no duplication with NATO (Dumbrell, 2006, p. 238). The British naturally had their own agenda in this matter as well, knowing that one-sided reliance on the United States was a problem but that a mediator role between the United States and the EU was ideal. Blair has been widely criticised over his seemingly unconditional support for the Iraq war, a support that ensured that his political standing would plummet in the last years of his premiership. 'Our special relationship is an illusion', it was said, and the debate along these lines continues under Gordon Brown: his dilemma is to retain the favour of Washington while deciding on troop withdrawal.

Apart from this, the role of Britain in the ESDP is now generally recognised as the major, or at least the pivotal one, for France cannot act without Britain. The novelty is the British position, not the French.

Niblett (2007, p. 628) points out that 'the UK is now a central player in efforts to develop increasingly activist foreign policies, whether these can later be coordinated effectively with the US or not'. This is an entirely new position compared to that of only ten years ago. The issue was then whether Britain should engage itself. Now it is a fact that Britain is the indispensable nation in the ESDP. The importance of the daily cooperation between French, British, and other EU states' officials is underlined: 'The constant participation of UK officials and ministers at the EU level discussion ... is building an new fabric of instinctive EU consultation at the heart of British foreign policy-making' (p. 639).

Realists argue that the national interest in security and defence policy equals the jealous guarding of national sovereignty in this area. As we argue in this chapter however, the so-called national interest is the key to understanding why states seek a pooling of sovereignty in this field. The national interest in security policy in Europe is no longer a matter of territorial interest and independence, but much more a matter of playing a role on the international scene. Thus, Aggestam (2005) finds that for Britain, participation in the ESDP was seen as a quest for influence Aggestam (2004).

Given the predominantly intergovernmental nature of the ESDP, there is little risk and much potential gain in this. In the British case, several reasons are given for the St. Malo turnaround in 1998: the need for European states to modernise militarily and be able to act as one; the fact that Britain is not in the other important core, the EMU; and the compatibility between a 'UK-model' of the ESDP and NATO/US interests (Haugevik, 2005). A supporting fact in this regard is the extensive British influence on the EU strategy document, the ESS. Christopher Hill analyses how the ESS was developed in reality and drafted in the British foreign office in a non-paper (Hill, 2004). He writes that 'it should be noted that the main drafter of the ESS in Mr Solana's office was Robert Cooper, who used to be Tony Blair's foreign policy advisor' (p. 1). The reason for writing such a strategy is also very attuned to British strategic interests, writes Hill – a major reason was to 'adapt to new circumstances and to convince the USA that Europe was not totally mired in delusional "soft power" thinking' (p. 2). Hill also points out that Britain, as a 'middle-range' power, 'has come to believe in the importance of the international community or society' (p. 3), hence the need for multilateral settings as a 'force multiplier' for own interest, as well as the need for international law as a set of rules that bind also greater powers.

Regarding the St. Malo turnaround, Hill attributes this to the pragmatic realism of British foreign policy: 'Blair came to the conclusion that Europe lacked credibility while it has no military teeth on its own, and also needed to reinsure against the possibility that the US on occasion might not wish to commit its own troops to causes which Europe thought vital' (p. 5). The main British concern, according to Hill, is that the EU be taken seriously as a political player on the world scene, and that this requires ability and willingness to be tough in military terms should the need arise. Other foreign policy tools simply lose their impact unless the military tool is present.

For the British, playing a lead role in the ESDP served several purposes: To enhance the general standing of the country in the EU – Blair had wanted to join the EMU, but was effectively barred from this due to public opinion and then chancellor of the Exchequer Gordon Brown's resistance; to enhance European military capacity 'to get more bang for the buck'; to stop French attempts at dominating the ESDP, and to develop a role for transatlantic bridge-building.

These driving forces continue to develop under the premiership of Gordon Brown. Although reputedly a Euro-sceptic, he has continued the close cooperation with the new French president, Nicolas Sarkozy, and with German Chancellor, Angela Merkel: 'Some officials already talk about a new triumvirate', reports the *International Herald Tribune*.[41] Dennis MacShane, former Europe minister for Britain, even called for a new *entente cordiale* because 'all three leaders realise that unilateral policies could not work successfully to benefit their countries' (ibid.).

There is thus a question of not only military 'critical mass', but also what we could term 'political critical mass': none of the great powers can act alone. As argued in Chapter 1, there is a very material side to this, namely the military needs in expeditionary missions where even large militaries need others. There is also the legitimation need: no European state can act alone in the defence and security field. These two demands have the effect of making even great powers interdependent. There is no way that is not multilateral, but inside a multilateral setting the real actors are the contributors to coalitions of the willing and able.

Miskimmon (2004, p. 273) concludes that 'strategic culture has not remained static in the British case, but has gone through a process of incremental change to meet new challenges and new circumstances'. He points out that the preferred way has been multilateral: 'It is through the UK's multilateral ties that Britain has been able to redefine the role of the British armed forces in the post-cold war area' (p. 278).

As Robert Cooper (2004) argued in his analysis of European foreign policy, Europe has to back its new value-based interests with military power. This was a central theme for Tony Blair, and his ten years in power showed an increased willingness to intervene militarily. His use of the 'force for good' meant that he needed multilateral legitimacy and multilateral forces. Miskimmon finds that the post-modern Blairite foreign policy contributed to the creation of the ESDP.

From unilateral to multilateral force deployments

Both France and Britain seek to enhance their *general* role in the EU. Security policy is one means to achieving this. Since contributions matter in an almost absolute manner in this area, both these states are able to play major roles as the two most important military actors in Europe. They thus share an interest in developing the ESDP. It is sometimes argued that one of the main reasons for the British willingness to engage in the St. Malo process was its lack of ability to join the EMU.[42] What remains clear is that states engage themselves where they can play a role, and the ESDP requires very concrete military capacities in this regard.

As pointed out previously, both France and Britain have opted for multilateral military deployments rather than unilateral ones. Both states have interests in Africa as former colonial powers. Treacher points out that French deployments have all been multilateral and UN-mandated after about 1995. It is also true that Britain had opted for this manner of interventionism after the cold war. The two have cooperated bilaterally on this, and often carried such bilateral schemes to the EU table where they also share an interest in making policy, including the military tool, for Africa. It is also noteworthy that Germany is very reluctant to deploy in missions in Africa. It had to be pressured to deploy its own battlegroup on rotation to DR Congo to provide security for elections. As a British interviewee put it 'Germany has to be dragged to DR Congo'. Germany likewise refused to join the EU mission to Darfur and Chad, and faced heavy resistance at home to African deployments. It was not part of Operation *Artemis*. (These cases are analysed later.) The point here is that African operations are the key issues for both France and Britain, and it is also recognised that the United States has less interest in this continent and welcomes EU/European engagements here. Africa has been that continent where the United States has had the

118 European Union Security Dynamics

least geopolitical interest in the post-cold war period. It is also where France has been dominant and kept a sizeable military presence, while Britain also has retained a role in former colonies. It thus seems to be a common interest to develop an EU intervention capacity, especially for African conflicts. In this area there is likely complementarity between US and NATO interests.

How can we assess the 'great game' being played at the EU table? As argued above, France and Britain share major interests, but also differ in their grand strategic visions. As one source underlines, the conflicting nature of the strategic visions of the two states has been a key characteristic of the policy outcomes so far. By that it is meant that cooperation follows from common interests in enhancing European military capacity, but that there is sharp divergence when it comes to the old French strategic goal of creating an independent European military capacity that will be able to balance US power. I have pointed out that developments in French policy are favourable to strengthening EU–NATO complementarity and that that French politicians now stress pragmatic attitudes much like the British. However, there is no contradiction between this and the outcome of the EU process, a *l'Europe de defense*, which by virtue of its very existence may come to be used as a balancing device. To speak of balancing here is not correct, however. There is no threat involving the United States and Europe, only possible disagreements on the use of force. But even such disagreement seems unlikely with regard to common security problems like terrorism or failed states. The major point of the French strategy is simple. Unless an actor commands also military power, it cannot act in normal diplomacy beyond Europe. Coercive power and the ability to project military power globally is a precondition for being a global political actor. Until the EU acquires such power, it remains handicapped in global politics. But once the EU also has military power which is commensurate with its other political tools, these tools are the more powerful because military power is a 'force multiplier'. This is also what Britain desires for the EU.[43] But the fact of Europe becoming strong also in military terms is a *fait accompli* – *accompli* in the sense that it automatically implies that such a strong actor has the strength and liberty to disagree with the United States and to pursue its own full-fledged global foreign policy. The obvious point is that *once the EU has its autonomous military capacity, European states are no longer dependent on the United States for their own security*, and are able to rival the United States if interests diverge. The British strategic vision is to ensure that the interdependence between the United States and Europe continues and that NATO therefore remains the key security organisation in the Western world, but a too successful strengthening of EU military capacity would undermine this interdependence in military terms.

In the following we investigate how these differences have influenced the ESDP. It is a fact that both the battlegroups, the EDA, the Iranian diplomatic venture, and the protocol on permanent structured cooperation are the results of bilateral French–British cooperation. But is also a fact that there have been disputes over the HQ question and other institutional issues, including how to interpret the 'rank' between NATO and the EU.

What explains the cooperation of France and Britain in the ESDP? Howorth mentions four factors: The need for European military capability in order to remain able to act and interesting to the United States; the personal ties between Blair and Chirac and their close-knit 'epistemic' community in the ministries of defence in both London and Paris which has worked on this from the early 1990s; a shared strategic culture of global force projection and intervention; and the needs for a European matching of the defence consolidation in huge American actors (Howorth, 2005b). When President Sarkozy made a state visit to Britain in March 2008, further cooperation in the security and defence area was announced, and 'traditional German ties played down'.[44] As we have seen, French ties with Germany have been strained after Sarkozy assumed office, and it is clear that security and defence cooperation with Germany is rather senseless because of the domestic constraints on the German government. For France, the ESDP is the most important aspect of EU policy development. Britain is the only possible partner. During the state visit, Sarkozy pointedly said that the French–German 'motor' was no longer sufficient to drive the EU, and that French–British cooperation was 'indispensable' in this regard (ibid.). Both PM Brown and President Sarkozy hailed this entente cordiale, and additional French troops to southern Afghanistan was announced by the French[45] who also plan to return to the integrated military structure of NATO. This fact also underlines the general point I make about the importance of participation in the inner cores of international organisations in order to wield influence. For Britian, it has to be in the inner core of the ESDP; for France, in the inner core of NATO. While these interests are common, there are differences in terms of the 'great game', as we will discuss later. First, however, we will analyse how French–British cooperation from 1998 onwards has changed the political dynamics of the ESDP in a major and novel manner. We do this through an analysis of the concept of permanent structured cooperation, the battlegroups, and the EDA. We then proceed to an analysis of this in the strategic setting of the 'great game', that is the Euro-Atlantic setting.

In all these policy developments it is typical that Germany has been included at a late stage in the process. Germany is a weak state in terms of executive autonomy in the security and defence policy field, as spelt out in detail in the next chapter. German national interests hardly exist in this field. The constraints on German policy in security and defence for historical reasons and the dominant role of domestic public opinion explains why Germany cannot play a lead role in the EU in this field. These are analysed in detail in Chapter 5. For as long as the French–German 'motor' was the key political dynamic in the EU, Germany was the indispensable nation in the EU. But that was before the ESDP came into existence. The German strategy for the EU has not included military power as a main asset, but rather a general foreign policy which would allow also Germany to have national interests. It was only in 1994 that the German constitutional court allowed for German deployments abroad. The German role in the CFSP has been important, but not its role in the ESDP. Germany has regarded NATO as the main security organisation in Europe and has traditionally vacillated between an Ostpolitik of appeasement and a pro-atlanticist stance.[46]

The main political dynamic: *Directoire* inside the EU

The decision-making process in the ESDP remains intergovernmental. But as we have seen, consensus is a major norm and voting ever hardly takes place (Thomson et al., 2006). Unanimity is so strongly ingrained that it takes exceptional cases to oppose and defect. 'EU personnel believe that consensus is the right decision mode' (p. 304). Thus, we can assume that Member States will not oppose the proposals made by the ESDP lead states, but we may also suppose that proposals that do not attract almost all states have little chance of being accepted. What does this imply for leadership in the form of a core of states? Can these states bank on support from other states because the consensus norm is so strong, or does the fact of such a strong norm mean that the lead states must make proposals that all can accept?

The Amsterdam Treaty of 1997 introduced the mechanism of 'constructive abstention' whereby fewer than one-third of Member States could opt out of a Joint Action under the CFSP without blocking it (Cini, 2007, p. 233). These negotiations took place at the same time as Tony Blair assumed the premiership in Britain, introducing ten years of pro-European policy. But Amsterdam made some modest improvements on the CFSP. Qualified majority voting (QMV) now applied not only to the implementation of 'joint actions' but also to the adoption of such when they resulted from 'common strategies' already adopted by the European Council, and states could distance themselves from CFSP decisions through abstention, as stated above. In a similar vein, states could invoke 'reasons of national policy' if they disagreed – seemingly a way to retain intergovernmentalism, but also a way to marginalise oneself. Clearly, states that forge ahead with a common EU action are seen to represent the EU as a whole, and those which abstain are regarded as laggards.

At Amsterdam there was also the naming of the High Representative for the CFSP and the creation of planning facilities and early warning capacity. Yet 'advances in the defence area were very modest' (Rynning, 2006, p. 486).

In the Nice Treaty of 2000, there was further development of the concept of enhanced cooperation. Article 42 of the Treaty on European Union (TEU) allows eight or more Member States to establish closer cooperation between themselves, but contains an exception for policy which has military or defence implications, as stated in Articles 27a–e. If states wish to cooperate in this policy area, they must first submit a request to the European Council. This is clearly a way of ensuring that intergovernmentalism prevails. The Commission and the EP play no role in this policy decision.

The major breakthrough for enhanced cooperation in the ESDP came in 2004 in the draft of the Constitutional Treaty. Here, France and Britain took the lead in designing a way for militarily ambitious states to move forward. After the experience of the Artemis mission to DR Congo (Bunia) in June 2003, the two states decided to formalise such 'spear-heads' in the EU. They proposed a new mechanism entitled 'permanent structured cooperation' which is only valid for the ESDP, that is, those parts with military implications. A Council vote based on a qualified majority must approve a proposal by two or more states for such cooperation, and there are requirements for those states that want to join . They must possess military capabilities and want to contribute with these. A Protocol annexed to the treaty specifies the military capabilities required. The Constitutional Treaty was not adopted, however, but delayed for several years after its rejection in the referenda in France and Holland. It was finally renegotiated in October 2007 at the European Council meeting in Lisbon. The resulting Treaty of Lisbon contained important paragraphs on the ESDP and 'permanent structured cooperation'. This treaty was finally ratified in Brussels on 13 December 2007. Ratification in Member States' parliaments is pending, and the treaty only enters into force when such ratification is finally approved.

The provisions on the Common Security and Defence Policy contains a new Article 28 which *inter alia* states that this policy also can contribute to strengthening 'international security'. This comes in addition to the familiar wording on crisis management (new Article 28A). Also, the wording on a progressive movement towards a Union defence policy is interesting: 'The common security and defence policy shall include the progressive framing of a common Union defence policy. This will lead to a common defence, when the European Council, acting unanimously, so decides' (ibid.). There is also a specification of something akin to an Article 5 obligation:

> If a Member State is the victim of armed aggression on its territory, the other Member States shall have towards it an obligation of aid and assistance by all the means in their power ... This shall not prejudice the specific character of the defence policy if certain Member States (here NATO is alluded to.

We see here that the ESDP expands into collective defence. This is also the case with the addition of 'terrorism' to the text: in a new Article 28 B, the usual crisis-management tasks are listed, but additionally: 'All these tasks may contribute to the fight against terrorism, including by supporting third countries in combating terrorism in their territories'.

The new paragraphs continue to list the demands made on states that wish to participate in 'permanent structured cooperation': They 'shall undertake work progressively to improve their military capabilities', and there follows a detailed list of things the EDA shall do as a leading actor in this regard. Then the usual unanimous rules for Council decisions in this field are reiterated, but with the important addition that 'The Council may entrust the execution of a task ... to a group of Member States' (ibid.). These states are required to be 'willing and have the necessary capability for such a task' (Art. 28 C). Then the main rule of permanent structured cooperation is introduced: 'The Member States whose military capabilities fulfil higher criteria and have made more binding commitments to one another in this area with a view to the most demanding missions shall establish permanent structured cooperation within the Union framework' (ibid.).

A protocol on Permanent Structured Cooperation details the demands made on states that wish to participate, and the tasks of such cooperation. The intention is to make states quicken their pace in developing their national military capacities as well as integrating them in international settings. These states must have the ability to 'supply by 2010 at the latest, either at national level or as a component of multinational force groups, targeted combat units for the missions planned, structured at the tactical level as a battlegroup ... ' (Art. 1, b). They shall also undertake to cooperate, and 'bring their defence apparatus into line with each other as much as possible, ... by harmonization, pooling, and when appropriate, specializing their defence means and capabilities, and by encouraging cooperation in the fields of training and logistics' (Art. 2).

This amounts to a very clear logic. *States that desire a stronger military role for the EU, can create such a role by themselves.* By making demands on states that want to participate in such core cooperations, one ensures that there are no laggards in the group. The entry requirements are clear: military ability and willingness to contribute, modernise, and integrate.

Can other EU states stop such core formation? The requirement for the establishment of a core is, as stated, QMV procedure and not consensus. This in itself makes it easier to arrive at a decision to form a core. As we have seen, the consensus criterion for enhanced cooperation applies in the other policy areas of the EU, as does the requirement that eight states or more form the core. But the permanent structured cooperation is exceptional in that only two states are needed and only a majority procedure is needed in the council. Further, clear demands are made on the states that want to participate. This decision-making mechanism is tailor-made for France and Britain – in fact, they are the architects behind it. The common interests of the two are military modernisation, effectiveness, and enhanced ability on the part of European states. The way to promote this interest is to put pressure on finance ministers not only through the old and not so effective arguments of the United States and NATO, but also through the more general process in the EU. If security could be seen as integral to EU foreign policy, it might be easier to extract more from the national coffers, it was assumed in London. At the same time, it was clear that only serious military actors could create EU military capabilities. Here, only France and Britain could lead. Furthermore, the importance of practice is undisputable in this area: the EU could only establish credibility as a military actor through *performance*.

Rynning points out that flexibility became an issue in the EU when defence and security became policy areas in the organisation (ibid., p. 495). At Amsterdam, Britain (which was pre-Blair at the time) opposed flexibility because it provided a 'short-cut' to more integration. One feared a French–German 'motor' towards a political union, something which is a traditional British concern. The first paper on flexibility was written by a German politician with an interest in federalism, Karl Lamers, whose ideas were seconded by Eduard Balladur. The main idea was that some states would form a core and integrate in the EU to a greater extent than others. The French never favoured supranationality like the German federalists, but did favour an EU consisting of cores of states that undertook common projects while retaining their national sovereignty. The model is one of several 'cores' led by willing and able states. Inside the EU, such cores then come to represent also the EU itself, which is a major point for France. The desired model is to retain the EU as a unitary actor on the world stage while retaining French national independence.

Traditionally, the British have opposed all core logics, as that could lead to integration: 'Britain preferred decentralized flexibility during Amsterdam to prevent the emergence of a hard core of pro-integrationist countries, such as the France-German couple' (Rynning, 2006, p. 495). But as Rynning also notes, 'with defence becoming an EU issue in 1999–2000, flexibility again became a key question' (ibid.).

The issue could also be adjudged in purely pragmatic terms: how can an EU development towards more usable forces be ensured? The answer must be through some kind of leadership on the part of the states that possessed the means of military force projection and intervention. With unanimity, nothing would happen in the EU. Britain therefore changed tactics, that is, its national position, aligning it with the French position, and developed permanent structured cooperation in 2003 and 2004 through bilateral negotiation.

The model was the EMU, a small group would initiate policy in a practical sense; others would qualify to be included once they met certain criteria. The articles in the Constitutional Treaty, later the Lisbon Reform Treaty, were opposed by many members of the constitutional convention. As Howorth reports, the British change of position was not without its doubts and difficulties. One feared that such a core concept would do major harm to the intergovernmental nature of the EU in high politics. Yet France managed to adjust to a compromise with Britain: 'After a successful meeting with defence ministers on August 29th, 2003, during which a number of misperceptions were dispelled, Blair, Chirac, and Schroeder set their "sherpas" working on a trilateral compromise which was duly agreed at a summit in Berlin on September 20th, 2003' (Holworth, 2005, 49). The compromise was that this core project would only concern capabilities and practical measures, not defence policy.

The permanent structured cooperation has worked in the two major cases of defence cooperation to date in the EU: the formation of the battlegroups and of the EDA. Let us now briefly examine these cases to see whether we can term this dynamic a *directoire dynamique*.

The battlegroups

The precursor to permanent structured cooperation is the battlegroup. This in itself is the result of the well-managed Operation *Artemis*. As has become usual in the French–British relationship, practice precedes theory, perhaps to the dismay of the French. Howorth emphasises the military hardware issue which is at the centre of British interest in the ESDP: 'All those proposals [at le Torquet in 2003] sought to precipitate and facilitate the development of serious military capacity. This was to become the UK's clear and unswerving focus thereafter' (Howorth, 2005, p. 47). Wallace also notes that 'The Franco–British strategy was to focus first on capabilities and only later on institutional reform' (Wallace, in Wallace and Wallace; 2005, 449).

As stated, Africa has remained a key interest for both states. They had showed their ability to aid effectively in conflicts where the UN has missions which were sometimes paralysed militarily. Thus, a small but very effective British force re-established peace in Sierra Leone in 2001, in a conflict where a UN force of 17,000 had failed. Similarly, they intervened in Côte d'Ivoire in 2002. The enmity that had prevailed traditionally between these two states was turned into close cooperation when in Africa; their foreign ministers travelled the continent together in 2002. The common interest in Africa was also rather unique among Western states – the United States, and thereby NATO, did not see Africa on its 'radar screen'.

However, in May 2003 a crisis was under way in the province of Bunia in DR Congo. The UN Secretary-General was on the outlook for an intervention force. The French, with their ample experience in Africa, were called upon. A British diplomatic source tells the amazing story in an interview with the author.

> The request from the UN came in the middle of an EU ministerial. The French said 'yes', but we will get a legitimacy problem if we go

alone, although this is not a military problem. Then we British told them, why not make it an EU operation, that will show the world that the EU is capable of sharp end operations as well provide a testing ground for such in Africa.[47]

This win-win proposal carried the day, and Operation *Artemis* was ready in record time under French leadership. The formal request from the UN came within days, and forces were also on the ground within days. It was prestigious to participate, and those EU states with serious ambitions in the security and defence field rushed to contribute. Non-aligned Sweden for instance contributed special forces.

Thus, the core logic appears to function as intended by both France and Britain: they are sovereign in deciding to launch a practical defence and security policy, but once launched, other states want to participate. Since one of the main aims of the ESDP is to promote military modernisation in Europe, this is exactly what is useful, as it is not the two leading states that are most in need of such modernisation.

As stated, the breakthrough in permanent structured cooperation was the agreement between the three major states in Berlin on 20 September 2003, where Britain gave up its resistance to core logic in the ESDP. It is clear that the success of Operation *Artemis* was important here. The British key interest has been and remains that of practical utility: effective expeditionary forces that can deploy rapidly around the globe.

Artemis, as we have seen, came about in an entirely informal manner, where the French needed legitimacy in the form of multinationality. Here the EU provided both – there was, of course, a UN mandate (Res. 1484), but deployment needed to be multinational in order to provide such legitimacy. The time line is instructive. Resolution 1584 was adopted on 30 May 2003. Within a week, EU troops were on the ground in DR Congo. Ulriksen et al. (2004) report that although the EU officially announced the mission on June 12, the first French combat troops arrived on June 6. The mission consisted of 1,700 French soldiers and 70–80 Swedish special forces. In addition, there were British support elements, including air lift. The British were otherwise heavily engaged, in Iraq and Afghanistan, but wanted to show participation through contributions also to this mission, as this was a major political point. All in all, 16 EU states participated, including three non-EU states: Brazil, Canada, and South Africa.

The timeline corroborates the information given in interviews, where the request from Kofi Annan led to the ad hoc decision by the French, with British support, of making this request a test case for a sharp EU operation far away from Europe. The fact that the French 'scouts' were in place before the EU officially had adopted the decision on the operation, further underlines the bilateral character of the latter. The date for the UN mandate also tells us that the real decision-making was made *prior* to the UNSC decision, that is the mandate came only after the decision on deployment had been made – something which is not uncommon.

To plan deployment of a multinational force usually takes months. In this case it took days. This was because the French provided the HQ and the bulk of the troops. The need for rapid intervention is a vital key to being able to prevent genocide (as was the threat in this case) and other humanitarian catastrophes. The military demands on such a rapid force are entirely different from that of so-called follow on stabilisation forces, they cannot be generated in a long-drawn force generation process where each state contributes what it can spare and what it wants. On the contrary, a rapid intervention force must be configured beforehand according to the exact capacity needs it has; it must be trained as a battalion or brigade, it must contain all the necessary support elements from the beginning, and importantly, it must have access to air and sea lift as well as a mobile HQ. The battlegroup must therefore be ready, and on call, at any one time.

Needless to say, nothing can be improvised in such a case. The major problem with European forces after the cold war has been that they are of the wrong kind – large mobilisation forces that have never been trained for real combat, that have never travelled, and that have been based on conscription and mobilisation. One example says it all. When a Norwegian battalion was deployed to Kosovo Force (KFOR) after the peace agreement was made, it took three months before it arrived. 'What took you so long? Did you walk?' mused the commander, British General Sir Michael Jackson.

The military transformation, as it is called, is about rapidity and ability to become expeditionary. As stated earlier, only between 5 and 10 per cent of European troops are usable in modern internal conflicts, and the major modernisation efforts in NATO as well as on the national level is about professionalising national forces while equipping them with interoperable means of communication. Until the end of the cold war, only France and Britain had global force-projection ability. No other European state is able to match this on its own, but together, in multinational forces, this is possible (Ulriksen, 2003a). NATO has developed its rapid reaction force, the NATO Response Force, and the EU its battlegroups.

The battlegroup is the main military capability that the EU possesses. It can be formed by one state alone as is the case with the larger states, or by a combination of states. There are today 16 such battlegroups, two of which are on rotation every six months. These forces cannot be otherwise employed during this time. They must be able to deploy in five to ten days' notice.

The decision to develop the concept was made at the previously mentioned Berlin meeting of the three states in February 2003, and the *Artemis* was a brilliant test case of the concept. The actual decision to launch the battlegroups was taken by France and Britain after bilateral negotiations and where Germany was invited at a later stage. The three great powers then proceeded to propose the concept to the Council of Defence Ministers where it was approved in June 2004. The role model *Artemis* and its success played a key role. This underlines the importance of experience, of having proved one's ability in the security and defence field. The fact that the EU could undertake a sharp mission was extremely important for the ESDP.

Once approved politically, the EUMC and the EUMS started to work on the modalities (EU battlegroup concept, 10501/04). Not surprisingly, as early as in 2005 there was operational capacity, because both France and Britain provided one battlegroup each on rotation. The EUMS designed battlegroup generation conferences starting in 2007. From this date there were two battlegroups on rotation simultaneously.

We see how the core logic has worked very well in this case. The decision to form battlegroups was taken by France and Britain, and seconded by Germany. It was then adopted by the whole of the EU. The initial formation of such groups was undertaken by France and Britain. Within a year, 21 EU states as well as 1 non-EU state, Norway, had joined to develop national or mostly, multinational, groups. Finally, the one example of a battlegroup sized operation, *Artemis*, was basically undertaken by France, seconded by Britain, but it very quickly attracted contributions from 16 states in the EU.

These facts show that a core logic is very functional in the EU. Instead of repelling others, it attracts them. We see the same with regard to the EMU: almost all states want to join once they are able to meet the criteria for so doing. The secret of why this happens lies in the main thesis of this book, namely the nature of what we term 'new national interests'. State need to *participate in order to shape decisions* and institutions and in order to gain international standing. Note that those states that do not try to join EMU, Britain, Sweden, and Denmark, are states where the chief executive, that is the government, is constrained domestically. Their governments mostly want to join the cores of the EU. This is also the case with Denmark where the government wants to lift the national restrictions on participation in the CFSP that resulted from a national compromise in 1992. However, as the only way to lift this is through a referendum, the government is unable to act unless public opinion changes.

The political dynamic seems clear: *Core logics in the EU are increasingly necessary for decisions to be made in a decision-making mode of 27 members.* Further, core logics work as engines of sovereignty 'pooling'; they attract all the members whose governments are free enough to join. In the following chapter we will see how those governments that are constrained try to play two-level games in order to be able to join the cores.

A study of the battlegroups concludes: 'the formation of EU battlegroups remains a remarkable achievement ... the tremendous speed with which the battlegroup concept has developed remains a remarkable EU achievement' (Andersson, 2006, p. 21). The battlegroup itself is a militarily impressive fighting force. It consists of three or four mechanised infantry companies, perhaps with as many as ten to twelve combat vehicles armed with cannon, accompanied by howitzers and heavy mortar. Helicopter gunships may also be added as well as air defence systems. The more modern the networked centric capacity, the more lethal the force. Yet size is a limitation also in terms of deployment time. It is only a battalion in size, which means that it remains a tactical unit.

The battlegroup is the realistic type of unit that the EU can field today. A much larger intervention force would be desirable, but has proven to be unrealistic. The Helsinki Headline Goals that were initially launched in 1999 led to impressive paper-tigers, but nothing more. Up to 15 brigades were committed, a total of 50,000–60,000 troops, but these troops existed basically on paper. They could not be deployed on short notice – something inherent in the crisis-management concept – and they were not trained as multinational forces. Moreover, the same forces were registered to both the UN, EU, and NATO. When NATO started to generate a much larger rapid reaction force, the NATO Response Force in 2002, it proved near to impossible. It was declared operational only some five years later, but this decision had to be reversed in 2007 due to troop overstretch in Afghanistan.

In a detailed analysis of the EU's history of security and defence, Salmon and Shepherd (2003) point out that two factors decided against a supranational or integrated military force. One was the lack of political will to abandon sovereignty, the other was the lack of interoperable forces. The only states that can provide full military 'leadership' are France and Britain, and the political will – as far as it goes – was added after 1998. 'Since only two states, the UK and France, have national HQs capable of running a multinational military operation on a reasonable scale, it seems logical that one or both of these states would form the core of the leadership' (Salmon and Shepherd, 2003, p. 43).

In sum, the British and the French are the key players in the generation of the battlegroups and their formation. Unlike these two states that have formed national battlegroups where they do not have to integrate with anyone, Germany has opted for multinational battlegroups only. This is probably in order to gain the legitimacy of multilateralism. If we look at the implications of pooling sovereignty in multinational operations, these are usually at the tactical level: states contribute various capacities and therefore depend on one another. This is true when the formation is more permanent. In battlegroups, states really have to integrate in terms of serious training before the group is ready to be on rotation. The states that only have national groups avoid the integration that other (usually smaller states) have to accept. Further, all smaller states usually have to accept that a large state fields the HQ as they themselves are too small to have one. Also here, both France and Britain can provide their own. There are thus no integrative or even 'pooling' implications of the EU battlegroup concept for these states.

The EDA and defence industry 'pooling'

The other major French–British decision is the creation of the European Defence Agency (EDA). The decision behind this is pragmatic from the British side, but may form part of a larger European industrial vision on the part of France. It is clear that there are compromises in the decisions that the EDA takes, carefully balancing between the French desire for a common European defence industry and the British desire for a common market in European defence procurement.

The EDA is potentially very important because the problems of European defence production are those of small scale, national champions, protectionism, and competition in a small market. These suboptimal structural conditions face dominant American companies that have completed their consolidation already. The US defence market is protected, but it is much larger than that of Europe.

In a discerning analysis, Guay (2005) provides a key to understanding the critical situation in which European defence production finds itself.

While the United States has retained its defence spending since 1989, albeit with troughs, average European spending is down 15 per cent from 1989 levels. For the three states France, Britain, and Germany, the percentages are approximately 10, 20, and 30 per cent respectively. Thus, the two major military states in Europe have decreased their defence budgets in the period, while this is not the case in the United States (Guay, 2005, p. 145). In absolute terms the US expenditure level is four times larger than the three European states put together. In addition to this, US politicians are fiercely protective[48] of their market. In 2003, Congress passed the infamous 'Buy American Act', while US defence companies merged throughout the 1990s to achieve economies of scale. Today, the world's three biggest defence firms are American (Lockheed Martin, Boeing, Northrop Grumman). The fourth is British (BAE – formerly British Aerospace), while the United States again dominates with Raytheon as the fifth largest and General Dynamics as the sixth. In the seventh place follows French Thales and European company EADS, while the rest of the top companies are all American.

It is important to note that the few European companies which make it to the list of world leaders in armaments are the results of mergers: BAE is a rare case of national consolidation and acquisition of an American company while EADS is a merger of French, German, and Spanish companies where the public share is 34 per cent. But 'there is little left to consolidate in Europe' after this (p. 143), and the problem is that of markets. The same holds for the consolidated American companies, but as stated, they have a large domestic market. In Europe however, each state continues to protect much of its defence sector. Article 226 of the EU treaty exempts defence from the internal market rules. But the creation of the EDA is a step in the direction of developing common rules for both research and development, and procurement.

There are already some important examples of common procurement. Airbus won a contract for transport aircraft (A400M) over Boeing. This is a seven nation cooperative project. Further, Britain is buying refuelling aircraft from EADS, another blow to Boeing. Britain has also chosen French Thales to design a new aircraft carrier and opted for a French–British joint venture in building these, dating from 2004.

The common procurement project Galileo is another example of European cooperation. Twenty-seven states, including non-EU members, participate in this satellite project and which aims to have 27 satellites in operation by 2008. The US-owned GPS system is not available to other states, although it is used by NATO allies. Guay remarks that the United States bars foreign states from the GPS for security reasons whereas the EU allows non-members in when they can pay, an indication that the economic issue is so important that it dominates the security issue.

Politically, EU actors like the Commission and the European Parliament have urged more common projects, arguing that they will be the basis of the ESDP. The EDA is the political platform for this. But the main driving force for all this is not political, but economic. European defence companies are barred from the large US market and face the dangers of takeovers if they remain small. Hence the need to consolidate. But the many small, protected markets for national defence companies that were typical in the cold war period are extremely dysfunctional today. There is no longer need for European states to be self-sufficient in defence as they are not a threat to each other. Agrell (2005) has shown how Swedish defence companies have opened up to foreign investors through a major process of privatisation in the 1990s. He concludes that competition, often involving civilian technology, is the key to success today. Thus, defence derives its products from dual-use technology, and this cannot and should not be protected. For the EU, the ability to compete meaningfully requires some kind of working market for these products. But how can protectionism in small national markets be countered?

'Within the EU, a growing chorus of voices is calling for a single, competitive market in armaments that is treated in much the same way as other economic sectors' (Guay, p. 154). This demand is enhanced by the isolationism of the US defence market and the small scale of the national European markets. The latter cannot sustain an industry for the future, and the former does not seem to change. This leaves European states with the horns of the dilemma: rely on buying American in the end, or develop a sustainable European industry.

The EDA is therefore a necessity at a time when markets are both too small and too closed in Europe. The beginning was slow, but by 2005 the EDA had adopted a Code of Conduct on Defence Procurement (21 November 2005) which very carefully established a voluntary cooperation among states in the EU. The wording of the code reflects the sensitivity of this field. While there is a 'need for decisive progress towards creation of an internationally competitive European defence equipment market' (Code, first paragraph), the text underlines that this is a 'voluntary, non-binding intergovernmental regime'. The procurement market over 1 million euros is to be opened to all states, and the EDA will monitor that this happens. Time and again, however, the scheme is emphasised as voluntary: each state can withdraw any time without penalty, and the EDA realises that 'this regime will not prosper unless all states find benefit in subscribing to it'.

Even with this careful tone, the logic of the document is crystal clear: it is in every state's interest to open up procurement in order to obtain better prices and stimulate competition which can ensure innovative industry. There is simply no other choice, given the parameters. However, as Guay points out, national companies often prefer national political protection, and only intergovernmental political agreement can change this.

In November 2007, the EDA adopted a 'Framework for Joint European Strategy in Defence R&T'. The intention is to achieve

> better collective performance from national R&T budgets, in turn linked to another EDA decision from May 2007 on a strategy to make a European Defence Technological and Industrial Base (EDTIB). The French strategic interest behind EDA is that of creating a common industrial base in the EU, sources in Brussels affirm.[49] The British, however, want a free market and for EDA to act as a 'clearing house' and 'facilitator.' There is full war in EDA between these points of view. (says one source jokingly)

The British underline the difference in French and British views of EDA: 'The British view is that EDA should be more like a dating agency, not an institution with power'.[50] Yet the compromises reached are a start towards a common market for defence. There is French–British agreement on common Research and Technology (R&T), but not common procurement. There is also agreement to abolish the very common offset arrangement between the two states – something which smaller states typically want to retain.

The EDA has a steering board consisting of defence ministers of participating states. Further, the EDA is a voluntary arrangement, a type of core integration. It has recently published a long-term strategy document, 'The Long-Term Vision' (2007), which looks at military capability needs in a Europe characterised by low fertility, post-national values, and a changing view of the use of force. This is a sophisticated policy analysis which fully recognises the new parameters for European military defence stating that 'defence will have to contend with public finances under pressure from a growing pension burden, a shrinking recruitment pool and societies increasingly cautious about interventionary operations ... and inclined to favour security over defence spending' (Executive Summary). The key issue for the EDA is the need to strive for European defence under the increasing economic strictures. Thus, we are faced here with another pragmatically motivated French–British initiative born of necessity rather than ideology.

Conclusions

The *Livre Blanc* for 1994 emphasised expeditionary forces and a common EU policy, and France pushed for crisis management to be added to the Amsterdam Treaty. In the negotiations for the treaty, France agreed not to push for a mutual solidarity clause in return for enhanced cooperation. France defines the Petersberg tasks to include *all but Article 5 operations, that is the sharp end of operations.*

The EDA shows the difference in French and British thinking. The French want a common European defence policy, the British a true market only. On the battlegroups, there was the Helsinki summit trade-off which made a compromise possible, and London and Paris made detailed plans in November 2003 prior to a tripartite summit with the Germans in Berlin. The French also made a proposal for a Gerdarmerie force in 2004.

Africa was the testing ground for EU expeditionary forces. When the Tervuren initiative – security cooperation between Belgium, France, Germany, and Luxembourg – was launched by Belgium, France was reluctant because their priority was the relationship with Britain. The demand for an EU HQ was dropped when a compromise with the British was possible. This indicates that the bilateral cooperation was more important.

The Constitutional Treaty, later the Reform Treaty, retained a national veto on defence. Both states agree on the need for efficiency and improved military capacity as well as an institutional presence. The French promoted both enhanced cooperation at Nice – which the British initially rejected but later accepted – as well as permanent structured cooperation in the Reform Treaty.

The French–British bilateral relationship is key to the ESDP developments. During the mid-1990s France revised its NATO policy, seeing it as a way to enhance the ESDP (, 2003). The Bosnian and Kosovo crises made it clear that it was impossible for Europe to fight, even in Europe. The focus became one of modernisation and so-called jointness. Without major change NATO would be dead, a key issue for Britain. Howorth notes a 'close-knit epistemic community between London and Paris' (Howorth, 2005, p. 174). Further, London realised that it might differ from the United States in the future, and therefore needed another leg to stand on.

But the St. Malo work slowed down with the advent of the chain of events following 9/11. There was a prolonged disagreement over the interpretation of the term 'autonomous'. The reality of the primacy of the military tool remains, however: there is no viable ESDP in military terms without French and British capacities. Thus, de Villepin stated that 'there can be no European defence without Britain'. As the Iraq crisis was unfolding, with disagreement between the two states, they continued to work as usual, reaching compromises on military planning cells in the EU and scrapping the Tervuren plans.

The inclusion of Germany in the defence core of the EU is both a goal for France, as well as a means. The French have traditionally led the EU, but not with regard to the ESDP. Yet France has continued to involve Germany as much as possible during early stages. During the Iraq crisis there was a strong alliance between the two, but lately both Merkel and Sarkozy have emphasised a good US relationship, thus making tripartite European leadership more likely as well as open to the United States for the first time in many years. It is the domestic constraints on Germany that prohibit a true development of such a relationship.

The *directoire* concept is key in the development of the ESDP. The idea is that a core that is an *avant-garde* also draws other Member States into its centre. We see this in the case of Sweden which punches above its weight in the ESDP, sending special forces and other forces to both Bunia, Kinshasa, and now Chad.[51] Both France and Britain want to break the political impasse in both the EU and NATO. Thus, the Berlin 2003 European summit was preceded by a directoire of the three which aroused criticism. This was repeated in February 2004 before an ECOFIN meeting, and was the format for agreeing on the EDA. We see that same format in the Iran negotiations, and during the years of the Bosnia crisis. The great power format was used in the so-called Contact Group.

The French and German interest in the *avant-garde* goes back to the Lamers-Schauble proposal of 1984. The French have always wanted the dynamics of a core in order to solve the problem of progressing without losing the national veto. At Tervuren, there was French reluctance as this was a group of states where only France could provide state-of-the-art military capacity. This did not include Britain and therefore was in direct opposition to the United States. Chirac later regretted having taken part . The French, logically, distanced themselves from the so-called chocolate summit.

The persistence of a French security strategy is clear: a multipolar world is only possible if the other pole – in this case Europe – has autonomous military capacity. As we have seen, the military gap between Europe and the United States has widened in the post-cold war period. While the US defence budget has remained stable after a 'dip' in the 1990s, the British budget decreased by about 20 per cent between 1989 and 2005 whereas the French decreased by about 10 per cent in the same period and the German budget decreased by 28 per cent (Guay, 2005). These figures speak for themselves: *they imply that autonomous military capacity can only be had in a coalition setting.* This must also imply some kind of institutional setting as common military capacities that are usable in modern internal conflicts far away from Europe can only be had when forces are trained together for rapid reaction. This kind of training is new in the sense that European forces have not been in distant operations before. The EU battlegroups and the NATO Rapid Response Force are key examples of this kind of expeditionary force. The follow-on forces that were planned under the Headline Goals are intended for much slower deployment.

As argued in this book, multilateralism in security and defence affairs increasingly means coalitions of willing and able states. We have shown how France and Britain formed a core in the EU in all-important political initiatives in this field after 1998, and that this kind of cooperation implies that participating states are able to contribute meaningfully. Words without contributions are empty. The lack of relevant military contributions is a clear and natural limitation of the ability of states to have a say.

This is also very true of NATO. Howorth points out that 'NATO appears, at best, to have an appropriate function as *a facilitator of coalitions*' (Howorth, 2003, p. 244). He continues: 'Unless the Europeans make themselves capable of fighting alongside US forces, the latter will have no alternative but to operate on their own. There is, therefore, a real danger that a "three-tier" alliance may emerge' (p. 245). The first tier consists of the British and the French, the second of most European militaries that have not modernised to become expeditionary, and the third consists of all the new members of NATO whose contributions are niche capacities at best.

The variable which can be termed 'relevant interoperable military capability' is thus of key importance. Without such capabilities, European states cannot operate alone – the French ambition – nor with the United States, which is the foremost British concern. The common French–British interest is clear here, but it serves both strategic visions. It is not surprising therefore that there are hard bargains and compromises behind their common decisions.

It is a fact that only those states which are militarily viable matter politically when a request for a PSO is made. In NATO, as well as in the EU, there are many states that make but token contributions to PSOs, even none at all. Given the admissibility of a core logic in actual mission formation, decision-making on such issues and questions lies with the states rather than with the EU. We therefore speak about a 'pooling' of sovereignty in this field rather than any form of supranational integration. But this having been said, it is a fact that the EU represents an attractive arena for PSOs for the Member States as it develops various capacities, including the EDA. Political risk-sharing is a central feature here, as is enhancing the EU's common actor role on the world stage and promoting more rational military integration than the current 'bottom-up' approach.

With regard to strategic thinking in the EU, it follows from this analysis that it resides with the two main states in EU security policy-making, France and Britain. The ability for bilateral cooperation between these two states ensures that major security policy initiatives are only undertaken when first developed between these two. Strategy in the practical sense of 'what to do' is therefore controlled by these two states. The main trust of EU security policy is pragmatic in terms of 'what to do' – if anything – once a crisis occurs. In other words, as an arena where 26 players have formal rights of a veto, the EU does not allow for forward strategic thinking like that of a major state. However, as we have seen, both. The British and France think strategically, mainly in terms of what kind of security structure Europe should develop. The great strategic game is between the French interest in Europe puissance and British Atlanticism, and this game is now played with both players at two tables – the EU and NATO.

5
Playing the Two-Level Game: France, Britain, Germany

In this chapter I analyse another major dynamic of EU security policy, one which is constituted by national government elites who seek a pooling of sovereignty in this field. My hypothesis is that even the major actors in security policy such as France and Britain take an interest in such pooling to an increasing extent. This is because the EU provides a shield against public opinion turned sour when an operation does not go well, or when there are national losses, thus making risk sharing – military as well as political – a reality. There is an additional reason in the need for military integration, as multinationality in this field becomes necessary and cost-effective. More 'steering' at the international level of the modernisation of defence forces also makes it easier to blame international actors when bases and jobs at home must go. Further, the most important rationale for pooling sovereignty in this field is influence. Through active participation and contributions a state carves out a place for itself because going it alone is no longer possible, even for great powers like Britain and France.

Even if security policy is the most traditionally sovereign of all policy fields, there are rational reasons why government elites seek more international pooling of sovereignty in this field as well. We have also noted that there is frequent disagreement between domestic actors in this policy field today as it has become 'de-securitised' after the cold war. Government elites therefore have several reasons for using the freedom of action that the international level offers also in this area.

Two-level games played

A set of hypotheses about interests and political integration can be developed from theories about two-level games as developed by

Putnam (1988) and Koenig-Archibugi (2004a). Putnam's general model suggests that governments seek international 'self-binding' when they are weak at home and desire changes in domestic policy. He suggests that governments may find it advantageous to present a 'tight mandate at the international level', here the EU, thereby constraining other states. The logic is that the other states then have to accommodate the lack of negotiating scope of such a state, so that it may be advantageous to the state in question. The advantage of this is that the government can get a 'better deal' at the international level in the international negotiation if its domestic 'hands are tied'. If it is domestically constrained, the other states must then grant concessions in order to secure an agreement for all. Conversely, if the government is constrained by an international agreement, it can impose this solution at home, arguing that 'the EU made me do it'. It is therefore advantageous to be constrained by the international negotiation if the domestic level disagrees strongly or is very volatile politically. States that cannot effect the desired changes domestically may therefore use international obligations and constraints in order to do so. Thus, at the outset we see that even great powers have a need for a multilateral framework. The Putnam framework of analysis postulates that states strong in the policy field in question – here security and defence – also can make use of the two-level dynamics (Putnam, 1988). The strong state can impact the more on negotiations and use the IO as a multiplier for its interests. Where the weak state can make use of its weakness to argue that others may accommodate it in order to an agreement to be made, a strong state can play games more freely.

The development of this theme is especially interesting in the work by Koenig-Archibugi (2004a) who advances the thesis that governments 'collude' in seeking a strengthened role for themselves vis-à-vis their own publics. He cites examples that show how the Italian government has opted for collusion in order to effect change at home, acting from a position of weakness: 'During the cold war, the government was quite happy to surrender sovereignty to international organisations if it meant removing defence from the political debate' (p. 173). This has also been the case with Germany in the security and defence field.

Thus, weak governments will welcome 'self-binding' at the international level precisely because the domestic level is so important in policy-making. Neither realism nor constructivism captures this. As for states with strong powers in a given issue area, they may need 'pooling' of sovereignty for other reasons, such as 'pooling' of risk and cost, and/or shaping of the IO in question. The importance of the EU means that also EU-sceptical states like Britain have to participate.

Thus, the new national interests we analyse in this book are very different from the static geopolitical interests of traditional realist security policy. Instead they are changeable and optional, but not more optional than the fact that a government that wants influence in NATO and/or the EU must be able to contribute relevant military capacities and take risk. What we see emerge here is a fascinating political dynamic: the domestic level now matters most in security and defence policy, but it often has different interests than the government. The government typically wants to make major contributions to operations under NATO and the EU in order to strengthen their hand in these and to maintain them as such, and governments regard security policy in the traditional manner of 'high politics'. Publics and domestic actors have little insight into and knowledge of this traditionally secret policy area, and are wont to use civilian yard sticks and criteria for making their judgements. There is controversy over risk and the fallen, over cost and longevity of operations, and over motivations. Why participate in optional wars, may be for the sake of gaining general influence? As we shall see, both weak and strong governments need the multilateral setting as arena, scapegoat, and as raw material for shaping their strategies.

The hypotheses that underlie this model are the following. Governments want maximum autonomy not only abroad, but also vis-à-vis their publics. Participation and even integration in international organisations tends to increase governments' power over domestic actors, and they may find the trade-off between domestic and international power in favour of strengthening their national hand through 'self-binding'. It follows from this that a government which is weak domestically in an issue area will seek international 'self-binding'. Such 'tying of hands' may make the government able to shift domestic agendas and marginalise various actors in pointing out that international obligations narrow or even determine national freedom of choice. The need to transform domestically as a result of binding agreements to NATO and/or EU criteria is one example of such an international argument, and one for which a study of Norway and NATO found evidence. Norwegian politicians argued for transformation of traditional mobilisation forces into expeditionary ones through the use of arguments from the NATO level. No domestic actor could question the demands made by NATO as they lacked information and independent sources of interpreting the latter. Two-level argumentation is therefore especially useful in the security policy area which is characterised by secrecy and discretion (Heier, 2006).

Do states play two-level games in security and defence policy? What do we know about this question? The question is whether major European states will adopt such two-level strategies in order to manage sensitive questions like military integration of national capacities, modernisation of defence sectors with large job layoffs, and so forth. The case seems a plausible one. Resistance to change is vast: decisions to cut jobs and bases are extremely unpopular.

The stronger the elite, the less such strategies are needed, but an 'EU cover' may nonetheless be useful at home. The Koenig-Archibugi framework suggests that states with a weak role in security policy (without the foreign policy prerogative – FPP) will adopt strong EU policy positions, that is, desire more supranationality. Two such states are Germany and Italy, both strong supporters of a common EU foreign policy as well as a common security and defence policy. France and Britain, however, are the only two states that retain the FPP, which means that the French president and the British PM themselves decide on the deployment of troops. Parliamentary control is very weak. Thus, we should expect them to be content with the intergovernmental model of EU security policy.

We see, however, this development from sovereignty hedging to sovereignty pooling clearly in both British and the French cases. The shift, which is tactical and not strategic, occurred in the late 1990s in both cases. In Britain, the Strategic Defence Review of 1997 and the St. Malo declaration of 1998 mark the shift. In France, it is the reappraisal of NATO that most clearly marks a tactical change. This occurred in 1995–6 when France returned to the political structures of the organisation.

The 'blame game' for post-modern use of force – in non-existential threat situations – is nonetheless a serious political business. As discussed in Chapter 1, legitimacy today is the key political resource needed for any military operation. Iraq and the legitimacy question haunted Tony Blair, and there is no EU or NATO actor with whom to share the blame in the case of the Iraq war. As I have shown, legitimacy for the use of this 'hard soft power' is increasingly important in Western states (Matlary, 2006). The modern open foreign policy debate in a culture that lacks 'the warrior ethic' may induce also strong governments to 'outsource' the unpleasantness of using force to the EU to an increasing extent (Coker, 2007).

Thus, there are two reasons why all states in Europe may desire the pooling of sovereignty in the security and defence fields. One can be referred to as the needs and benefits of military integration; the second is related to the benefits of sharing blame, risk, and having a 'multilateral' cover for unpopular military deployments.

As Wagner notes, the increasing degree of integration in European militaries will lead to a stronger role for the international level in the 'two-level games'. Not only will 'self-binding' occur, but so will real integration, 'real binding'. 'The general trend of privileging the executive in the process of Europeanization is exacerbated in security and defence policy by the integration of military forces on an international level' (Wagner, 2005, p. 5). The battlegroups of the EU illustrate the discrepancy between the military integration commitment and the intergovernmental nature of political decision-making as a state that participates in a battlegroup cannot opt out of a decision to deploy. If it does, it has to leave the battlegroup which has to be reconstructed (and probably cannot deploy as planned), and we may safely assume that the state in question will not be invited to participate in any more battlegroups. If we add a strong domestic dimension to this, it is clear that governments may find themselves politically impotent, squeezed between negative publics and real military commitments in international organisations. The management of the domestic and international levels in the two-level game metaphor is challenging, but rewarding in terms of power and autonomy for a government, yet it also entails ties that may bind more than intended. We return to this at the end of this book.

The other reason mentioned for 'pooling sovereignty'– having a multilateral cover – deals with the precarious balance between commitment in ongoing operations and domestic public opinion. Western elites increasingly lack the experience of war and a 'war ethic', and the same must be said for Western publics (albeit less so for the United States, Britain, and France) (Coker, 2007; Vedby-Rasmussen, 2007). When the media report from the battlefield, criticism mounts, and NGOs and the media request detailed information on targets, weaponry, calibration, and so forth. (Frantzen, 2005; Schmitt, 2005). They demand the right to change views on deployment as fighting progresses, and are often easily swayed by day-to-day events in the field. Only in operations without much media coverage can one still maintain elite control – political and military. But almost all military operations today are highly focused in the media. Media are often 'embedded' in operations themselves, and in general, operations must count on much media interest once military force is employed.

Do EU governments play this game in security policy? Such 'self-binding', also called 'executive multilateralism', appears an attractive strategy to governments that are deeply constrained by parliaments in deployment of military force. Here, only France and Britain have retained the FPP whereas most other EU states labour with elaborate procedures for decision-making in this area. A major difference is between states with an FPP and other states, and the main difference is evident in the role parliaments play.

There is not much research on the democratic accountability of military force in terms of political processes, but rather more on the formal accounts of rules for democratic accountability (Born and Hanggi, 2004). This is at least a start, but much more needs to be done on the actual two-level game processes. The research on this theme is also quite often normative because it assumes that there should be maximum democratic control with all aspects of an international operation. For instance, there is a research institution, the Geneva Centre for the Democratic Control of Armed Forces that is committed to increasing the domestic, that is the democratic control, of the military tool. A major publication from this research group is in fact entitled *The Double Democratic Deficit: Parliamentary Accountability and the Use of Force under International Auspices* (ibid.). The assumption is that is it a democratic problem that publics and parliaments do not have all control over international deployments. Yet, this kind of control requires extensive expert knowledge of how modern wars are conducted, of the interaction between political and military factors, and also of the ability to refuse to respond to short-term and partial political concerns. It is for this reason, among others, that the FPP has existed in this policy field. Yet today there is, as argued in this book, no turning back to less democratic practises as security and defence policy has become 'normalised'. Whatever one thinks about the normative issue, the empirical issue is what is of concern here.

Domestic political processes

What do we know about domestic level policy-making? In the studies by Bono (2005), Wagner (2006), and Born and Hanggi (2004, 2005), we have the major work that is done on the formal aspects of this. The latter three scholars all take the normative view that the more parliamentary oversight and control, the better, but Bono's work is much more balanced than the other two.

Wagner's main theme is that the ESDP is undemocratic: 'This article argues that the ESDP, though not challenging civilian control of the military, does warrant concerns about the democratic control of defence policy in Europe' (Wagner, 2006, p. 201). The article goes on to argue that the Europeanisation in general diminishes democratic control, and that military integration in Europe contributes to a worsening of this situation. Citing Moravcsik that 'international cooperation tends to redistribute domestic political resources toward executives', he points out that parliamentary control of international operations tends to be weak at the outset, and that the current type of tightly integrated missions makes this an even more serious problem. There is no discussion with this logic; it is clearly a relevant issue that integration leads to lack of real control the more integrated an issue area is, but it is not necessarily good for military effectiveness to have constant intrusion by politicians that for the most part know very little about this issue area.

Wagner points out that there are major differences in national political systems. Whereas the French, British, Spanish, Greek, and Dutch governments can deploy on their own, a two-thirds majority is needed in the Hungarian parliament. Parliamentary approval prior to deployment is needed in most other European states. Many states have a special foreign and security committee in parliament that must approve such deployment, and where discussions are confidential. Wagner's conclusion is very clear, admitting also the normative gist of his research: 'From the normative viewpoint which has inspired much of the civilian power literature, the democratic deficit in the ESDP must appear alarming as the democratic control of security and defence policy has frequently been counted among the defining features of civilian power' (ibid., p. 212). Using the example of Germany, he interestingly points out that executive power has increased because of the two-level game logic: 'Opposition against the use of force is easier to overcome for executives if security and defence policies have been internationalised' (ibid.). The concrete case is the Airborne Warning and Control System (AWACS) decision in 1993 when NATO flew these reconnaissance aircraft to enforce the 'no fly' zone over Bosnia, something which met major opposition at home. Yet the argument about NATO commitments and consequences of a withdrawal were much stronger because the AWACS depended on German personnel, and withdrawal would have severely hindered the operation.

In the work of Born and Hanggi, we find detailed data on the formal and informal powers available to parliaments in security and defence affairs. The normative concern is the same as that of Wagner: the already weak parliamentary control in this field is further weakened when military force is integrated in multinational operations. This is because there is much more room for the executive to play two-level games. Only the executive has information, and it controls the access of parliamentarians (Born and Hanggi, 2005).

The 'collusion thesis' introduced earlier – that governments cooperate at the EU level to offset criticism at home and to change domestic politics – is even less democratic than the two-level game. If executives collude among themselves, they agree to devise policies that help each other against own domestic opposition. Yet we see that the normal diplomatic practise acts like this: visiting ministers typically praise any government they visit, and will refrain from critical comments on a country for fear of intervening in internal affairs. Likewise, the EU or NATO will always praise the government in power, regardless of other political forces in a country, and diplomatic norm is to relate to the government of a given state only, never to other actors. It is common to offer 'help' from the international level if a government has a hard time at home, and NATO or EU officials will always be very positive about any contribution made by any government. In short, government executives have tremendous advantages over opposition and parliament in any democracy when the issue area is international. These advantages are strengthened by their membership in international organisations where all governments see advantage in mutual assistance. If we add to this that the security area is special because of its secretive and specialist character, and because it deals with the very core of a state's survival, we see that the strength of governments is very considerable.

In a detailed study of parliamentary power resources, Bono provides a very useful analysis of actual decision-making at national level, to be discussed for each state below. Her conclusion supports the argument that governments can play two-level games more easily in this policy area than in others: 'The results of this investigation demonstrate that national parliaments are either constitutionally and procedurally unable or politically unwilling to exercise supervision over EU-led military engagements' (Bono, 2005). What is of normative concern to these scholars – the lack of democratic accountability – is empirically a verification of the 'collusion hypothesis'. There is a so-called double democratic deficit at work in the ESDP, as well as in NATO for that matter. Parliamentary control with international deployment is weak, and even weaker the more integrated and multinational the operation is. Let us look at this in more detail.

Weak governments: Italy and Germany

We now examine two-level game playing in security and defence policy in the case of two weak and two strong executives, all four major states in Europe and the EU. The thesis is that weak governments have the more to gain from such political tactics, but as we will see, strong states also play this game. The Italian case is included here in order to provide a broader picture of the situation of weak governments in the security and defence area. As stated, two strong cases are France and Britain. By including another case of a weak executive we hopefully get more information of typical security policy dynamics.

Italy

If we take a brief look at Italian defence policy, we see that its parliament is in much firmer control than in the French and British cases. It must approve deployments prior to sending troops, which is not the case with the other two states. It must also approve the mission mandate, the budget of the mission, the longevity of the mission, and it also has the right to inspect operations in the field through visits. But it does not have the right to approve or change the Rules of Engagement (ROE), which are the detailed rules for using force that soldiers follow and which differ from operation to operation (ibid., p. 205). As regards the common foreign and security policy of the EU, the Italian parliament has a committee of foreign affairs, but it is only informed at the discretion of the government. Bono notes that in the security and defence area, the British and French parliaments are weak and the Italian is strong, whereas the opposite obtains in the case of EU policy.

In the Italian case, foreign policy shifts with majority governments, and there is evidence that the mechanism of 'collusive delegation' was at work: ' the government was quite happy to surrender sovereignty to international organizations if it meant removing defence from the political debate .... It has exploited its international commitments to legitimize defence activity domestically, while it has justified its minimal commitments to international bodies on the grounds of internal weakness' (Andreatta and Hill, quoted in Koenig-Archibugi, 2004a, p. 173).

This pattern has continued until the present: Italy wanted the military dimension included in the treaty revision of the Treaty on European Union (TEU) in 1990 because it 'would improve the domestic legitimacy of Italy's participation in the military coalition against Iraq' (ibid., p. 174).The author continues 'Also the integrationist position held at the intergovernmental conference in 1996/97 was due at least in part to the desire to avoid damaging domestic political conflicts by Europeanizing foreign policy decision-making' (ibid.).

Bono has investigated two cases of parliamentary control of the ESDP decisions to launch missions: operations *Concordia* and *Artemis*. In the Italian case, she concludes that despite the important parliamentary powers in security policy there was no consultation with parliament prior to the Italian decision to contribute to *Concordia*. The issue was neither debated in the European Affairs, the Defence nor the Foreign Affairs Committees (Bono, 2005, p. 213) despite the formal powers that suggested that parliament be involved prior to the decision to contribute troops. The reason for this, says one of Bono's interviewers, was that 'the lack of political pressure' (p. 213). As Bono sums up

> The Italian government sought parliamentary approval for Operation Concordia once it had already committed itself to taking part in the operation. Parliament approved Operation Concordia on the same day that the operation was launched and without asking any substantive qualitative questions. Italian parliamentarians had formal powers to provide monitoring of the operation, but decided not to use them. (p. 214)

In this case, it is abundantly clear that formal powers meant nothing to real decision-making. As discussed, security and defence affairs are complex, often characterised by secrecy, distant from the general population's interest and no vote-winner. It is therefore conceivable that such an issue was of no interest to parliamentarians as they would not get any credit from voters or media for taking an interest. We may thus witness a two-level game played also by parliaments. They may engage in issues that are high on voter and media agenda, and foreign affairs are generally not in this category.

Bono also investigated the decision-making on the sharp Operation *Artemis*. In this case, her findings are similar. The Italians sent only one person to this operation, but this is still a contribution. Nevertheless, there was no discussion of the operation in parliament before or after it took place.

A study of Italian public opinion and the use of force reveals that the Italian public is generally in favour of international operations as long as they are multinational and have a humanitarian purpose . But Italians have a lower tolerance of casualties than public opinion in other European states (p. 110), and more importantly, Italians do not accept any loss of life, be it enemy or their own. There is, in other words, evidence of the post-modern political culture that is risk-averse in the extreme in the findings by Isernia. This is also supported by my interviews.[52] As Vedby-Rasmussen argues, modern society is so risk-averse that risk-takers are unable to find a role unless it is in the military (Vedby-Rasmussen, 2006, p. 189), and as the former chief of the British defence staff, Sir Charles Guthrie, put it 'The simple truth is that late 20th century Western society is not very well adjusted to the prospect of fighting' (cited in ibid., p. 175). As a result, humanitarian missions with good and noble purposes are acceptable, but not war-fighting for security interests. The Italian data show very clearly that *warfare for security interests is met with very low support*. Another implication of this general culture which is so risk-averse is that casualties, be they their own or the enemy's – even a journalist who has taken the risk to go into a war zone – cannot be accepted. Everything must be done to save a life, however culpable the person in question is, and whatever the tactical cost to the operation. Furthermore, in general the government cannot rely on a 'rallying around the flag' syndrome in Italy. The use of force must be legal, humanitarian, incur no losses, and involve no actual use of force to be sustainable over time. Post-modern publics do not accept the characteristics of the military tool any longer. This presents the government with formidable obstacles and promotes two-level game playing.

Thus, in the Italian case we see a pattern where there is very little parliamentary interest in security and defence issues in general. Yet, when an issue is highly media-focused, there is a major national debate and the government is forced to become engaged. This was the case when a well-known Italian journalist, Daniele Mastrogiacomono, was kidnapped by the Taliban in 2007. The fact that he was so well-known and a media figure resulted in massive pressure on the government. In fact, the government almost collapsed over the issue.[53] It had to pay ransom, conduct talks with kidnappers and most importantly, swop hostages with the Taliban, freeing one of the most wanted Taliban leaders, the brother of Mullah Dadullah (ibid.). This action is a major violation of all rules of international politics and diplomacy in such cases, and undermines NATO solidarity directly. Yet the survival of the government was the number one priority: 'In Italy, the kidnap revived misgivings about any involvement in Afghanistan, increasing the risk of a government defeat in the senate' (ibid.). We thus observe the commonsense chain of events: parliaments become interested (and interesting to the government) in cases where the public and media are engaged. The trigger for public engagement is drama in the war zone, which involves nationals – be they kidnappings or killings.

The paradox in the field of security and defence policy is as follows. As long as the events in the field are undramatic, there is less than normal engagement by domestic actors because security policy does not deliver votes, but once dramatised through death or horror, the public is more than normally engaged. In essence, this means a populist engagement as opposed to a serious and in-depth understanding of a policy area that calls for responsible decision-making.

The Italian government therefore has much to gain from two-level game playing. It is too weak to manage its domestic forces, and must 'import' decisions in order to participate in them. In the Italian case, it may seem that 'executive multilateralism' has succeeded without too much conflict, although the public continues to be strongly anti-war in most cases, most clearly the Iraq war. One wonders how the executive had managed to balance two irreconcilable positions for so long, as seen above, but the then prime minister, Berlusconi, opted for the domestic preference as election neared. Again, domestic political survival trumped serious security policy.

Germany

The German case is that which best illustrates the dilemma governments increasingly face in this field. But here, we see a well-organised and mature democracy where democratic control of deployment decisions is very strong. This is the direction that we must assume that other European states also move in, given the importance of legitimacy in all phases of an operation and the roles that new actors assume in the security and defence field. In Germany, there is a strong emphasis on democratic control of the military tool as well as a strong scepticism towards it. This is naturally based in the historical legacy of the Second World War. There is also much more pacifism in the attitudes of publics in former East German states (Juhasz, 2001, p. 80), correlated with leftist political orientation. With unification in 1990 one could therefore assume that the generally pacifist political culture of Germany was strengthened.

The German parliament has the right not only to give a mandate to deploy, but also needs to check on an ongoing operation as it unfolds. In a comparison of parliamentary powers over deployments in European states, Germany scores highest together with the Netherlands (Born and Hanggi, 2005, p. 6). These two states have parliaments that have the right to prior approval to send troops abroad, approval of a mission's mandate, approval of ROEs and command and control as well as risk assessments, and the right to visit troops abroad as well as right to terminate a mission. It is very noteworthy that parliament can micromanage a mission down to the ROEs and tactical issues in the field. ROEs are usually a matter of military assessment and competence, and not a political matter. In addition to these two states, only Denmark has similar parliamentary rights of approval.

In Germany, however, the constitutional court in Karlsruhe plays a major role in deployment abroad because the German constitution forbids German troops to participate in foreign wars. The ability for Foreign deployment became possible only after protracted political battles in the mid-1990s when the German constitutional court made the final decision that German troops may be deployed abroad, but only with parliamentary approval, and only in peacekeeping missions. The battle over German participation in NATO missions with AWACS aircraft in 1993 was a turning point. After having refused Bundeswehr contributions to the Gulf in 1991 due to strong domestic opposition, the German government was able to get a court ruling to contribute the AWACS aircraft. Their turmoil surrounding this had a considerable 'cost side' in NATO: Was Germany still an ally that could be trusted? The government realised that 'similar behaviour in a future conflict would probably result in a crisis with its major allies' (Wagner, 2005, p. 7). Therefore, government arguments about integrated force structures, alliance solidarity, *Bundnisfahigkeit* and *Integrationsfahigkeit* were used, referring to obligations in NATO and the EU. By a narrow margin, the constitutional court voted that the government was able to deploy German military personnel in the AWACS aircraft, and the consideration of alliance obligations played a key role in the decision: 'Allies and European neighbours would inevitably lose trust in German policy; the resulting damage would be irreparable'. In the end, the major decision on whether the government can deploy troops beyond Germany's borders specified two exceptions: in the case of existential defence of the country, and in cases where Germany has alliance commitments (ibid.). With regard to the Rapid Response Force of NATO, the German government launched a process for increasing the speed of the parliamentary process, this time in close cooperation with the United States.

German troops have strong limitations on what they can do. They have an unflattering history of being reticent to fight in situations where it is needed, such as in Prizren in Kosovo in 2004 when they were accused of 'hiding in the barracks like frightened rabbits' in a German police report.[54] In ISAF, the small Swiss participation which was embedded with the German PRT in Kunduz had to leave because it could not get its job done: 'The two Swiss officers (that remained) could no longer carry out their mission effectively because of the measures taken by the troops for their own protection', said an army spokesman. The Swiss depended directly on the Germans, and could not move about to carry out humanitarian projects because the Germans refused to move outside the camp.[55] Another unflattering indication of the lack of a warrior ethic in the German armed forces was the report on the physical condition of the army in March 2008. 'Germany's defence ministry said today that it would take very seriously a parliamentary report showing that the nation's soldiers are more overweight than the average citizen'.[56] Forty per cent of all soldiers in the age bracket 18–29 are overweight compared to 35 per cent in the general population, the study conducted by Cologne University found. The reason for this truly shocking state of affairs is seen by the MOD spokesman Thomas Robbe to be a 'passive lifestyle encouraged by military officers (!) and an excess of bureaucracy' (ibid.).

The German case is special in the sense that it rests on a very antimilitaristic political culture, but it is of general interest in the sense that parliamentary control of defence is well developed. This is a condition that we can expect will obtain also in other EU states. Koenig-Archibugi remarks that 'what is interesting here is the use of the EU, the WEU and NATO by the supporters of a more activist role for Germany' (Koenig-Archibugi, 2004a, p. 169). In addition, the international organisation in question also 'interfered' with strong arguments to such an extent that the government used 'help' especially from the EU in the domestic debate. 'Gaining influence by appealing to the legitimizing effect of the EU was especially significant in the German case. The CDU leadership argued that a German refusal to take on an active military role would endanger the European integration process' (p. 170). Because of the strong degree of internalisation of European integration as vital to German status and foreign policy, this argument resounded well in the debate.

The case of German military contributions to ISAF in Afghanistan in 2008 shows that domestic politics determine security policy to an almost total extent. The German case is the best documented in Europe although also Italy shares in much of the same political logic. According to Marina Nuciari, professor at the Italian Military Academy and the University of Torino, the Italian public is ill-prepared for war-fighting, and losses incurred are routinely presented as accidents and exceptions in the public debate.[57] Politically, military affairs have a low standing in the hierarchy of political issues and no politician therefore wants to jeopardise re-election by being engaged in this area. In brief, security and defence policy is highly unpopular with the public and therefore the political class will avoid these issues. This is a pervasive phenomenon in European politics, but it is not well documented or analysed yet. Consequently, the German case is particularly interesting because it clearly shows political logic at work.

At the beginning of February 2008, American Defence Secretary Robert Gates sent letters to European NATO members asking them to contribute troops to the dangerous southern district of Afghanistan. The letter addressed to the German government was particularly sharp in tone, and was leaked to the press. This happened right before the NATO defence ministers' meeting in Vilnius and the famous Munchen conference on security policy that followed immediately.

The leaked letter caused a major debate in NATO and particularly in Germany. The United States had just pledged another 3,200 soldiers, this time war-weary marines that came from Iraq for an emergency tour of a further seven months in the south of Afghanistan where the forces of Canada, Britain, Denmark, and Holland had already suffered several losses and were ready to be relieved. The troop contribution was already extremely unevenly distributed: Germany with its population of 80 million contributed only 3,200 soldiers, and they were in the relatively pacific North and had very constrained ROE. They could not engage in combat or any other dangerous activity. This 'double' caveat was one of the most constraining in NATO. The government had to agree every detail of the mandate with parliament, and public opinion remained extremely hostile to any use of military force. The Gates letter triggered a major reaction, as was intended.

German public opinion differs from that of other European states. For instance, as much as 48 per cent think that the United States is a greater danger to world peace than Iran;[58] 58 per cent think that the United States should not have a leading role in the world; only 55 per cent think that NATO does not play a central role for German security. Whereas 74 per cent of Americans think that war may be necessary in some cases, only 32 per cent of Europeans think the same, and only 25 per cent in Germany (ibid.). From these statistics it is clear that German public opinion is extremely pacifist. The percentage who oppose that the Bundeswehr should engage in war-fighting stands at 86, which tells a lot.[59] These realities, stemming from historical experience, are not attempted to be changed by the political leadership. The public debate does not contain the normal terms for war and war-fighting; the German chief of defence is merely named a 'general inspector' (*Generalinspekteur*), and discipline in the curriculum in the officer's education is called '*innere Fuhrung*' (internal leadership). The lack of realistic terminology leads to excessive political correctness in the debate. The editor of *Sud-Deutsche Zeitung*, Stefan Kornelius, calls for '*Mehr Ehrlichkeit*' ('more honesty') in an editorial on this topic.[60] He analyses the motto of the German army '*Schutzen, vermitteln, helfen, kampfen*' ('Protect, Communicate, Assist, Fight'), pointing out that the last part of the motto is always ignored in the public debate – it is taboo! There is a '*Scheinkonsensus*' – a pretence of a consensus, he says, which forbids speaking about fighting. The political parties do not dare to break this consensus, they have avoided realistic talk for years, and to speak about fighting has become completely impossible.

Other commentators agree. Hebestreit concludes that the terms of the 'permissible' public debate has been cemented for years, and that it is a 'make-believe' world about Germans helping the Afghans in their development only.[61] 'There is never talk of danger, of violence, of fallen – because here in Germany no-one wants to hear this.'[i] The security expert of *Die Welt*, Michael Sturmer, calls his admonition 'Because they do not know what they do in Afghanistan'.[62] 'It is time, in Berlin and elsewhere, to call War, War.'[ii] The German public has simply not been told what goes on there:[iii] (ibid.).

Given this state of public opinion, what happened when Gates called for German support in a very difficult situation for the alliance? No states were ready to replace those in the south, all of which have rotated several times. The United States had nearly 30,000 troops there, and had suffered 483 fallen; Britain had 7,800. The Germany contingent (of only 3,200) was deployed in the relative safety in the north.[63] The reply to Gates's request was very swift. Within hours, Chancellor Merkel's spokesman had replied that no change in the German mandate or in its contributions in ISAF would happen. The matter was simply settled. Defence Minister Franz Josef Jung seconded her. Germany already carried a heavy burden; it would be folly to move any troops to the south, he said, stressing how very important the German work in the north is.[64] There was no discussion of extending the number of troops

---

[i] '*Von Gefahr, von Gewalt, von Toten ist seltsam wenig die Rede – weil es bei uns in Deutschland auch niemand hören will.*'
[ii] '*Denn sie wissen nicht, was sie in Afghanistan tun.*'
[iii] '*es wird Zeit, in Berlin und anderswo, einen Krieg einen Krieg zu nennen.*'

at all. Instead, Jung proudly pointed out that Germany would assume responsibility for the Norwegian Quick Reaction Force (QRF) in Masar-el-Sharif in the north. This force, on 60 minutes readiness, should assist all other NATO troops and civilian actors in the entire northern region. It comprised only 250 soldiers. The desire to have this role came from the German army as officers were keen to do real soldiering and to get realistic counter-insurgency experience. By not talking about the offensive operations that this force had undertaken over the last months of 2007, the German government was able to get this proposal through parliament without a renewed debate about the mandate for German ISAF troops. The Norwegians had been in several dangerous operations in the fall of 2007, including a major offensive against the Taliban, the Yarekate Yolo II, but this was not generally known in Germany. By managing to place the QRF mission within the existing mandate from parliament, Jung could offer some active soldiering capacity to NATO. This was presented as a major contribution, but only German eyes could possibly view it in this manner. Norway, a country of just 4.6 million people, had operated the force for two years. Germany, with 80 million people and an army of 250,000 troops thought it a domestic 'victory' to be able to field a combat force of 250.

As stated, the Gates' letter was made public in the beginning of February 2008, at the most opportune time, immediately before the NATO meeting of defence ministers in Vilnius and the Munich security policy conference. In the letter, there was sharper language about the need for German contributions than had been used to other NATO states. Gates made an 'urgent appeal' to Germany to contribute more and in the south:[65] 'The US demands war fighting from the Bundeswehr. Pentagon expects helicopters and parachuters to the South of Afghanistan.'[iv] The demand made was in line with the military needs. Gates commented that states which were so constrained as to not be able to take risk, could at least send helicopters and other materiel which was much needed.

The US pressure put on Germany was strong, but not unusual. It is common that the United States approaches NATO countries inturn when it seeks to exert maximum influence prior to NATO meetings. That such bilateral pressures are also leaked is a matter of routine as well. In this case, it is not known who leaked the letter to the German press, but it was said to stem from the MOD itself. It could have been a German

---

[iv] 'USA fordern Kampeinsatz der Bundeswehr: Pentagon erwartet Entsendung von Hubschrauber-Einheiten und Fallschimrjagern in den Suden des Afghanistans.'

MOD official or politician interested in getting as much leverage as possible out of the situation, on the logic of two-level games.

The US demand for increased German contribution was also supported in a more diplomatic way by the NATO secretary-general. It acted as a missive into German domestic politics, and created a major debate, as we have seen above. But the remarkable result of this debate is that this strong international pressure had no result. The government, led by a Christian-Democrat and pro-NATO politician, Angela Merkel, moved extremely swiftly to reject the call for more troops. Only some hours after the letter was made public did she address it through her spokesperson. He simply rejected it, saying that Germany had already made important contributions. Simultaneously, Defence Minister Jung gave a press conference where he detailed German contributions and argued that they were so important in the north that they could not be moved south. While an editorial the *Wall Street Journal* referred to 'so-called NATO allies' like Germany 'that fill up lots of air space at policy conferences in Brussels talking about Europe's readiness to play a prominent role in world affairs', there was almost no nuance in German public debate on the matter. It amounted to a unanimous rejection of the US call.

'Politicians who wish to have a future in German politics cannot say anything', said an editor, 'The only one who has had a different view, Klose, has no such future'. Hans-Ulrich Klose is a social-democrat (SPD) politician who is also the deputy chairman of the parliamentary committee on security affairs. He is the only German politician who is positive to German deployments in the south.[66] All others called upon to respond said that Germany must remain in the north only. A general, who for obvious reasons wanted to remain anonymous, said 'We import security from the Americans, and one gets sick when one sees how the Germans in Afghanistan are restricted!' (ibid.). *International Herald Tribune* commentator John Vincour adds 'What we are dealing with is a truly pathological situation'.[67] An expert commentator, the director of the German Institute for International and Security Affairs, Volker Perthes, says that German politicians run for cover and fear the next election: 'In game theory, that is called a "game of chicken" for cowards'.

The only expression of disagreement about the issue appeared to be the commentators and academics. Two of the latter made a strong plea for sending more contributions, also to the south. Jan Techau and Alexander Skiba from the German Council on Foreign Relations in Berlin published a strongly worded article in *International Herald*

Tribune on 8. February 2008: '*Germany must pull its weight...*' where they diagnosed the situation as one of 'paralysis'. In fear of being rejected by the electorate at the ballot box, 'they (the politicians) compromised on following through on the country's strategic interest'.[68] In a longer paper in German, they explained that German elites have refused or neglected to speak about hard power for so long because public opinion still suffers from the complex created by two world wars. The domestic foreign policy debate has therefore been unreal, dishonest, and largely non-existent. A false image of Germany as a peace nation has been created to avoid talking about when and how to use military power. 'We demand an honest debate domestically', they conclude. When I asked Defence Minister Jung what he planned to do about the lack of realism in the German public debate on Afghanistan, he simply referred to the special situation in Germany due to its past.[69]

Thus, the response to Gates' request was remarkably uniform. The commentators were also unanimous in their analysis of why. 'Merkel's election fear drives Afghan refusal', *International Herald Tribune* succinctly summed up 'Security analysts and legislators here in Berlin stated that one of the main reasons why the German government would not send any of its 3200 troops in Afghanistan to the south was that combat losses would be exploited by the pacifist wing of the Social Democrats as well as by the opposition Left Party'.[70] The political situation is the cause of the reticence and lack of leadership on the issue, German editors concur. The editorial in *Frankfurter Allgemeine* is entitled 'Eyes Left!'[71] and points out that the unusually quick response by the chancellor (in the negative) has 'everything to do with the election in Hesse' (ibid.). In two state elections (Hesse and Lower Saxony) just prior to the Gates letter, the party of Merkel, the CDU, suffered major losses. With a public opinion that maintains spending on defence to be a waste, and the United States is the culprit in Afghanistan, the editor comments, speaking about strategic issues that involve German military risk is equal to political suicide. Like Schrøder before her, Merkel may have to not only play down, but also play against the ISAF mission's war-fighting aspects in the campaign to be re-elected.

The political dynamic that explains this startling situation is one where domestic concerns of re-election now completely trumps any consideration of security policy. As discussed above, there is great variance in the role that domestic factors play in security and defence policy in Europe. Three sets of variables make up the power triangle. One is the strength of domestic opposition to or support for deployments; the second factor which is ultimately a function of the first, is the strength of the government in this policy area; the third factor is the strength of international pressure on the country in question. The first factor, essentially the role of public opinion, can be highly critical of a given deployment without having much say if the government enjoys the FPP, as in France and Britain. Yet ultimately also these governments must adjust to the prevailing opinion in the electorate. But when the FPP exists, there is a time-lag of considerable importance before unpopularity matters politically, sometimes for the entire period of the presidency. Unpopular decisions in security and defence therefore do not have much importance for the presidential election unless a war is unusually politicised. In addition, systems with the FPP tend not to invite public discussion of routine deployment, such as French and British use of force in Africa. The situation has to be extraordinary, as in the case of Iraq, in order to get the public's engagement. In the Iraq war, it was the issue of the UN mandate that caused the first major transatlantic debate, and only much later the lack of success of suppressing the insurgency. The domestic variable is thus much more important politically in systems that have formal powers in the security and defence field vested in parliament. When a committee has to endorse all aspects of an international operation, much public debate ensues. The influence of public opinion is therefore translated directly into the formal channels of parliament.

It follows from this that international pressure is harder to exercise. The normal channel of secret diplomacy – including 'arm twisting' – is harder because politicians cannot make decisions freely. The press is much more alerted when an issue is a matter of domestic controversy, while it is considerably less interested when it only concerns foreign policy. The government in a political system where domestic factors determine much of security policy will have little choice but to accommodate public opinion. They dare not exercise leadership on controversial issues that will lose them votes.

The German case is at the one extreme of domestically dominated security policy systems; France is at the other – it is a president-dominated system. The governmental prerogative is total in the French case. But in the German case it is the opposite: there is total domination of domestic factors, defined as a combination of public opinion and parliamentary powers.

The conclusion that *domestic factors now completely trump international pressure seems a very solid one.* The loss of international standing that Chancellor Merkel suffers when she refuses to engage in a meaningful debate about German contributions to ISAF is obvious, and noted by the international community. To refuse to act in solidarity when NATO is in a crisis, is naturally a serious matter. Yet, it is equally obvious that the choice in this case is between loss at home and loss abroad. The fact that it is presented as a victory when Germany takes over the QRF from small Norway underlines how far away from great power status this country still is. The QRF decision was contested by the Left Party as well as by leftist politicians in the social-democratic party (SPD) as being beyond the mandate given by parliament, as it involved war-fighting.[72] In the light of this, the question of going south was understandably not something any German politician wanted to discuss only one year before the election.

As we have seen, the power of the German parliament in international deployments is extensive. This means that the power of public opinion is the main factor in determining policy. It is significant that Gates addressed the publics of Europe directly in his intervention at the Munich conference.[73] Normally, this is not acceptable for diplomatic reasons, as ministers or diplomats always address their counterparts only. To speak directly to another state's population is a form of interference in domestic affairs. This can be seen as the ultimate attempt to engage publics in Europe when their governments will not listen.

While the Afghanistan war has resulted in the 'highest number of Military Crosses awarded since WWII'[74] awarded to British soldiers and much recognition for their bravery in war-fighting, the German debate about decorations at the same time was characterised by denial of any aspect of fighting and war. The need for some kind of decoration for bravery was recognised when the German president approved a new medal,[75] but the condition for such approval was that this medal in no way should be seen as the continuation of the German Iron Cross,[76] the traditional medal in German military history. Moreover, the new medal was hotly debated in terms of whether it should be called a medal for bravery. It should not be only for military personnel, some politicians thought, but also a peace medal for aid workers, police, and soldiers.[77] 'For what, for which scenario should such a medal for valor serve?' asked one politician. 'Does the government imply, that the Bundeswehr is engaged in war fighting?'[v] This statement is extremely clear in its expectation that the army will not fight. The contrast to the British understanding of why military medals are given, is total. In the

---

[v] 'Wozu , wann, fur welches Szenario soll so eineAuszeichnung verleihen werden?' ... 'Will die Bundesregierung implizieren, dass sich die Bundeswehr schon in Kampfeinsatz befindet?'

British reporting on decorations, it is the exercise of military virtues like bravery and risk that are lauded. The Military Cross is given for exceptional bravery, often posthumously. In the German case, there is not even the recognition that there is a distinction between military and civilian activity. This shows 'how distant Germany remains from normality when it comes to the military'.[78]

Strong governments: Britain and France

In France, the president effectively decides on the use of force in his 'nuclear monarchy'. The Fifth Republic has concentrated power in the presidency's *domain reservee*: 'Parliamentary committees are weak and ill-informed' (ibid., p. 167). In Britain, the same power applies to the prime minister. The defence budget is only summarily examined by the Select Committee of the House, and foreign policy is formally still under the FPP or Royal Prerogative, which means 'the residue of discretionary or arbitrary authority which at any time is legally left in the hands of the Crown' (p. 171). In addition, foreign and security policy are not of much interest to the British public: 'Except in moments of extreme crisis, the British public has never been much interested in foreign affairs.' (p. 172).

However, with the Iraq war, also the French and the British publics – the latter belatedly – became active on the question of deployment of own forces. Thus, whereas the institutional set-up for deciding on deployment is still on an FPP-model, publics are now more concerned about the issue. This means that eventually the role of parliaments, NGOs, and publics, also in Britain and France, will become more similar to the rest of EU states.

Britain

In the security and defence policy area, the British parliament does not have any formal powers. It does not approve sending troops, the mission mandate, the mission budget prior to the launching of the operation, the ROEs, risk assessment and command and control, the duration of the mission, but is allowed to send visitors to the operation in the field (Bono, 2005, p. 205). In a comparison with other states, the British parliamentary control is the weakest in Europe. The French come second, but the French parliament must approve the budget prior to deployment.

Under New Labour, Britain changed policy on Europe, away from the hostile stance of the Tories to a policy aimed at being 'at the heart of Europe', as Robin Cook put it . The intention was to establish a position in the EU equal to those of France and Germany. Here we encounter a paradox: the British government is weak in the area of general EU policy as domestic opposition and media are very negative concerning the EU. But in the security and defence field, the government is one of the strongest in the EU.

As we have seen, the impetus for the changes that led to St. Malo were practical ones. The experiences of European impotence in the Balkans and lack of military modernisation, When the Kosovo situation arose, 'tensions between the US and Europe simmered throughout' (p. 119). In addition, African conflicts were increasingly dealt with bilaterally with France. Robin Cook and Hubert Vedrine even went to Africa together. As noted, during the very noisy disagreement over Iraq between France and Germany on the one side, and Britain, Spain, and the United States on the other, 'their (French and British) officials nevertheless continued to discuss the creation of a common European armaments agency and cooperation on proposed new aircraft carriers' (p. 125).

Yet there is also evidence of two-level game playing. Blair arranged for the referendum on the constitutional treaty text as the last state among the EU members, thus hoping that some other state would fail to ratify first, thereby leaving the problem with Britain. Fortunately (for Britain) this is exactly what happened. But with regard to decision-making on sending troops in EU missions, there is no evidence of consultation with parliament or of any domestic debate.

Bono's findings on the processes leading up to operations Concordia and Artemis show that the Foreign Affairs and Defence committees were not consulted and, as indicated, they have no formal rights to be. However, the Select Committee on European Security followed the cases closely, as it has the right to see all documents related to the ESDP. But the British government agreed to operation *Concordia* before this committee had seen the documents on it, and it does not have a right to express an opinion. The decision in the EU Council of Ministers was made on 4 February 2003, whereas the Select Committee was only informed on 12 February. Once an operation is launched, the issue moves to the Defence Committee. But also here there was no active policy-making. Bono concludes that 'the Foreign Affairs and Defence Committee did not show much interest' (Bono, 2005, p. 211).

In her investigation of Operation *Artemis*, Bono made similar findings: there were no formal discussions in any parliamentary committee, and the decision in the EU was made on 5 June 2003, but only reviewed by the committee on 25 June. By this time, the operation was far advanced. The Select Committee on European Affairs should have been consulted, but was not – something which was regretted by the Minister for Europe, Dennis MacShane (p. 216). The committee protested, arguing that it had the right to review such decisions, but this was notably contested by the government. The decision not to debate these two operations were excused by committee member Bruce George as natural because the operations 'did not amount to much' (p. 217). Deployment abroad is, after all, the normal thing in the British case – the troops are always abroad, and the global scope is the normal scope, as is the expeditionary mode. Thus, what is considered an aberration and as new policies in most other states in Europe is simply the norm in Britain. This explains why there is no public debate about these operations and why parliament still accepts the FPP. Only in the case of Iraq is there a pronounced public dissatisfaction with the military failures of the war.

British public opinion is generally favourable towards their military, and also proud of their achievements. This was evident when Prince Harry returned from duty in Afghanistan. The media, which had agreed to keep his commission secret until he returned, all praised his courage and military ability. In Britain, a 'covenant' exists between the people, state, and army: 'It is an informal understanding, rather than a legally-enforceable deal, but it is nevertheless treated with great seriousness within the services'. The army doctrine publication says[79]

> Soldiers will be called upon to make personal sacrifices – including the ultimate sacrifice – in the service of the nation. In putting the needs of the nation and the army before their own, they forgo some of the rights enjoyed by those outside the armed forces. In return, British soldiers must always be able to expect fair treatment, to be valued and respected as individuals, and that they (and their families) will be sustained and rewarded by commensurate terms and conditions of service. this mutual obligation forms the military covenant between the nation, the army and each individual solider; an unbreakable common bond of identity, loyalty and responsibility that has sustained the army and its soldiers throughout history.

In the British case, there is thus a military culture that respects and supports the work of the soldier. Most deployments are uncontroversial, and parliament takes little interest and has few powers in security and defence policy. The only reason why British governments play two-level games is in their general problems with EU-scepticism. As we have seen, both Blair and Brown have had to resort to this. Thus, the general thesis holds: when a government is weak, it plays two-level games, when it is strong, it has no need to do this.

France

The French case is the one where executive power is the strongest of all the states discussed here. There is no need for parliamentary approval of any aspects of sending troops abroad – including mandate, budget prior to deployment, ROEs, or duration of the mission.

In the cases of Operation *Concordia* and *Artemis*, Bono found that there was no discussion of either operation at any stage of their duration. On Concordia, it was reported by the parliamentarians that 'there was an overall consensus on the importance of the operation for the development of European defence and the shaping of the EU–NATO relationship' (ibid., p. 212). On *Artemis*, the French parliament was informed only by default: 'The French parliament was informed about Operation *Artemis* one day before the European Council agreed to the operation because one MP put a question to the Minister of Defence' (p. 218). Thus, there was agreement domestically on both operations, but parliament was not consulted, and its knowledge of both was coincidental.

As stated, the French constitution of 1958 places all power for foreign and security policy in the hands of the president. The French parliament is not involved in ratification of defence treaties, military cooperation agreements or any other treaty related to security matters. This is a very comfortable position for the president. He can simply make the decision himself, aided by his own advisers. The role of public opinion is equally unproblematic: it is mostly not able to play any role for presidential decisions. La Balme (2005, p. 201) observes 'Public opinion is indeed not completely irrelevant in the foreign policy process in France' By this she means that public opinion can be constraining in some cases in the sense that the president has to accommodate it. President Mitterrand had to accommodate a critical public opinion when he refused to name the Serbs as aggressors in the Bosnian war, and made some conciliatory gestures to that effect (p. 199). Public opinion allegedly also played a key role in deciding on Operation Turquoise in the case of Rwanda, but this is not very well substantiated beyond public statements (p. 198). It is also clear that presidents, especially Mitterrand, paid close attention to the need to mobilise public opinion in support of defence policy.

In the French case, however, is it very clear that the public approves almost all use of force. As reported in the previous chapter, up to 80 per cent approve of deployments, including humanitarian interventions. And as La Balme notes, French presidents use public opinion to play two-level games. When a mortar hit the Sarajevo food market in February 1994, it was not public opinion that 'demanded that something be done' in France, but French politicians who used this argument to push for air raids from NATO. As a US diplomat at the time remarked, the market massacre 'helped the French argument' (La Balme, 2005, p. 201). The massacre also made the United States make up its mind. We thus see that a strong executive may make use of public opinion in order to present it as a constraint on its own freedom of action as in this case, where it is useful at the international level. Further, Rynning's (2001) detailed analysis of domestic security and defence policy in France demonstrates that various presidents have played two-level games to an extensive degree in order to effect change at home:

The agreement between NATO and France in 1967, under de Gaulle, 'not only defined practical ties between France and NATO, but also allowed de Gaulle to establish his conception of French–NATO relations firmly on the domestic political stage' (Rynning, 2001, p. 111). De Gaulle had failed to shape NATO, the EU, and in general, the European security architecture to his advantage, and needed this agreement to offset left-wing criticism at home.

Further, Mitterrand succeeded in 'connecting domestic military reform to international agreement' (ibid.). The military reform changes adopted in his presidential period were 'the underpinning of the renewed Franco-German partnership', and here the importance for Mitterrand was the international level. A balance-of-power strategy was evident in consolidating a partnership with a Germany that might turn in a 'neutral' direction with regard to the USSR.

Rynning notes that 'Giscard had less success in using allied cooperation to protect and promote his doctrinal ideas', he 'effectively lost the ability to forge prominent allied agreements that could have a decisive influence on the domestic political stage' (ibid., p. 112). But he was not alone in failing to utilise the second level. Also Chirac 'mismanaged reform and made himself vulnerable to political attacks' because he did not succeed in creating a multilateral platform – neither in the EU nor in NATO – for the new French policy of multinational deployments (p. 113). In general, 'The ESDP is an attractive wrapping for the new (domestic) doctrine because it is based on cooperation partly outside the Atlantic alliance' and therefore this has been 'a means by which Chirac could point to political benefits of his reforms and tie the left-wing government of Jospin' (ibid.).

In these passages we see that the major driving force of French politics is domestic. The main concern is how to influence and shape domestic security and defence policy. The basis for doing so has been excellent in France because of the strong role of the president in this policy area, as argued before. Rynning is very explicit on the connection between the management of international politics and the effects at home: 'When the dimensions of doctrinal change ... (such as) allied cooperation, were poorly managed, doctrinal change was either prolonged or rendered impossible' (p. 114). In other words, the power to be had from the international level was essential to success on the part of the president.

This year a new French defence study (*Livre blanc*) is published, and will serve as the basis for a new French defence plan (*Loi de la programmation militaire*). This occurs at long intervals in France; previous White papers were published in 1972 and 1994. The chairman of this work, Jean-Claude Mallet, remarks that the key issue is to develop and solidify the ESDP:[80] 'France must take the lead inthe EU in defence matters.'[vi] We can assume that this will serve as the basis for the proposed changes in French security and defence policy.

With the Iraq war, both the French and the British publics – the latter belatedly – became active on the question of deployment of national forces. Thus, whereas the institutional set-up for deciding on deployment is still on an FPP model, publics are now more concerned about the issue. This means that eventually the role of parliaments, NGOs, and publics, also in the United Kingdom and France, will become more similar to the rest of EU states.

Weak state elites must play two-level games

In sum, there is clear evidence that weak state elites take advantage of the two-level game possibility, even to the point of 'collusive delegation' as in the case of Italy. But also German governments used international obligations and expectations as their main argument for domestic change.

[vi] '...la France devait mener de front la relance de l'Union europeenne en matiere de la defense.'

Bohnen (1997, p. 62). concludes that 'Pressures emanating from the European level coexisted with wider international and domestic pressures. In many cases, it was these other, alternative pressures which exercised the overriding impact on defence policy'. 'In sum, NATO pressures and expectations implied the need to change German reticence towards sending troops abroad, whereas participation in the ESDP was part of the general foreign policy imperative of Germany'. Combined, these two international organisations exerted fundamental influence on German defence and security policy: 'Europe ... represented a useful means of circumventing domestic pressure' (ibid.).

If domestic opposition to the use of force increases – as predicted here, also for reasons of unfamiliarity and media coverage that results in resentment of warfare – we can expect governments to seek 'hedging strategies' through more EU burden-sharing and possibly integration. As stated above, weak governments are most likely to be willing to engage in 'self-binding' in the form of integration. But also for Britain and France there are gains in sovereignty 'pooling' in the EU.

Strong state elites sometimes play two-level games

This analysis above has brought out a number of possible reasons for more EU integration in security and defence policy. For governments that are weak in their control of this field domestically, there is a rationale for 'self-binding', that is integration. For governments that are stronger, it may be sufficient to have access to the EU as a 'cover', as a resource in terms of capabilities, and as a venue for military and political risk-sharing. As seen in the French case, there is rather systematic use of the ESDP as a rationale for domestic change.

In the British case, this is less so because the general view of the EU is very negative. David Allen's research on Britain concludes that its government elite is 'Europeanized', that is it perceives advantages to British interests as well as to a common European interest in being an active EU Member State. However, the British public is characterised by the most deeply anti-EU attitude of any Member State (Allen, 2005, p. 139). The change to a more pro-European policy stance came in 1997 with the election of Tony Blair. In security and defence, 'the EU's traditionally most reluctant Member State has become gradually more European regarding security and defence issues' (Haugevik, 2005, p. 82). In political speeches held by Blair in the period 1998–2004, the links between European and British security have been highlighted (p. 83). But invoking the EU as legitimacy for effecting domestic change remains highly risky, given much of the anti-EU stance in the press.

As Wagner notes, the increasing degree of real military integration in European militaries will lead to a stronger role for the international level in the 'two-level games': not only self-binding will occur, but also real integration, 'real binding': 'The general trend of privileging the executive in the process of Europeanization is exacerbated in security and defence policy by the integration of military forces at an international level' (Wagner, 2005, p. 5). The battlegroups of the EU illustrate the discrepancy between the military integration commitment and the intergovernmental nature of political decision-making. If we add a strong domestic dimension to this, it is clear that governments may find themselves politically impotent, squeezed between negative publics and real military commitments in IOs.

There is the added problem of democratic accountability at the international level: How can governments justify 'outsourcing' their power in creating more 'self-binding' when the democratic accountability is non-existent at the international level? Neither the European Parliament (EP) nor the parliamentary committee of NATO has any real say in defence and security (ibid.). Forster (2006) further notes another problem: that at the domestic level, parliamentarians with experience of war and/or of military duty are shrinking to 'historically low levels' and that expeditionary warfare in far-away places remains distant from everyday politics; in fact, it constitutes something entirely unfamiliar.

If domestic opposition to the use of force increases – as predicted here, also for reasons of unfamiliarity and media dramatisations that create resentment of warfare – we can expect governments to seek 'hedging strategies' through more EU burden-sharing and possibly through integration. As stated above, weak governments are most likely to be willing to engage in 'self-binding' in the form of integration.

Part III

Incurring Security Policy Dependencies?

6
Coalitions of the Able: The Pooling of Military Capacity in the ESDP

In this chapter we investigate how important the military need for multinationality is in Europe. The objective is to assess how the need for cooperative and even integrative arrangements impacts on the freedom of states. Throughout this book we have argued that two factors are parameters for the ESDP: military capacities and political legitimacy. The state that commands the most military capacity as well as strength in terms of the FPP has greater freedom in its dealings with the ESDP. Such a state does not incur the dependencies that smaller and weaker states do. In our analysis, we have seen that France and Britain are both global military players and strong states in security and defence policy, whereas Germany is extremely handicapped by its domestic politics.

The point of this chapter is to look more in detail into the dynamics of military cooperation in Europe. In Chapter 7, we look at the political implications of this for the ESDP and the EU as a strategic actor in coercive diplomacy.

As discussed in Chapter 1, the paradigm shift that has occurred in security and defence policy in Europe after the cold war has profound implications for the national defence tradition in Europe. The so-called peace dividend that occurred as a consequence of the end of the cold war resulted in a reduction in national defence budgets in Europe by approximately 30 per cent, with ever-mounting pressure for lowering the budgets each year as there was no longer any territorial threat. Budget constraints coincided with increased costs of modernisation of traditional armies that were set up to counter an invasion. The new uses of military force are, however, very different. Modernisation here means not only new procurement, but a major change away from mobilised, stationary forces.

As stated, few, if any, European states can afford such monumental changes alone. They therefore seek multinational cooperation and integration both in terms of use of equipment, maintenance, forces, and occasionally personnel. This process is a bottom-up, *ad hoc* process spearheaded jointly by some states, but encouraged by both the NATO transformation process and the EU development of battlegroups, an armaments agency, the EDA and processes of capability building. Bilateral and multilateral cooperation among states in Europe now takes place as a matter of economic necessity, bottom-up, initiated by states themselves, but also with the general coordinating role of NATO and the EU.

If we assume that defence budgets remain stable, modernisation for all but the large states will only be possible through more integration. This is logical but will *predetermine more than today which military coalitions are possible*; meaning that politics follows military integration (assuming that there is no total 'fit' between military and security interests on the one hand, and general political interests on the other).

As France and Britain are the key military actors in Europe and therefore in a class by themselves, it is mostly the smaller and medium-sized states that have to find partners in cooperative arrangements. Only these, in some cases including Germany, are big enough to act alone. Yet also they need to cooperate closely with others in the operative stages of a deployment, and increasingly also for procurement and maintenance, as we will see.

In previous chapters we have shown that the major powers dominate the ESDP, in particular France and Britain. But despite this dominance in the policy-process, we have pointed out that in the EU the main decision norm is consensus because states do not leave the EU but are members in close cooperation in almost all policy areas on a permanent basis. The case studies based on rational choice models conducted by Thomson et al. (2006) concluded that self-interested actors which pursue their own interests also agree that a certain regard for consensus is in their own long-term interest. The reason for this is that an EU which is not consensual weakens itself – and thereby the EU policies that are created by states in the organisation. If a *directoire* becomes too obvious as the main political dynamic, EU states outside this constellation will protest and thereby destroy the legitimacy created by the consensus itself. It is therefore in the interest of major states also to retain consensus and therefore legitimacy to the extent that is possible, while simultaneously leading the policy-process themselves. Such leadership gives momentum and direction to EU policies but cannot move too fast or radically if this alienates other Member States.

In the case of the ESDP, the dominance of the two major states, France and Britain, is very clear. They have initiated and carried out major new policy initiatives such as the battlegroups, the EDA, the deployment of *Artemis*, and so on. The question now is how much this leading role also entails interdependencies.

The first question is whether the pressure to integrate militarily will result in interstate dependencies. Are they emerging as a consequence of military integration and the specific needs of military cooperation in theatre? This topic has not been exhaustively examined by any scholar as yet. There exist, however, empirical 'mappings' of this phenomenon, and some tentative conclusions.

The second question is whether political interdependencies arise in the security policy field from the EU system itself, despite the great power dominance and the 'core logic'. As argued in the beginning of this book, states have 'new' national interests. One of these is to act with multilateral legitimacy, another is draw on the EU as a power 'multiplier' – France and Britain alone amount to much less impact on the global scale than does the EU as an actor. The major powers cannot act alone as in traditional international politics. When they act, they do so in coalitions, often within an international organisation.

Military integration in Europe

The military integration that currently takes place is primarily driven by budgetary considerations, but the process is nevertheless a dramatic one that is only now starting to become recognised (Matlary and Østerud, 2007). To take one example, in his annual briefing on the status of the Norwegian armed forces, Chief of Defence General Diesen , made it clear that unless the budget line starts to follow the real cost of procurement, up to 25 per cent of Norwegian military capacities will have to be discontinued in the near future, and the whole military structure will disappear in the next 25–30 years. But the history of Norwegian defence budgets does not suggest that increases are likely, and this is not atypical of other nations in Europe.

Traditionally, military officers will set the lowest level of multinational integration at the corps or brigade level. In the cold war period, there was no integration below the corps level. Each NATO Member State maintained its national forces, and these were stationary. After the cold war, there has been a major shift in all aspects of the military's functions, as discussed in Chapter 1. Today expeditionary forces are much smaller and may be up to battalion size for most states. Even these occasionally consist of multinational units. The French military doctrine is that multinationality should only be used at the strategic level, and not below (Weber and Haddad, 2007, p. 53). Cooperation below this is only possible 'when the situation is very secure'. They add 'For a coercion force, the most effective level must remain the brigade or even the division' (ibid.). Multinationality should never happen at company level and rarely at battalion level. Likewise, the British have a clear rule: multinationality will not work and is dangerous 'when bullets are flying'. They often cite the tragic example of 'Gloucester Hill' from the Korean war where an American commander misunderstood British understatement. A British regiment was surrounded by superior North-Vietnamese guerrillas and the British officer in command told his American superior that the situation was 'a bit sticky'. This in fact meant that the situation was close to desperate, and that the British should have been ordered to retreat. Instead they ended up being massacred (ibid.).

However, in Europe today with its small national militaries, multinationality takes place at much lower levels than what is traditionally recommended by military experts. Ulriksen (2007) details how military integration now takes place also below the corps level after an initial period of creation of multinational corps like Eurocorps, the first German-Netherlands Corps and the Multinational Corps Northeast. These corps have been deployed in several operations, especially in the ISAF and on rotation in NATO's Response Force (NFR). Ulriksen remarks that these two tasks have put concrete and heavy demands on the multinational corps of Europe, and this in turn means that they train together in a much more committed and well-defined way than hitherto. *The lower the level of integration, the more co-training is needed. Further, the sharper the operation, the more co-training is needed prior to deployment.* In short, European forces must be integrated in a new and deeper way today than hitherto. Multinational forces have moved away from the drawing board into the field. This makes for real integration in action, especially when we move to the lower level of battlegroups. But the key states are not pressed to integrate militarily at such low levels. France and Britain opt for national contingents and have their own HQs. Thus, the smaller the state, the greater the burden of integration placed upon it. This makes it especially difficult for small EU and NATO members to manage the modern sharp operation. The only way is to find some partner states with which they can integrate more or less permanently.

Integration in the battlegroups

The EU decision to form 16 battlegroups and to rotate them two by two biannually was spearheaded by Britain and France, which also have lead nation roles. In addition come Spain and Italy: 'One should note that the four states that provided national battlegroups (in the EU) are also lead nations in NATO deployable corps', Ulriksen (2003b) points out. This implies that these states are able to dominate a military deployment and in a sense, to gain maximum influence within it. A lead nation role in command and control is not realistic unless one contributes significantly on the ground, as in the case of command of UNIFIL II in Lebanon in 2006 where France initially offered only a couple of hundred troops while wanting command of the mission. This was heavily criticised, and France had to 'increase the offer' tenfold in order to be lead nation. Thus, a certain size of the military contribution is needed for states to be eligible to hold lead nation status. *This privileges major states.*

The four states in question have clearly understood this principle and, as stated, are contributors in such a manner as to make lead nation status warranted. This means that the four enjoy a political lead nation role as well. Large states are dominant in military integration schemes because they can offer HQs as well as entire units such as battlegroups. But being on rotation also implies responsibility to act, and thus binds states within the EU and NATO. Ulriksen mentions the reluctance of Germany to lead the EU mission to DR Congo for the election observation in June 2006: 'Since a German battlegroup was on guard in the readiness rotation cycle, Germany was expected by its European allies to lead the operation' (ibid., p. 10). But domestic resistance in Germany finally required that both France and Britain assume major responsibilities in the mission. Ulriksen's assessment is that 'influence depends upon contribution, competence, and credibility' (ibid.).

We see that even 'bottom-up' military integration initiated by states themselves has important implications in the form of 'self-binding' as battlegroups bind contributing states, especially small ones which do not contribute a full group by themselves. It is politically impossible not to participate if one is on rotation in a battlegroup and the decision to deploy is taken. Although there is the formal veto right of each EU Member State, it is clearly not feasible for only one or two states to veto a decision that the others agree upon. But also great powers incur obligations to deploy, as was the case with a reluctant Germany with a lead role in the battlegroup on rotation during the DR Congo election period in 2006. Should a state in a battlegroup on rotation refuse deployment, the whole concept of the battlegroup is lost and both the EU and the state in question lose credibility and standing.

Integration through procurement and planning?

There are attempts at 'top-down' military integration in both the EU and NATO. As stated, in the EU the creation of the EDA is intended to result in a rational process of common planning for both the R&D and the procurement as well as military modernisation phase, whereas the NATO process of setting up the NRF and the defence modernisation process led by Allied Command Transformation (ACT) have the same purpose. By being on rotation, be it NRF or the battlegroup, state contributions must be interoperable and co-trained. This works to create real military integration as well as a real political obligation to deploy, regardless of individual states' national interests.

Further, the driving force towards multinational cooperation and even integration in military procurement, training, and operations discussed above, contributes to sovereignty pooling. The EDA in the EU and the NATO 'transformation' process are loci for directed change, and the usefulness of some kind of direction to multinational integration is obvious. European states are now on the verge of realising this. The bottom-up process is dysfunctional, and EU states, especially small and medium-sized states, stand to lose if the bottom-up process continues.

The EDA is intended to direct the process of rationalising military planning for research, procurement, and cooperation. There is a clear incentive to match the dominance of US actors in this field – the United States exported weaponry to the value of 18.5 billion USD in 2005 while export sales in the three European states discussed in this book totalled 7.2 billion USD. The EDA has proposed a common research fund 'to give up the last remnant of national sovereignty in this field' (ibid.) in order to counter the market dominance of the United States. Although there are many obstacles to such a development, it is clear that both the weapons industry as well as military integration among two or more states is the way ahead for European states (Agrell, 2005; Khol, 2005; Matlary, 2005; Sköns, 2005).

Few, if any European states can afford such monumental changes alone. They therefore seek multinational cooperation and integration both in terms of use of equipment, maintenance, forces, and sometimes personnel. This is a bottom-up, *ad hoc* process, spearheaded by some states in cooperation with each other, but encouraged by both the NATO transformation process and by the EU development of battlegroups, the EDA, and capability building.

The battlegroups of the EU illustrate the discrepancy between the military integration commitment and the intergovernmental nature of political decision-making. Although the EU council will decide on deployment by consensus, only those states that are military contributors are likely to matter in real terms. We know that the coalition of leaders regarding the use of force in the EU consists of France and Britain with the support of Germany, but that no request for an EU deployment arises without prior consultation with troop-contributing states. In the case of Operation *Artemis*, the UN knew that France would bear the brunt of such deployment, and asked for troops once this was agreed (Ulriksen, 2004b). We can assume that the EU will remain vague on the question of 'grand strategy', and will be willing to deploy only on an ad hoc basis as in the case mentioned. Thus, the consensual character of the decision-making process will remain in formal terms, but the *real decision-making will evolve around those states that are on rotation with a battlegroup, always involving the major states France and Britain*. These two states are therefore dependent on each other: no major decision on the ESDP can be taken without the other.

In the case of multinational battlegroups, all contributing states are bound to deploy together even if the formal option of defection exists. As Andersson points out in his study of the Nordic-Baltic battlegroup, even non-EU member Norway is formally 'consulted' on the decision to deploy (Andersson, 2006, p. 39). In theory, states can withdraw their contribution: in reality, this will be a total blow to credibility for the battlegroup Member State that does this. In sum, whether it is 'bottom-up' or 'top-down' military integration, *European states incur political obligations to deploy as they co-train and rotate in fixed military units such as battlegroups*. Such obligations are greater for small states than for major states for two reasons. First, small states integrate in the battlegroup itself, thus not having full battlegroups. They therefore depend both on partner states within the battlegroup as well as on the IO for which they rotate. Second, major states usually also field HQ capacities, thus commanding their own forces, for example, their own battlegroup. Even if this is not the case, major states are much more likely to be in lead positions than small states. Further, the rapidity of deployment in both battlegroups and the NATO NRF implies that there is no time for the usual, slow political process. Crises that demand responses are not plugged into political cycles of intergovernmental decision-making. The use of force may therefore come about with much more *rapidity* than anticipated when these organisations were designed.

Finally, since both the NRF and the battlegroup have a deployment time of only a few days, these units have to be on high readiness, meaning co-trained to a very high standard. This factor means *real military integration*, which in turn demands that politics follow military facts. The fact of rotation means that specific states are under obligation to contribute at specific times. One cannot 'free ride' or opt out as before.

As states integrate in common R&D procurement and maintenance schemes, they consolidate military integration for the longer run and commit to common deployments through such common capabilities and their interoperable systems. Military integration in Europe, driven by cost factors, will likely continue and deepen with regard to both these aspects. The political level continues to work on formal intergovernmental terms while the military tool is increasingly and rapidly integrated. Moreover, political sensitivity about sovereignty precludes any principled discussion about political integration in this field. These developments mean a loss of national control of own forces, but it is also the precondition for gaining influence, as argued above, albeit in a mode of interlocking interdependence.

These are the military dynamics of today's Europe, and they have direct consequences for the political dynamics of the ESDP.

Military capacities: Who depends on whom?

'Europe is weak in terms of military ability' is the standard argument, most forcefully expressed by Robert Kagan (2003). The American model is seen as the only one when this argument is advanced. However, this is not an accurate assessment unless one adopts the United States as the standard, argues Ulriksen (2003a, 2004a). On the contrary, whereas the United States is No. 1 in terms of 'commanding the commons', it has weaknesses in 'contested areas', in the opinion of Barry Posen (2003). How the gap is seen is partially a reflection of different military cultures, and partially one of what kind of military preparedness to arm for. Typically, US commentators emphasise the technological gap that separates the United States and Europe. But European forces are trained for crisis management and for combining the military tool with others in the toolbox, making for a strong force in this area. Europe is best at crisis management; the United States is best at high-intensity warfare – a simple conclusion would have it. But this is too simple. The Europeans can perform most operations and in a few years' time will have acquired much of the missing capacity (Ulriksen, 2003b).

Yet even when we allow for more diverse views on how to modernise, it remains clear that most European states have to modernise their militaries more rapidly than today's pace. They have to transform mobilisation forces into expeditionary forces and acquire all the capacities needed for interoperability within a networked system. They also need force protection, including ABC (atomic, biological, chemical) weapon protection, intelligence that is state-of-the-art, and sea and airlift. All this costs far too much, given the state of defence budgets. The only solution is some form of integration.

As stated, two European states stand out in military terms, Britain and France. Both have long military traditions of high-intensity warfare as well as of 'imperial policing' where local and political knowledge are keys. They can field HQs and assume 'lead nation' roles for multinational operations, and committed ground troops in both Bosnia and Kosovo. The view of risk in these key European states is thus very different from the maximum force protection that US forces demand. As a rule, Europeans are better at post-conflict tasks and PSOs than the Americans. European states seek to integrate in bilateral and multilateral country groups in order to decrease costs, for example, Norwegian partners in the so-called North Sea Strategy which consists of states like Germany, Denmark, the Netherlands, and Britain, or the Dutch–Belgian integrated navy. Niche specialisation will most likely increase in some states whereas others, such as Norway, choose to keep as many capacities as possible and instead seek internationalised procurement, maintenance, and support functions. However, states seek to resolve the modernisation-*cum*-transformation task; it is certain that they have to internationalise much more than today in order to achieve this.

The capacities that EU–Europe lacks are well defined: 'EU forces lack the combination of projection, mobility, precision firepower and force protection together with a sophisticated, robust command chain and communications network capable of operating for sustained periods in dangerous environments' (Lindley-French and Algieri, 2004, p. 30). NATO and states such as France and Britain offer HQs and command and control capacity, but European states *inter alia* lack intelligence capacities for sustained operations far from home as well as fast sea and airlift. But for simpler missions the EU can do without such capacities, which only the United States currently has.

EU states can undertake limited high-intensity war-fighting against organised forces and extensive peace operations in not so permissive environments. The detailed Venusberg report provides data for each military capability for each EU Member State. The general conclusion is that very much must be done to move from stationary, mobilised forces – of which about only 10 per cent are usable in modern combat and/or PSOs – but that most European states can together undertake Petersberg tasks with medium intensity. When one moves beyond that, to advanced expeditionary warfare including special forces, sea control, air support, strategic lift, and so on, only France and Britain have sufficient capability.

The imperative to integrate militarily is particularly pressing for small and medium-sized states:

> Given budget constraints, if the EU is serious about building a force that is capable of operating without US support, it will have to experiment with new ways of carrying out the military tasks it cannot afford to replicate. EU members may have to relinquish some national autonomy. They will certainly need to pool resources to buy the necessary equipment and systems. And they will need to integrate their forces multi-nationally; to a far greater degree than is already done in NATO. (Schake, 2003, p. 117)

The lack of money for all the state-of-the-art military technology may lead to a 'European way of war' – based on the particularly British tradition of sophisticated cultural knowledge of the world and risk-willingness – in what amounts to 'an internal dynamic of autonomous EU military action (that) will encourage the development of a unique EU approach to warfare' (Schake, 2003, p. 118). Military modernisation and integration take place in two processes, the NATO one which is the most important, and the EU one, more at the planning stage. Yet, important decisions such as establishing the EDA have been taken. We have also seen that the budget limitations in Europe as well as military traditions that are more risk-prone than the American perhaps point in the direction of a so-called European way of war.

The processes of military modernisation are however not directed in any firm 'top-down manner', informed by political strategy. Rather, they are the result of advice and consultation in NATO's transformation command, but advice to Member States remains just that – advice! In the EU, there is no 'grand design' so far in this area, although the EDA may come to play such a role. But for the time being, the processes that integrate and cooperate in military transformation are voluntary and 'bottom-up', something which constitutes a considerable problem from a cost-effectiveness and rationality point of view; not to speak of the political point of view (Camporini, 2005). There is much unnecessary duplication in present-day Europe, but the political sensitivities here are of capital importance. Even more seriously, there is military integration without a strategic culture and planning on the political level.

As Ulriksen (2003a) points out, it seems rational with a full political integration of European forces, but this is very far indeed from any political realism and barely has advocates beyond perhaps the Belgians. There is at present no weighty political process dealing with military integration. In NATO there is open and widespread discontent over the lack of political 'muscle' and direction: The Secretary-General, Jaap De Hoop Scheffer, voices unusually blunt criticism of this, saying that the relationship to the EU was unsatisfactory and void of content, and that unless military transformation was accompanied by political transformation of NATO, there was little point in the former. He was seconded by the then two top generals of NATO, Jones and Giambastini, who in their addresses called for a political reinvigoration of NATO. Having the NRF was one thing, but the key thing was using it, as they remarked. In its conference discussion paper, the Royal United Services Institute (RUSI) in Britain concluded that unless NATO revised its 1999 strategic concept, there would be a major gap between the degree of military transformation and strategic political culture: 'As the NRF approaches scheduled operational availability, the need for political guidance is becoming increasingly clear' (RUSI, 2005).

There is, therefore, a dual problem of strategy and modernisation: unless the 'top-down' leadership of transformation in the EU and NATO has a clear political strategy for the use of the military tool, there is not the necessary direction to the process. But as we have seen, the EU has a very general security strategy and lacks a politico-military one, whereas political direction in NATO is far from uniform. Military modernisation and integration thus happens in a *political vacuum* when it comes to multinationality. Each state continues to work at its national level, making changes from a national point of view.

The calls for the 'political transformation' of NATO are becoming louder; including the surprising statement by former German Chancellor Schrøder at the *Munchner Konferenz fur Sicherheitspolitik* in 2005, where he stated that NATO is no longer the key forum for security policy-making in Europe. This was not news. The news was that he said it on such an occasion. The Europeans expect the

United States to show an interest in decision-sharing and in giving the alliance new political lifeblood, while the United States seems to prefer a two-option situation with coalitions of the willing alongside NATO. Meanwhile, the EU develops on its own and does not coordinate this development with NATO. To some extent the NFR and the battlegroups overlap, and the new EDA may be the 'missing link' in actor coordination in the EU if it succeeds in planning and procurement. The lack of burden-sharing in ISAF, as evidenced in the US call for contributions to the south of Afghanistan, threatens to undermine the alliance (Gates, 2008).

In sum, Europe – including both NATO and the EU – undertakes a process of military modernisation and integration, but is at present without any common strategic culture. With regard to NATO, this has mainly to do with the United States and its preferences. In the EU, there may be an embryonic political culture for using force, to be discussed below. However, European states possess the necessary military capability to undertake PSOs, both for fairly high-intensity operations but certainly for simpler stabilisation tasks and post-conflict management. Missing capabilities will be procured, and the economically driven military integration, especially among small and medium-sized militaries, implies a need for political governance beyond the state. At present, it is undecided whether the EU or NATO (or both) will develop more political 'muscle'.

The developments suffer from a lack of political direction and the EU's lack of unitary decision-making capacity in security policy constitutes a problem. The urgency of political management and planning from the top down of the military integration process is clear. As a typical example of how military leaders diagnose the situation, the Swedish chief of defence, Håkan Syren, concludes that 'In many ways our national defence is reaching a stage where it is sub-critical, that is each capacity is getting too small to be useful' [My translation] (Syren, 2005).

In the words of Naumann and Ralston

> Currently, national decisions regarding defence capabilities are being made largely in a vacuum, with little or no consideration of what might be most useful for the EU as a whole. National, bilateral, and multilateral initiatives are launched virtually every month but none of them is part of a broader strategic plan. (ibid., p. 60)

In a pessimistic assessment, Biscop (2007, p. 268) concludes that the current process towards military multinationality is 'one of fragmentation, duplication and very low cost-effectiveness'. The state of national militaries in Europe today is one of 'mini-mass armies' where each state guards political sovereignty and tries to keep as many capabilities as possible for as long as possible. The result is very dysfunctional, for once a capacity falls below the critical mass needed to operate it, it is useless. As an example, a state which cannot afford more than one submarine cannot have any, because one vessel cannot justify the maintenance and training costs of crew, bases, and so forth. Most overhead costs are fixed.

The same problem occurs in deployment: in order to deploy one battalion one needs at least four, preferably five others, in order to rotate soldiers and officers at a normal pace, which ideally should be in the ratio 1:6. The sustainability of forces is necessary, especially when deployed far away. Biscop makes the very interesting point that the small size of European militaries makes for *an illusion of independence while in fact it creates more dependence:* 'In reality, no (EU) Member State has the capacity to mount any sizable operation on its own, except for France and the UK, and even they need others' assistance in specific fields' (Biscop, 2007, p. 269).

The painful process of *ad hoc* multinationality, at best, leads to clusters of states which are co-trained and have pooled some capacities. The Dutch and Belgians have a common navy, the Norwegians have common F-16 units with Denmark and the Netherlands. The six states Belgium, France, Germany, Luxembourg, Spain, and Britain have developed the transport aircraft A400M, while some states have abandoned key capacities altogether, such as Denmark which no longer has submarines, and Belgium which has no tanks or artillery in order to afford armoured vehicles. In an international operation, tanks are rarely used, and artillery is hard to use when the enemy is a guerrilla force as in Afghanistan. Yet tanks are used in offensive battles, and have major deterrent value in stabilisation operations.

The EU has decided on developing its own satellite, the 'Galileo'. This, and other projects of a common European nature, have been spearheaded by France, which has the aim of independence from the United States as a stated goal with regard to this capacity. As quoted in Jones, a French minister states that Galileo was needed so that 'the EU could liberate itself from dependence on the American GPS system' (Biscop, p. 162). Jones interprets most European defence cooperation as a strategic move to decrease such dependence. However, it is a simple fact that the Europeans must have their own capacities in order to be able to inter-operate with the United States. They have no choice in this matter: in order to operate in far-away theatres, states must have state-of-the-art military technology.

The same argument holds for the long-range transport aircraft. Unless Europeans can transport their own troops, they rely on Russian or Ukranian Antonovs. The United States cannot cover the needs in Europe. The realist argument about power balancing in this case is not correct. The developments of military technology as well as the demands for global power projection add up to a practical need of having real-time intelligence, air transport, logistics that can move around the world, and so forth. Further, the way one fights in asymmetric warfare puts specific demands on communication and other networked ability: patrols on the ground must be able to call in air support, and for that they must be interoperable to the highest communication standards with Americans and others.

Importantly, because the value of Western lives is so high in postmodern risk-averse society and the deployments in non-existial wars, the military demands for intelligence and force protection must be the best available. It should also be added that the Western main tool in the fight against insurgents and terrorists is intelligence, which largely means 'SigInt', (signals intelligence). A final aspect of this type of warfare is that civilian lives must be protected as much as possible while the enemy naturally hides amongst the civilians. Western forces are under strict rules to observe the Geneva convention. This has the implication that air power must be as precise as possible, which in turn demands PGM-missiles (Precision Guided Missiles). In light of this, it is clear that there is no choice on the part of European states. If they wish to participate in modern international operations, they simply have to equip themselves with the most advanced military gear. As the UN High Level Report concluded, military robustness is necessary also in more peaceful operations because it deters spoilers, in addition to being useful if there is any fighting.

The key explanatory variable for the ESDP is therefore to be found in the military needs of modern operations. This factor is easily overlooked because it is so technical and as yet, there is little analysis of the demands that modern warfare makes on military capacities beyond specialist publications. Yet the crisis of European militaries is a double one in both military and political terms. First, they lose purchasing power while having to renew their capacities under an entirely novel paradigm, as discussed in Chapter 1. Second, they are individually far too small to accomplish such modernisation and therefore have to integrate in multinational clusters. But the tragedy of this is also a double political deficit: they lack political leadership which acknowledges that political integration is essential if military integration is to be planned, and at the international level – in the EU and NATO – there is no political power to direct such integration.

As in most such cases of uncertainty and belated recognition of changes to old paradigms, actors that have to act, do so, but in an *ad hoc* manner. This is the situation at present. As Biscop suggests, the logical course of action would be to 'shift the focus from the national to the European level: the objective should be to have full military capacity at the aggregate level of the EU' (ibid., p. 271). He continues to suggest that the most expensive capacities, such as space-related assets, which are extremely capital-intensive, should be financed in common for the EU. Other capacities such as aircraft could be owned by clusters of states that decided on common use but also retain national air capacity, whereas capacities like infantry battalions could be maintained nationally, but be pooled at brigade level if necessary.

This is not only a logical way of thinking, but a development that forces itself upon smaller and medium-sized EU states. Smaller states in Europe can contribute battalions, but not brigades, to international operations. A battalion deployed far from Europe requires very extensive support elements, from hospitals to engineering, to supply. For instance, a small state like Norway has the political ambition to deploy one battalion, but falls short of this because there are not enough battalions in the force structure for rotation over a long period of time. Thus, the need to integrate below battalion level, as discussed earlier, is a reality.

The urgency of modernising European militaries is a fact. This is above all recognised by the key military actors in Europe, France and Britain. As I have pointed out, this is the main explanation for the ESDP developments after 1998 when these two states took the lead. Other motives, such as balancing the United States and creating autonomy vis-à-vis the United States, seem logical from a general, deductive analysis of security policy, but have no empirical support. Jones's otherwise excellent analysis of European defence pooling fails to provide proof of such strategic thinking beyond the general rhetorical level of French political statements, for example. A modern European military capacity which can act globally will of course have autonomy and power as a consequence, but the need to modernise is something that is necessary if European militaries are going to continue to exist. Only a military that will never be used can continue old-fashioned mobilisation defence. The most traditional military in Europe today is the Finnish, based on reservists, conscription, and mass army mobilisation. But when Finland wants to be in ESDP missions, a very different force structure is produced, in fact a modern intervention battalion.

The conclusion so far is that the objective reasons for military modernisation in Europe – lack of money and technological imperatives – imply a radical overhaul of cold war militaries. We have seen that 'necessity is the mother of invention'; ad hoc integration in clusters consisting of states that can save by matching capacities is gradually taking place. We have also seen that there is clear lack of political attention to this urgent issue. The explanation for this is simple. It is very difficult for any national politician to acknowledge that some form of international integration of national force structures is necessary. Yet, the driving forces in this direction will not change. The only alternative to international integration is a massive increase in national defence budgets which will not happen in 'relative peacetime'.

The political process: Does it create integration?

The NATO process of military transformation is the most important of the two European attempts to direct change. Yet the process in NATO does not yield rapid results and remains intergovernmental. The process commenced in 1999 with the so-called DCI (Defence Capabilities Initiative) which aimed at facilitating cooperation between the European allies in modern warfare. The American technological leadership was clear already at this time. As Ron Asmus, former deputy assistant secretary, put it 'If NATO does not address the central strategic issue of our time ... it will cease to be America's premier alliance' . The American National Security Strategy of 2002 also emphasised this need. At the NATO Prague summit the same year, a decision on concrete capabilities was taken. The four areas that were singled out as the most pressing, were CBRN (chemical, biological, radiological, and nuclear) defences, rapid transportation, communication and information systems, and modern all-weather weapon systems.

On the American side, the slogan was: 'Out of area or out of business'. Congress passed a resolution that concentrated on a concept of NATO as a launching pad for coalitions of the able.[81] The Prague meeting also adopted the goal of 2 per cent GDP defence spending for Member States, but as we have seen, this goal is met in but a handful of Member States. In 2005, only France, Britain, Turkey, and Poland spent more than this.

The results of the DCI initiative were meagre. The United States pushed for integration of capacities, but this proved to be politically very sensitive. Testifying before Congress in 2006, then SACEUR general, James Jones, concluded that the goals of transformation were not being met: 'Our efforts to procure agreed upon strategic capabilities, such as strategic lift, the Alliance ground surveillance system, computer information systems and the like, have not been funded adequately, thereby perpetuating shortfalls within the Alliance'.[82]

During this period the DCI was relegated to the sidelines and the Americans tried to forge transformation through the creation of a rapid reaction force, the NRF. The Europeans were supposed to make up the force; the Americans would supply only marginal capacities. But as of 2007, the NRF must also be termed a failure. It has proved impossible to field sufficient capacity from European states for the force to be on rotation, and as needs in ISAF mounted, the force was no longer sustainable in its original form. While the NRF was intended to be the vehicle for transformation, lacking contributions to the force reflect lacking funding. Although the NRF was not declared operational until the Riga NATO summit in late 2006, there was still no agreement on when to use this force, and by then it was clear that NATO members needed to make additional contributions to ISAF. With serious shortages in ISAF, the NRF has now been redefined at a much lower level. The political strategy for the force remains unclear.

As of 2008, NATO finds itself in a crisis over ISAF. The work on transformation within the alliance is no longer at the forefront, as the mounting military needs in Afghanistan must be met. US Secretary of Defence Robert Gates addressed a very sharp letter to his German counterpart in late January calling for German troops to fight in south Afghanistan. This was an unusual move and met with resistance and sharp reactions (ibid., 2 February 2008). Canada, which has suffered heavy losses there, has signalled withdrawal of its forces by 2009, and the Dutch, in the same situation, withdrawal by 2010. No states have come forward to promise replacements, and the Germans have so-called national caveats that prevent them from fighting. In this context, the issue of NATO solidarity comes to the fore in a dramatic manner.

The political crisis in NATO over this shows how much disagreement there is on political strategy in Europe. The consensual system which has worked so well in former times is now a way to stall changes. States that do not wish renewed strategic discussion can ensure procrastination, but it is now clear that the Strategic Concept of 1999 will be renegotiated at the 2009 NATO summit. Yet there is no indication that states plan to increase their defence budgets. The losses in ISAF will contribute to less willingness to deploy in most Member States. Polls show that support for ISAF is low in almost all states.

In light of this, what can we conclude about the EU process of military modernisation? As discussed, the EDA is promising as it deals with all aspects of defence planning, from research to development to procurement, but as we also have seen, the only way the EDA can influence state choices is through offering a 'clearing house capacity'. The agreement text on opening markets for some types of procurement is very careful to underline that national autonomy remains, and that it is only when states find it to their advantage that they should use this mechanism. This careful language underlines how modest the EDA effort is, and how sensitive the issue of procurement remains in terms of national sovereignty. The EDA is still a very young institutional set-up, but 'the first experiences demonstrate that it remains difficult to persuade Member States to commit to necessary but expensive measures' (Biscop, 2007, p. 280). There are some few small projects in the communication area, but this does not detract from the conclusion Biscop makes 'member states are very reluctant to consider the much larger investment required for strategic transport and air-to-air refuelling' (ibid.). There are some successes for EADS, however: Pentagon opted to buy their tanker aircraft over the Boeing alternative in 2008, a decision that caused outrage in Congress and in the American public.[83]

The dilemma states face is the same in NATO and the EU; they plan according to national defence needs and do not take the point of departure in a common European need for military capabilities. Therefore the political level remains the main laggard compared to the military level. Officers in planning positions simply have to make decisions that are within the budget line, whereas politicians can use two-level game playing to speak for common security and defence policy in NATO and the EU while avoiding this at home where it is naturally a sensitive issue as it involves giving up elements of sovereignty. The military paradigm shift is taking place, but there is no sign that a political paradigm shift is on the way. As one defence minister of a small state said 'What do you want me to do? Tell Parliament that we should give up sovereignty in the defence field? This is a recipe for losing the next election'.[84]

In conclusion, we see little political will to face the core issue of integration in this field. The result is that there is no strategic planning at political level, only formal intergovernmentalism whilst cores of able states form clusters of military cooperation. These states in turn decide on deployments in the sense that they offer contributions. Unless an operation is extremely controversial, other states in the organisation in question – be it NATO or the EU – will not put obstacles in the way. After all, active policy-making enhances the stature of the IO, and may also solve real problems on the grounds that are common to all.

But what does this situation mean for EU security dynamics? It is this to which we turn in the concluding chapter.

7

Coalitions of the Willing: The Pooling of Sovereignty in the ESDP

The issue discussed in this chapter is whether this largely intergovernmental political structure – the ESDP – has an effect in an integrative direction. This is not conceived as integration in the form of supranationality, but as the question of interdependencies. To what extent do states incur interdependencies through their multinational cooperation? In the security and defence field, there is the 'hardware' question of military integration as well as the political issue of how free states remain in an international organisation like the EU or NATO. The EU is obviously much more close-knit than NATO.

The lack of unitary decision-making capacity in security policy constitutes a problem, but it may not be insurmountable. It is most likely that groups of states which are willing to contribute militarily will press ahead, such as in the case of battlegroups, the intervention in DR Congo, and in the gendarmerie unit established in 2004. The right to abstain from enhanced cooperation functions as a way to allow others to form cores, and the permanent structured cooperation of three or more states is the key to further development and integration in the EU. Extensive use of such may however lead to a weakening of the EU as such, introducing *directoire* elements. In NATO[85] as well as in the EU, the able and willing undertake missions. In the EU, this is now the rule rather than the exception, being characteristic of the EMU, the ESDP, and the above examples.

We can assume that being in the 'cores' matters in ESDP as in other fields, like EMU. This implies that those that go ahead with military lead roles – primarily France and the Britain – will have little difficulty in getting support and participation from other states provided a practical policy proposal is 'covered' by policy documents already adopted. But even with new policy ideas, it is likely that much will be acceptable as long as other states do not have to participate. Thus, an EU mission somewhere in Africa does not really effect states that do not participate. Further, as we have seen, the idea of abstaining or even vetoing a core proposal is mostly theoretical as it would carry a big political cost to the state involved. Furthermore, especially when it comes to military commitment, there is a one-to-one relationship between contribution and political influence, on the political as well as military levels. This is known from UN and NATO operations.

The unanimity requirement becomes very important, however, when we deal with treaty changes or solemn policy commitment. For this reason we cannot expect any major common policy developments that imply a formal transfer of sovereignty in the security and defence field. But the 'core logic' described above will most likely function in questions of deployments as long as there is a UN mandate. The issue of whether to deploy will thus not be decided by formal political rules of the EU but by the question of whether the purpose of the mission is seen as legitimate.

As discussed in Chapter 2, the ESDP has developed in a short timespan, starting in earnest with the TEU in 1992 and the St. Malo agreement in 1998. The 'Petersberg tasks' have become acceptable to all Member States, even states with a strong reluctance to use force (Germany) or with a policy of neutrality (Sweden, Finland) have, in fact, changed their domestic security policy because of EU developments. This empirical evidence of 'Europeanisation' shows that state elites use the EU arena in two-level games, as analysed in Chapter 5. Although unanimity remains the key decision-rule, even neutral states like Sweden and Finland take great pains to be in the forefront of developing the ESDP, that is, in its inner core. As seen, Sweden has shown ability and willingness to participate in the sharp operation in DR Congo and elsewhere in Africa as a way of showing that 'we are serious about military participation and thus are allowed into the core of the ESDP development'.[86] It is extremely illustrative of this strategic policy choice that Sweden has sent special forces not only in the Artemis operation in 2003, but also to the DR Congo in 2006 and to EUFOR in Darfur in 2008. The latter force was heavily debated in the Swedish parliament when extra money for a three-month prolongation has to be found. It seemed that the government had rushed into the deployment in order to show the flag, the opposition insinuated.[87] *The willingness of neutral Sweden to deploy in dangerous missions in Africa where it has no national interests shows that general standing in the EU by belonging to 'cores' is what really matters.*

A similar reason was given about Swedish participation in the Barcelona process: one becomes a 'good EU citizen' by being in the cores and showing an interest in geographic areas far from one's own national interests. This kind of political logic is official Finnish policy – by seeking to be in the 'cores' in the EU where one has national interests, one gains influence, but also incurs obligations.

EU as an arena or an actor?

So far, it would seem that this analysis implies that EU institutions themselves do not matter in the policy-process. Great powers seem to determine everything, and smaller states can only follow the lead they offer. The latter gain by being able to participate in global security policy, something they could not do alone. But where does this leave EU institutions?

In EU scholarship, it is clear that the EU is much like a system of Venn diagrams in formal logic – there are overlapping areas demarcated by policy area. In Pillar One, economic issues are determined by the decision-shaping and formal agenda-setting by the Commission, the role that the European Parliament plays in accepting or rejecting directives, and by the majority voting logic of the Council of Ministers. In Pillar Two, the CFSP, the formal rule is intergovernmental, and in Pillar Three, Justice and Home Affairs, there is a mixture of community institutions and member-state decision-making. We have also pointed out that even where the decision-making is based on formal majority rule, voting almost never takes place in any policy area. Instead, there is a very strong norm of consensus. This has the logical implication that 'cores' of states cannot race ahead with policy that is unpopular or resisted by the others.

What does this mean for the ESDP? I have identified two types of policy-processes in this area. The formal one of agreeing to major policy proposals such as treaty changes or new strategies remains characterised by consensus. There is a formal negotiation, and long-drawn consultations with capitals. But once adopted, a legal text in solemn form, such as an EU treaty, leaves ample room for interpretation. This is particularly the case when it is the states and not the European Court of Justice that interprets it. Fielding a 'European security and defence policy' can mean any number of things. When states propose something under this umbrella, it is hard to argue that a proposal is not included in the formal documents. Moreover, we have shown how important military contributions remain in the ESDP. In a very basic sense, *nothing can happen unless there is willingness to contribute*. We have also seen that there are very many international missions that seek contributions today under the UN especially, but also under NATO and the EU. There is also a much higher 'demand' for new missions in the world's many trouble spots than what is possible to realise. Thus, there is a continuing unfulfilled need for relevant military contributions. These are far too few, and are costly in terms of both military hardware, risk, and political support domestically. Relevant military contributions in today's very dangerous international operations are therefore truly a 'scarce good' as the economist would say. It follows that such a good is more valuable politically.

The scarcer the good and the higher the demand, the more powerful the owner of the good. This is a good metaphor for the position in which France and Britain now find themselves. Where and when the EU contemplates fielding an operation, it has to draw on the military resources of these states. We can assume that all EU states as well as all EU institutions desire a major global role for the EU in the world because it enhances the standing of the organisation as such. After all, the EU has slowly worked itself into a global role in economics and politics, but not yet in security policy. Leaving the safe democratic region of Europe behind in going global, the EU knows that it must have teeth. In the light of the scarcity of relevant military force, the states that possess this are the more powerful. From this is it clear that EU states and institutions are critically dependent on the few states that can field a HQ and project power globally whenever an international operation involves military forces. We have also seen that they increasingly do so as peacekeeping has given way to peace enforcement.

ESDP policy involving military force is therefore in a class by itself in the EU decision-making system (Eriksson, 2006). Relevant military force cannot be substituted by any other policy tool – one cannot offer money or diplomacy as a substitute. The forces needed have to be state-of-the-art, co-trained, risk-willing, and deployable globally. These requirements leave out large parts of existing European militaries.

Which interdependencies are incurred by the lead states France and Britain? As discussed in the previous chapter, both states need other states in deployments. They have a military need to involve others as no state but the United States can field a major mission over a long time alone. 'US army stretched thin by war', reports the *Financial Times* on

19 February 2008, 'nine out of ten officers said the war had stretched the miltiary dangerously thin' (ibid.). France does deploy alone in Chad,[88] but does so with small forces for a short time. The same was true of Britain in Sierra Leone in 2001. But these small rescue interventions are generally the exception today. In planned peace-enforcement missions, there is a need for pooling contributions. Moreover, great powers today need political legitimacy.

The EU has an *arena* function in terms of decisions to launch missions, but offers the best 'menu' of civilian tools 'in the market'. NATO is the more efficient and proficient military actor, but lacks the civilian tools. However, the EU is not (yet?) an actor in this field. Decisions to launch an EU mission are taken by states, and states decide on military contributions themselves, even if they come from the EU force registers.[89] But when missions involve non-military political tools, EU actors play independent roles. The commission is in charge of civilian aid, and plays a key role in this. The ESDP is therefore not to be reduced to the interests and powers of the main military actors in Europe. As almost all missions today are both military and civilian in nature, EU actors will play roles in the running of them.

In bello decision-making matters increasingly

What kind of actor capacity does the EU possess in PSO? Here one must distinguish between the political decision to deploy force and the actual management of the PSO itself, both on strategic and operational level.

The political decision to deploy is intergovernmental, but the core logic works strongly as has been demonstrated in this book. In the case of the *Artemis*, it was the UN Secretary-General who asked for an EU contribution, and France was in the lead in suggesting the intervention force, also assuming the major military responsibility. The many EU states that did not participate were only asked not to oppose this, something which was easy as the case was one of halting genocide, and the mission had a UN mandate. However, as the Iraq case evidenced, there was major disagreement among EU states. We can assume that PSOs that are without a mandate and which involve a 'competition' with NATO, that is, in cases where NATO has not declined to send a mission – will involve the same major disagreements.

In the case of the EUFOR to the Republic of Chad, France is again in the lead. It has already deployed to its former colony, and will be the main contributor to the force with 2,100 of a total of 3,700 troops. The fear that this peacekeeping force that will assist in the protection of refugees from Darfur who cross the border into Chad may get involved on one side of the conflict is expressed by some EU members. The Austrian chancellor, Alfred Gusenbauer, defending a rare Austrian contribution of 160 troops to this mission to his domestic public, pointedly remarked that France has assured the EU that it has no political agenda beyond the mission itself. The mission is led by an Irish general based in Paris(!), but on the ground it is commanded by a French general, Jean-Philippe Ganascia. He assured the concerned Austrians that the force has no mandate to take sides or intervene in a conflict.

From these two examples we see that the country with military contributions, and political interests to warrant such – France this time – also plays the key role in commanding a mission. We also see that small states without a history of using the military tool, such as neutral Austria, can take advantage of the opportunity to change domestic resistance by participating on the logic of two-level games. In this case, Gusenbauer had to contend with major opposition at home, but argued that the good intentions of peacekeeping and humanitarian purpose warranted Austrian participation. In fact, a mission to the unruly and conflictual Sudan–Chad border area is extremely dangerous. This is hardly old-fashioned peacekeeping. But the Swedes also participate in this mission, their third precarious deployment to Africa with the French. Both Sweden and Austria are neutral states with opposition to military roles in their publics. The EU thus functions as a source of authority for changing domestic policy. This is one of the *new* national interests of European states discussed in this book.

These two examples thus also illustrate that the ESDP *means different things to different governments*. The driving forces of the core remain the leading military actors, but smaller states with weaker governments in this area are only too happy to have this opportunity to make smaller contributions. This logic happens in both NATO and the EU. There is 'a rift within the EU with regarding military capability'(Berger, 2006, p. 53) as we have discussed in Chapter 6. This difference in military capability determines which states are able to operate at the most sophisticated level of modern military operations, and therefore limits the range of states that are 'able', if not 'willing'. But when it comes to political will, there is a connection between the 'able' and the 'willing': The states that have modernised to the state-of-the-art level are also those that anticipate participation, otherwise they would not be so keen on modernisation. As Berger puts it, 'Future combat operations will come from selected allied forces ... in coalitions of the willing under American command' (p. 53).

The logic of the ESDP is similar to the logic of NATO. The states that are able are also likely to be willing. Unless they had the *political* ability to engage in serious military action, they would hardly have managed to effect *military* modernisation at home. *Thus, the able are also states with strong governments in the military field.* The counter-factual is well illustrated by the German case: the army has *sui generis* problems of morale and ability, as discussed in Chapter 5, and the army is constrained by ROEs that hinder it in undertaking normal soldiering in the sense of war-fighting. It follows from this rather logical connection that states that are politically willing and militarily able are also those states that will have military success in solving the operational goals of a mission. I have not included an analysis of this, but clearly success or failure in this most important sense will have major implications for the relative power that various states will have in the EU and NATO. States that are reluctant to take risk and that deploy in order to have some nominal contribution to an operation – a criticism that can be levelled at Germany – cannot get political returns on their contributions. On the contrary, military contributions that are not very helpful or counterproductive are a liability to an operation and eventually an even greater political liability.

As for the EU's political dynamics, we have seen that less important states in this regard, such as the small, the neutrals, and those heavily constrained by domestic actors, also find the core logic to be advantageous. They can 'opt in' and use an existing core as an argument to effect changes at home. In the NATO setting, these are the states that more or less 'free ride' in the military alliance. They may sometimes be able to contribute in non-essential ways, but they provide political legitimacy and show that the alliance comprises of many. In the EU, the same effect is in evidence: many members that politically back an operation is a valuable political asset, especially when the mission is sharp.

In sum, the analysis in this book has pointed to the key importance of two factors in explaining the political dynamics in the ESDP: military capacity and political ability. The former often indicates the presence of the latter, and is a necessary although not sufficient condition for it. The states which fulfil both criteria are very clearly France and Britain. Germany, the third major state, is handicapped in terms of political ability, and the dominance of the domestic political logic over the government has become increasingly clearer in this case. The electoral cycle with parliamentary elections in 2009 explains German ISAF policy totally, to such an extent that we can talk about a single-variable case. There is no attempt to play two-level games on the part of the German government in this case: NATO demands are simply rejected without further ado, as we saw in Chapter 5.

In the ESDP various states play various games – governments dare to participate in years where elections are far off, some try to change risk-averse foreign policy cultures or neutrality; others seek new roles in the EU because they cannot be big players everywhere. Britain excels in the ESDP, but not in EMU.

The core logic is typical of many policy areas in the EU, but it is particularly acute in the military field because contributions are not subject to substitution. Also, the political risk is very special; it demands a corresponding political seriousness without which much damage can be done to a government.

Coercive diplomacy: Another area of core logic

In the last part of this chapter we turn to the political 'superstructure' of the EU. We have seen how some few states have initiated EU missions. But can the EU act as one in foreign policy when it needs to be coercive? In the previous chapter we saw that military integration is *ad hoc* because there is no political strategy at the EU or NATO level to direct it. We have argued that a main reason for states to 'pool' sovereignty in the security area is that they are able to play a much greater common role on the world stage than the sum of their powers in concert. The EU as the actor is something different from France and Britain as actors in a bilateral relationship. For small states this 'power multiplication' is even more spectacular. It is therefore of great interest to know whether the EU, as a common actor, is able to play a role on the global scale, especially with regard to coercive diplomacy. Coercion need not be military; it can just as well be political and economic.

The EU has a major 'portfolio' in using political conditionality through the policy tools of enlargement as well as economic and political agreements with third countries. The human rights dimension in this is of growing importance, but it is used unevenly and inconsistently. The criteria for EU membership are very clear, and major structural changes in candidate states have been effected through the threat of non-membership and the occasional suspension of negotiations. However, there is a principled difference between such conditionality and the threat of use of military force; and the

EU and the United States have traditionally differed in their foreign policy approach to 'rogue' states. The EU prefers engagement and the building of interdependence whereas the United States prefers a tough attitude that often implies *ultimata*, such as in the cases of Cuba and Byelorus.

But also in this area there is great power *directoire* in evidence. Jones's study shows that sanctions policy in Europe developed from bilateral to EU mode in the 1990s (Jones, 2007). The EU was the preferred forum for launching coercive diplomacy for the major states in Europe, often in collaboration with the United States. The Iran negotiations are a very good example of this. The United States kept 'all options on the table' in the background while Britain, France, and Germany negotiated on behalf of the EU. The soft power of the EU thus had a 'back up' in the form of possible use of hard power by the United States. This pattern has been common after the cold war. The EU provides a multinational 'shield' of legitimacy while major powers are free to act, beyond the strictures of consensus. The rest of the EU and the EU institutions themselves benefit from the enhanced role of the organisation.

There is remarkable shift from sanctions imposed by great powers in a bilateral mode to sanctions imposed by the EU itself, as Jones shows in his analysis. This shift has occurred after the cold war. The explanation, I would argue, is that of legitimacy and impact. When the EU imposes sanctions, it is much more important politically than when France and Britain do so. The EU 'label' has become increasingly important in world politics, and therefore states seek to have their political interests promoted under this label. The EU label is also seen as more legitimate than great power action, as discussed earlier.

In a study of coercive diplomacy by EU–US efforts, Berger finds that 'carrots' worked for both actors in the Libyan case (1999–2000) when they combined this with growing pressure. In this case, the EU was able to act, but in reality the actors that carried out EU action were the major powers again. Britain and France. In the case of Iraq (2001–3), there was also transatlantic cooperation. Here, France and Germany played the role of 'gradually turning the screw' while the United States and Britain applied classic ultimatum tactics. Yet again in the case of Syria, there is a 'carrot' approach by the EU and pressure applied by the United States (Berger, 2006).

These cases show that European states are able to perform the various types of diplomacy that exist, including the coercive form. As stated, they increasingly opt to do so in the EU format, as in the Iran case where again the *directoire* of the three was the actor, cooperating with the United States which applies pressure to the extent of allowing for military options.

We should not make too much of this, however. The EU, via the *directoire* of the three states of this study, has only a few cases of coercive diplomacy to show for itself. But coercion as well as using the military tool is possible, as we have seen. The EU is no unitary actor in terms of strategic action (Hyde-Price, 2008). There is persistent and deep disagreement on what role military power should have in EU foreign policy:

> the EU remains ham-strung by many of its member-states' illusions about the virtues of 'soft power' and by a failure to develop a common strategic culture that goes beyond the platitudes of the ESS. (Hyde-Price, 2008, p. 205)

It is only when strategic leadership and direction has been provided by the major powers in the EU that a policy emerges where EU actors partake. Even in the case of the civilian mission to Kosovo in 2008, it was the directoire of the three major states that decided to grant diplomatic recognition to the new state on the first day of its unilateral declaration of independence. The mission to assist Kosovo is backed by many other EU states, but the strategic direction to the resolution of the Kosovo case came from the great powers, not from the EU. The lack of unitary action on the part of the EU is further underscored by the fact that several EU Member States have chosen not to recognise the new state. Thus, the EU sends a 'law-and-order' mission to the new state, consisting of 1,800 police, judges, prosecutors, and customs officials, while six EU states do not recognise Kosovo (as yet).

Today, both the EU and NATO seek similar roles, such as in the Middle East and Darfur. There is also military overlap as the same forces make up national contributions to the RRF as well as the battlegroups. Such problems can and will probably be overcome by common planning and coordination. The mechanisms for such are now in place.

The United States shows no particular political interest in making use of NATO as a principle, but rather as a pragmatic choice when it is useful. The political weakness of NATO continues for this reason, and there is clearly competition between the two organisations in the PSO area.

From the angle of coalitions, we see that it is the same states which make up the cores of each organisation: Britain, France, Germany, the Netherlands, Spain, Italy, and certain smaller states. Given the ability of a core logic in actual mission formation, decision-making as such lies with the states rather than with the EU or NATO. The existence of many tools may make the EU a preferred organisation over NATO when the issue is integrated missions.

The question of the EU's future in security policy depends very much on the larger question of the transatlantic relationship. There is a large literature on this subject, much of it of a very general nature. The realist is right to note that the external threat is gone and that NATO has a new role. In this new role that NATO competes with the EU, but also complements it. Even without major US interest in NATO we may see a complementarity continue, at least for some years. However, if duplication continues and the EU succeeds in building up its military capability further, it stands to win in the long-term. It has all the other tools in the 'toolbox' and plays a key role in world politics already.

But can it act as a strategic actor? By this we mean the ability both to threaten the use of force through coercive diplomacy as well as the ability to actually deploy such force. Both aspects of strategic action demand political will and ability as well as military capability. Logically there is no political action in this field possible without the corresponding military capability. Also threats to deploy force must be credible.

Some years ago experts would readily have dismissed the idea that the EU would ever develop in this area. However, they are forgetful of the history of the EU. The European Defence Community (EDC) was aborted because of the emerging cold war. Now, in the post-cold war period, the EU has emerged as a security actor in a very short time.

We do not expect that the EU will imitate US strategic culture or tradition. On the contrary, the question with regard to the EU is whether the 'soft model of hard power' is a *contractio in termini* or not: *Is a strategic culture at all possible within the constraints of liberal, democratic politics that 'speaks softly and carries a big carrot?'* The EU has been eminently successful in structuring the new democracies of the East through political conditionality with either membership or close trade and cooperation agreements as the incentive. But this is different from threatening the use of force. Thus, the prospects for coercive diplomacy on the part of the EU seem bleak.

As stated, the intriguing issue is not whether the EU can or will imitate the rather blunt style of US foreign policy where coercive diplomacy is invoked all too fast and easily. The Europeans and not the Americans are the masters of the art of diplomacy, and one main rule is not to escalate until absolutely necessary. The diplomatic 'overkill' of the young and simple US diplomatic tradition is no role model for 'old Europe'. The question is rather whether the Europeans will be able to agree on common diplomatic ventures when they become 'hotter'. It is easy to do least common denominator *démarches* – quite another to play the high risk games of *ultimata*. One case of common action in the name of the EU – but carried out by France, Britain, and Germany – is the ongoing effort to persuade Iran to allow IAEA inspections of all sites. But in this case there is a US threat behind the effort. Without an agreement the Security Council is the next step, and beyond that possible military action. But it is not the EU that poses the military threat; it relies on the United States to provide such a threat and assumes that Iran knows this. We may therefore assume that these EU states know that coercive diplomacy without the possibility of 'all options on the table' remains illusory.

This 'bad cop–good cop' model is also useful in the case of Belarus, where the EU has a softer approach than the United States, but where policies are coordinated. In this case there is no military power threat, rather the hard power of visa bans and the like.[90]

In a provocative article, Ulrich Beck argues that the new 'religion of human rights' leads to the emergence of a 'new kind of post-national politics of *military humanism*' (Beck, 2005, p. 9). This is deeply troubling for liberal democracies, Beck argues. The good and the bad become confused, and the use of military power is legitimised through ethical arguments. In contrast to this view, British PM Tony Blair argued that the military tool can and should be a 'force for good'. The same phrase is found in the EU's Security strategy. But Blair's greatest liability in his third re-election was precisely the military tool applied to Iraq.

Using military force does not go down well with democratic publics when the issue is not existential survival, unless there is an imminent humanitarian crisis or genocide with heavy media coverage which is unfolding. Perhaps the use of military force is ultimately impossible in democracies that lack both the FPP as well as a 'warrior ethic' Or might it be that a new strategic culture is emerging, one in which the use of military force must be calibrated to European publics and their media's demands for what we will call the 'soft power use of hard power?'

Security policy in Europe is both *de-territorialised* as well as *de-nationalised*, as discussed in Chapter 2. Most use of European military power takes place far from national borders and does not involve territorial expansion, occupation, or conquest. Although holding and controlling territory is part of the mission in a peace-enforcement operation (at least to some extent) territorial expansion or conquest is no longer the goal of or reason for the use of military force. The PSO does not fit in with the laws on traditional state-to-state war. This factor further unravels the Weberian state and its inside–outside premise. When the use of force is de-territorialised in interventions that are undertaken for reasons that have nothing to do with traditional conquest; the traditional legitimacy basis for its use in defence of national territory disappears. The rules for intervention are modified to fit accordingly, with a clear weakening of the intervention norm in the 1990s. One has moved from 'humanitarian' to 'democratic' intervention, mostly benign, but with the danger of giving pretexts for a new Brezhnev doctrine (Matlary, 2006).

As discussed throughout this book, the precariousness of using military force today implies that governments always demand an international cover for such use. It is a well-established fact that all PSOs are multinational today, either as UN, NATO, or EU missions. Further, the military superpower, the United States, desires the 'multilateralisation' of political risk through 'coalitions of the willing'. This is done more for political than for military reasons, and the political aspects of burden-sharing today play a key role in NATO (Cimbala and Forster 2004). This logic is one captured by the metaphor 'two-level games' (Putnam, 1988). A government wants to have multilateral cover for sensitive political actions such as the use of force; it wants to be able to blame failure on the EU, NATO, or the UN, and it wants to be able to argue for continued use of military force in the face of domestic opposition. 'The EU made me do it' is indeed a commonly observed logic in national capitals when things go wrong, while national praise is equally normal when EU policies go well. I have argued that this fundamental logic is at work when European states consider whether to develop EU security policy further for the following reasons. First, publics are capricious in their support for ongoing military operations: opinion shifts with media reports; there is thus much risk for the individual government which cannot exit military commitments easily. Second, the EU is better able to integrate civilian and military tools more so than any other international organisation. And PSOs demand such integration to an increasing extent, making the EU a useful arena for states.

The FPP obtains only in France and Britain today and will probably weaken as democracy 'invades' also the security and defence field. In most states of the EU, parliaments and publics hold strong reins on the decision to deploy military force and may thus act as unpredictable constraints on government obligations in military missions (Wagner, 2005). Further, EU governments now use military force for general foreign policy aims of gaining international influence (Matlary, 2005; Ulriksen, 1996) and see EU membership as such also in this perspective: 'The main concern of foreign policy-makers was not the defence of national independence but the quest for influence' (Aggestam, 2004, p. 16). This general motivation of seeking influence was also valid for British (Haugevik, 2005) and French (Rieker, 2004) EU policy. In this perspective, we may assume that also the militarily strong and self-sufficient states in the EU find increasing interest in a strong EU security and defence policy.

As of today, there is no supranational decision-making procedure for this field of the EU, but the realist model of sovereignty hedging does not seem to explain why. Rather, the reason is that the EU policy has not been developed very far yet. In the context of the question of strategic culture, this is an important point because it is commonly held that the security field is one where the pooling of sovereignty will not happen.

Legitimacy is tied both to ethics and to international law, that is, to internationally recognised norms, and less and less to Westphalian state interests. The advent of a right to humanitarian intervention in the 1990s has put the emphasis on human security rather than state security. This development is continuing with the emergence of 'integrated missions' in the UN context (Eide et al., 2005), and is evident in the crisis-management policy of the EU and NATO. The EU as a law- and norms-based international actor seems well positioned to achieve legitimacy in this policy field. Thus, the EU may be at an advantage in developing a post-national security and defence policy despite the lack of unitary action capacity.

In the cold war period, strategic thinking concerned how to avoid war whereas now, as in earlier historical periods, it is about winning wars of a special kind – the PSOs. Although the notion of 'soft security' has been developed, that is a security policy based on interdependence, membership, political conditionality, and common values, to date there has been very little European thinking on the military aspects of such a security policy.

As stated, there is a growing, but not very developed literature, on the EU as a 'different' foreign policy actor in the sense of being a post-national actor, one that does not look like a Westphalian state and one that is not an intergovernmental organisation. This 'governance system' is, however, distinct in its basis in treaty law and international legal norms. The EU is based on and held together by law.

Why is this important for security policy? If *legitimacy* for using military force matters increasingly in the post-national paradigm, then any actor who deploys such force must heed this fact. The difference between the US National Security Strategy and the European Security Strategy is not one of threat assessment or of policy response, but one of difference in terms of what constitutes *legitimacy* for the use of force.

The two strategic documents largely share the threat assessment and the need to deploy force in cases where other tools do not deliver, but there is a clear difference between them on what constitutes legitimate criteria for deployment. The ESS demands a multilateral political process before deploying force, and underlines the importance of a UN mandate as the main rule. The US strategy, as is well known, opens for unilateral pre-emptive and even preventive use of force.

In short, the EU stresses international legal norms; the United States stresses a Westphalian view of security policy (threat to national interests and values) and of legitimacy for using force. The EU defines itself as an international actor according to the Copenhagen Criteria: it is based on democracy, the rule of law, human rights, and market economy principles. Both membership as well as cooperation with third countries are premised on this. Whereas a traditional state is based on the concept of a specific nation with a common history and with '*national* interests' – notably not '*state* interests' – the EU is defined in terms of its underlying values, cast as the Copenhagen Criteria. This is an important point with regard to security policy: if the 'new' security policy is one based on these values rather than on territorial interests and state-to-state conflicts, then the EU is logically at the forefront of this development.

EU strategic culture: A contradiction in terms?

By strategic actor, we mean the ability both to threaten the use of force through coercive diplomacy as well as the ability to actually deploy such force (Hyde-Price, 2004; Johnston, 1995). Both aspects of strategic action demand political will and ability as well as military capability. While France and Britain are strategic actors, can the EU become one?

The classics from Clausewitz to Brodie were concerned with war as an instrument of policy, as a political tool. The clue to an EU strategic culture is to understand that 'war' in this context will mean the military tool integrated with other tools. The ongoing work on civil–military integration, the stress on crisis management and a 'European way of war' (Everts et al., 2005) point in the direction of a carefully framed use of force. The Kosovo experience showed how strong the political constraints on using military force are, both inside the military mission – where much more force could have been used with a quick result – and from the outside, from the constant interaction in the 'iron triangle of public opinion' between publics, press, and politicians.

Coercive diplomacy gives strength and conviction to the other instruments of statecraft and is, of course, far preferable to actually using force. Averting war is often the result of effective coercive diplomacy, hence the paradox that effective coercive diplomacy enhances peace by preventing conflict. Carl Bildt, former Swedish PM, remarked that it was the tragedy of the EU that it was unable to use coercive diplomacy in the case of Milosevic. We now know this diagnosis to be correct. If Europe is to be effective as a foreign policy actor beyond the states that may aspire to membership (and which are therefore coerced by economic and political tools in a very effective way already), its politicians must be able to employ coercive diplomacy, as has been pointed out by Robert Cooper (2004).

What are the requirements of a strategic actor? First, there has to be a strategy; second, there has to be actor capacity. The latter has to be fairly unified in order to allow for strategic thinking and acting, which often involves coercive diplomacy as well as rapidity. The EU does not score highly on either variable: it is typically not able to act quickly in foreign policy and it has no tradition in coercive diplomacy.

The concept of strategic actor as applied to the EU is awkward. There is a major debate about the concept of 'actorness' itself in the EU literature, on whether the EU is an actor, a 'presence', or an arena (Bretherton and Vogler, 1999; Laffan et al. 2004). Both the EDA and 'permanent structured cooperation' are methods of making the 'bottom-up' process less dysfunctional, but in the realm of 'strategic culture' the intergovernmental method is the only relevant one.

In short, the 'actorness' of the EU is being built from the bottom up in various ways that do not involve sensitive questions about national sovereignty. The EU has the EDA, permanent structured cooperation, has developed much crisis-management capacity in both the Commission and the Council Secretariat, is developing the battlegroups, and so forth. However, this does not add up to 'actorness' and even less to a strategic culture. We should therefore treat the question of whether the EU is a strategic actor with a strategic culture in a manner distinct from the incremental capacity-building process. There is no logical connection between the two, although a strategic actor cannot act without capacities.

Regarding the military capability to act, there is a constant and relevant build-up of EU forces, both in terms of rapid reaction (battlegroups), follow-on forces, etc., as well as civilian–military interface, as discussed briefly in Chapter 3. The EU has shown that it is possible to build more than 'paper-tigers'. The problem with regard to strategic culture is not primarily military capacity, but political will.

The French have always promoted the model of an EU strategic culture: the use of force must be a possibility as both a deterrent and active policy tool if the EU is to move beyond peaceful Europe. *L'Europe de défense* is indispensable. This view is now shared by Britain. But this force will not be used unilaterally or in traditional great power politics, but within international law and by a multilateral actor. The common French insistence on a multipolar world is toned down, and the terms pragmatism and complementarity with NATO emphasised. Needless to say, this strategic vision is very acceptable to the British and also to the United States. With the election of Nicolas Sarkozy as President, 'France joins US fan club as Britain slips leash', whereas the French–German relationship 'is under the worst strain in a decade as a clash of visions takes its toll'.[91]

Capability, legitimacy, but no political will

An apparent paradox consequently arises. The EU can be expected to be able to deploy force with increasing capability and legitimacy; but it cannot be expected to threaten the use of force effectively. The Achilles heal of coercive diplomacy in the EU lies in its need for multilateral legitimacy in using force as well as in its need to achieve unitary actor status before a threat can be launched. Current debates among policy-makers and academics disagree strongly about whether the EU is able to develop a strategic culture (Heusgen, 2005; Lantis, 2005; Naumann, 2005; Toje, 2005). Solana himself calls for 'the need to develop a strategic culture that fosters *rapid* and when necessary *robust* intervention' (quoted in Toje, 2005; my emphasis). The difficulty of developing a strategic culture, given such constraints, is obvious.

We have argued that there is no major constraint on EU actorness, neither in military nor political terms, when we speak about deployment in PSOs that do not involve high-intensity warfare. Once a political decision is reached to deploy, there are military resources in Europe for most relevant purposes. The bottleneck is not procedural rules in the EU, but rather political will. The EU's lack of a developed strategic culture has been noted as a drawback in this regard: it is embryonic and in the process of development.

Notwithstanding, the basis for a post-national security policy is developing for several reasons. Absence of existential territorial threat, economic imperatives for military integration, loosening of the citizen-state social contract in general terms are all factors that make for nothing less than a paradigm shift, also in terms of legitimacy. This prepares the ground for an EU role in this field. The 'human security' basis for the use of force is being developed at the UN in the form of a 'responsibility to protect'. The EU's own security strategy adopts the concept and embeds it firmly in international law and the UN system. The concept 'weds' human rights to security, including military security.

In this analysis, we have argued that the EU, being a non-Weberian polity type, is well positioned to develop a strategic culture for the 'limited wars' of PSOs. Not only does its own value basis in the Copenhagen Criteria fit with its non-national security make-up, but it also possesses all the necessary tools in the PSO tool box.

Thus, the argument is that the EU has the capacity, both military and political, to deploy force in PSOs. It also has the 'human security' basis for so doing, and the argument is here two-fold. First, human security replaces state security in post-national wars, and second, the normative changes towards such a basis are evident, especially in the recent UN process. Further, the need for stable support – legitimacy – for the use of force once deployed is a reason why governments may want to strengthen the EU's role in security policy.

However, potential legitimacy does not equal actual legitimacy. Blair's 'force for good' can easily backfire, as it did in his own re-election campaign. There is no reason to believe that the EU's necessary conditions for strategic culture will translate into military activism. There are inherent contradictions in the 'soft power model of hard power' – only cases of clear, persistent, and well-publicised breaches of human rights are candidates for PSOs. As Beck points out, 'intervention, like non-intervention, produces resistance and de-legitimation' (Beck, 2005, p. 15). The risk involved in using military force is high, and when the threat is non-existential, hard to legitimise to own nationals, some of whom risk their lives. The EU lacks a *traditional* strategic culture, as we have shown above, and a strategic culture cannot be not risk-averse to using force precisely because the threats are presented as non-existential. These facts may make the use of force by the EU seldom and sparse in PSOs, and as argued, non-existent in coercive diplomacy.

In his study, Dutch scholar and diplomacy expert, Rob de Wijk (2004, p. 259) concludes that in Europe, 'Coercion is conceptually difficult ... this is extremely demanding for political decision-makers. They often lack basic knowledge about the use of power instruments in foreign policy. Crucially, most decision-makers lack basic knowledge of military doctrine as well' (p. 259). He adds that post-national states are particularly problematic in this regard. They are unable to use coercive diplomacy and thus, effective use of military power – which equals the deterrents and threats, not deployment.

Conclusion: A French model for the EU?

The political dynamics of EU security policy outlined and analysed in this book are clear: the Member States differ widely in terms of military ability and military culture for using force. Governments also differ very much in how strong they are as actors in security and military affairs. They use the EU level in various ways: some to enhance their general standing in the EU, to offset the dominance of the other major powers in this policy area, to shape the EU to their strategic model, to offset and change policy at home, and so forth. It would seem that participation in the ESDP has something to offer everyone, even the passive Member State that simply lets others contribute. This state partakes in the common EU role in exchange for its political support for the mission in question.

Moreover, as we stated at the outset, France and Britain did not renounce their national security and defence policy to the EU. They retained their seats at the UNSC, their NATO-membership, and their nuclear power. The ESDP was added to this, and could at any time be exited.

How does this empirical situation fit with international relations theories? In Chapter 3 we criticised EU integration theory, especially constructivist versions of institutionalism. We argued that national interests drive the ESDP, but that these take on various forms. The 'two-level game' as well as the 'great game' provided useful metaphors.

We also criticised those scholars who argue that the ESDP is explained on the basis of realism's logic, as a balancing act to meet American power. There is no evidence for such. On the contrary, France and Britain both seek the closest possible relationship to Washington. After the election of Sarkozy, there is almost competition between the two in this regard.

As we have seen, the race to modernise militarily is the key to meaningful military participation. The political ability to do so is the other key, one which Germany rarely possesses but which the other two states in the *directoire* have. The German 'no' to the Gates request for more troops to ISAF directly detracts from Germany's political standing not only in NATO, but in Washington and in coercive foreign policy. '(Merkel's) current course devalues Germany's word: When (she) says that Iran's acquisition of nuclear weapons is "unacceptable", does that mean just intellectually repugnant? Or is it a guarantee ... that Germany is capable of concrete military action if the circumstance so require?'asks a commentator pointedly.[92] He adds that the dominance of domestic factors in German security policy implies that no coercive diplomacy undertaken by Germany is credible. The enemy will, of course, know that military action cannot be taken when 86 per cent of the population is opposed. This effectively answers the question about EU strategic culture. It is plain logic that only those states that can use force are able to plan for and threaten such use. We are back to France, Britain, and some few others.

The importance of the domestic factor in security policy becomes very clear at this point. A weak government can only be a follower at best at the international level of coercive diplomacy and military deployment. As stated, a government bound by a pacifist public cannot use coercive diplomacy at all because threats they may make are not credible. It can only deploy militarily when all sorts of conditions are met, such as the German caveats in Afghanistan. In the analysis of the German case we have seen how the German government has moved from playing a meaningful two-level game in the 1990s towards an increased dominance of domestic factors in security and defence policy. The Gates demand for more troops in February 2008 showed beyond any doubt that domestic politics now trump security policy completely. This fact pre-empts the possibility of playing two-level games for the government as it has nothing to offer at the international level. In the German case, the implications for both NATO and EU membership is that Germany cannot be trusted to withstand populist demands for caveats or even retreat from operations, something which makes it impossible to plan for military integration with German troops. The stronger the role of domestic factors in decision-making, the weaker the standing of Germany in the ESDP and NATO.

In our analysis we have found that domestic factors have started to play a role in the British case. This is evident in the heavy criticism of former PM Blair over the Iraq war and the growing unfamiliarity with the military profession on the part of a post-modern British public. This was expressed in such cases as harassment of British soldiers who wore their uniform in public because people disagreed with the Iraq or Afghanistan engagements and the major debate which ensued when the army desired all personnel to wear uniforms in public as a rule.

The terror danger from the IRA years explains why they usually do not do so. These cases point to a certain distance between the public and the military. However, there is recognition of the bravery of British soldiers in the dignified and impressive press coverage of military crosses awarded, something which contrasts very sharply with the corresponding German debate which refuses to recognise military bravery at all. We have also seen that the British government can decide on deployments without parliamentary consultation. The only problem with regard to domestic factors is the strong anti-EU attitude, probably the strongest in the whole EU. The government is therefore constrained by this general anti-EU sentiment rather than by constraints on security and defence policy.

In the French case, there are no domestic constraints at work, neither in terms of security and defence policy nor in terms of EU policy. The French government, which in reality means the French president, is free to decide on all matters of the ESDP without having to consult anyone else. This allows for an unprecedented degree of strategic planning. As one of the respondents to a major survey of who wields most influence in the ESDP responds 'French thinking is probably shaping this debate most (because) France has articulated a relatively clear vision for the future of the ESDP' (SDA-report, p. 35). With Bernard Kouchner as foreign minister, the 'values' part of security policy has a clear exponent. Like Blair's Britain, France wants that military force should be a 'force for good' in Africa and elsewhere. France has been in the lead of all African deployments, from *Artemis* to Chad. The *Realpolitik* of creating security in failed states in the face of possible terrorism is indistinguishable from the idealism of humanitarian intervention. The multilateralism of the ESDP provides legitimacy for the creation of *L'Europe de défense*, which will be a 'force multiplier' for the EU in its global role once accomplished.

In March 2008, French President Sarkozy made a state visit to Britain. In his address[93] to Parliament he outlined the political rationale for the *an entente amicale* between the two states and underlined their common interests in developing a strong EU policy in security and defence. He rejected the common assumption that the two states have different strategic visions and underlined their friendship with the United States and the necessity of NATO:

> One says that Britain and France have different visions of Europe and that these differences are structurally given. I disagree; I profoundly think that we are allies. I believe in the necessity of NATO.

I believe in the historical friendship with the US and noone can make me chance this conviction.[94] President Sarkozy

The state visit was a success, and there was a clear conclusion by both PM Brown and President Sarkozy that the French–British defence cooperation would continue and develop.

Some days after the state visit, NATO met at its summit conference in Bucharest. A major novelty was the French willingness to deploy combat troops to the south of Afghanistan, something which made a big difference at that moment. The French offered one battalion to be deployed quickly to assist the hard-pressed Canadians. President Sarkozy also announced the French intention to return fully to the military command (SHAPE) of NATO, thereby reversing de Gaulle's policy choice of 1967.[95] The offer of additional troops came at the best moment possible for France, and which could 'save' ISAF from a crisis over lack of troops in the south. The announcement of the return of France to the military structure was, as we have seen, a policy chance talked about for some time in Paris. It was also announced when it was most opportune. In 2009, NATO will elect a new Secretary-General, a post that France now probably can claim, should it wish to. With the much sought-after troop contribution, France has 'drawing rights' in the organisation.

Two reactions to the French policy move are noteworthy: The American president announced his support for the ESDP on the eve of the NATO summit, something which was interpreted as 'an early down payment from Mr Bush to a pledge last year from President Sarkozy'.[96] The other reaction came from the Socialist opposition in the French parliament. It was against both the troop contribution, the alignment with the United States, and the return of France to NATO's military structures.[97] The domestic debate centred around the question of whether France was giving up Gaullism in return for Atlanticism. Few seemed to heed the argument made by Sarkozy about the need to participate in order to wield influence.

There was also opposition to PM Brown's French *rapprochement* at home. Shadow defence secretary Liam Fox warned that too much emphasis on the ESDP would lead to serious domestic consequences: 'If Gordon Brown undermines NATO, he will have a fight on his hands', he wrote.[98]

Yet the domestic protests in both states led to little change. They were basically not important. The French president is early in his term and has the power needed to direct security and defence matters. PM Brown is also able to continue the pragmatic cooperation with France. This will intensify during the French presidency of the EU in the latter half of 2008.

The British warn that there are limits to the use of enhanced cooperation and state that they will not accept the creation of an EU military HQ.[99]

In sum, the French appear to benefit most from these developments. They will enjoy full participation in NATO as well as the EU. Britain is in the same position, but it is the French who have a strategic interest in the ESDP. If the United States accepts the latter because it needs all the European military capacity it can get, while France opts to forge a close bilateral relationship with Washington, we will see that the French strategic plan materialises. In this scenario, NATO and the EU are both autonomous military actors and the EU will relate directly to the United States as a counterpart.

The road to this state of affairs is paved with good intentions on the part of all actors: Britain, France, and the United States sincerely desire more able military capacity in Europe and see that only added work in the EU can bring this about. In this sense, there are new national interests that are common to these states. But if the ESDP succeeds, France also succeeds.

What can we conclude regarding our hypothesis that military capacity is a necessary but not sufficient condition for using military force in postmodern Europe? We have seen that all three major powers in this study have the necessary military capacity to act, but that only two of them project force globally. France and Britain are thus in a class by themselves. We have also seen that only these powers have strong governments in the security and defence field in the sense that domestic constraints play little or no role. But we have also pointed out that without legitimacy, defined as the general political support for an operation, none of these powers can act. They therefore ensure that all their deployments have a UN mandate if at all possible and that they always are launched by an international organisation. Iraq is the exception to this in the case of Britain, and this case led to unprecedented criticism of (then) PM Blair with regard to both the *ad bellum* and the *in bello* phases.

Thus, the new national interests argued for in this book seem to be important. Yet the question remains: How important is the ESDP as such as a security policy for states?

At the outset we stated that the ESDP is just an *addition* to national security policy. Ripsman and Paul (2005, p. 199) analyse whether postmodern security policy has replaced traditional realism in a comparison across regions. The authors looks at the globalisation thesis that 'the national security state has been weakened under globalisation'. They find little proof of this. In fact, it is *only in stable regions* – like Europe – that security policy tends to be pursued through regional organisations (p. 221). In stable regions, there is also recognition of new threats such as failed states as well as a shift to defensive postures. But in the larger global picture, there is no change away from traditional security policy. As the authors put it 'There is little evidence that globalisation has transformed the pursuit of national security ... Only among stable regions do we find a clear trend away from offence' (p. 220). They add that 'except in stable regions ... there would appear to be little support for the proposition that states rely on regional security organisations to achieve their security goals. Great powers look to these organisations, but only to a limited degree, and states in conflictual regions find them to be largely irrelevant'. Realism and its stress on territorial security and geopolitical structures therefore appears to be highly relevant in many regions of the world. The ESDP is therefore not only an addition to traditional national security policy: it is also the *exception* in a world where traditional security policy continues to dominate in many regions, alongside the security risk of asymmetric warfare. Our ESDP case is therefore of particular importance because it combines post-modern peace politics, as played out in Europe, with the global terrorist battle which is de-territorial and where deterrence tied to geopolitical structures does not work.

We have seen that traditional theories of EU integration do not apply to this case, but also that the traditional security policy theory of realism does not fit either. It appears that great power politics is pursued, but constrained by the demands of multilateral legitimacy and military dependencies. *France and Britain depend on each other not so much militarily as in terms of legitimacy* – one that can only be achieved in a multilateral organisation. The choice of the EU for making an ESDP is largely that of France; but France cannot create an ESDP without British military capacity and its political will to use it.

How should one pursue the study of European security policy? It displays a *combination of modern and post-modern elements*. France and Britain are modern states in the traditional sense with regard to their nuclear power and veto power in the UNSC, but depend on multilateral legitimacy and use military power as a 'force for good' as well. Other European states are post-modern in terms of all aspects of their security policy, among them Germany and partially the Nordic states, Spain and Italy. In these states domestic factors play such an important role in security policy that coercive diplomacy and dangerous peace-enforcement operations are almost impossible to sustain.

The effect of this constellation of modern and post-modern politics is that *Europe cannot act in a unitary manner*, be it in the EU or NATO. We are left with core logics and groups of states. Neither realism nor institutionalism are suitable theories for the study of European security policy. We need to focus on governments and their strategies as well as their power to achieve their goals. The indirect strategy of institution shaping that Barnett and Duvall emphasise is promising, as argued here. We need further studies of the various states in the EU and in NATO that trace their political processes at home and in the international organisation.

There is also a clear need to distinguish between the political dynamics of *small and large* states. The former are followers and can benefit from smart tactics in this regard. The larger are leaders, and eye each other as they plan their moves. The need to act within an international organisation invariably entails interdependencies. Also these must be studied.

It makes sense to study the security dynamics in Europe through a two-level game logic. We must not only include the domestic level, but analyse its interaction with the government as well as the government's use of second level power to influence it. Only through analysis of the simultaneous or sequential interaction between these levels is it possible to unearth which dynamic works in which case. It goes without saying that only a government which possesses power to threaten the use of force in a credible manner – that is unhindered by domestic interference – can conduct coercive diplomacy. This gives the rather strange result that those *states that are the most post-modern in Europe are also those most unable to make use of force in a peaceful way, as a deterrent or as a threat.*

The political dynamics at work in asymmetrical warfare are even more complex than those that concern crisis management and peace enforcement. We see the contours of this in the ISAF case. Terrorist attacks against post-modern publics are likely to effect these much more than modern publics that have retained a military culture and stamina in the face of danger. Asymmetrical warfare will strengthen the role of domestic factors even more and make it even harder to argue that military force is but a 'force for good'.

Notes

1. See the NATO document *Comprehensive Political Guidance* (CPG), adopted at the Riga summit in November 2006, for a good and recent assessment of threats.
2. Robert Gates (19 February 2008). The Future Development of Afghanistan. Address at the 44th Munich Security Policy Conference.
3. I was deputy Foreign Minister of Norway at the time, and recall how extremely difficult it was to keep the alliance united throughout this military campaign.
4. Norway, Ministry of Defence (2004). *Force and relevance*.
5. Canada. Prime Ministers Office (2005). *A Role of pride and influence in the world*. p. 12.
6. Lt. Gen. Mackenzie. Quoted in Ulriksen (2003, p. 8).
7. UN Human Development Report, 1994. This lists various threats to human rights and human dignity, none of them military. The report was made in preparation for the UN Social Summit in Copenhagen in 1995.
8. This part draws on my article 'The EU and human security'.
9. Bailes, A. (2008).
10. This part of the chapter draws on my article 'Much Ado about Little: The EU and Human Security', *International Affairs* 84(1), 116–31.
11. A report commissioned by the High Representative of the ESDP, Javier Solana, as a policy development based on the ESS (European Security Strategy). www.lse.ac.uk/Depts/global/publications/Human Security Doctrine.pdf
12. Report from the EU Institute 2007.
13. EDA press release 13 October 2005.
14. Ibid.
15. It is beyond the scope of this book to discuss the details of the various EU capacities, but useful analyses include Cameron and Quille (2004); Hanggi and Tanner (2005) and Matlary (2005).
16. See 'A Regime Saved, for the Moment', *The Economist* (9 August 2008), p. 43, and 'A Peace-Keeping Puzzle for Europe', *The Economist* (12 December 2007), p. 44.
17. 'Londres s'éloigne de Paris sur l'Europe de la Défense', *Le Figaro*, (13 November 2006).
18. Report from the EU institute 2007.
19. *Le Monde*, 10 February 2008.
20. Cited in Haugevik, K. (2006). 'Middelvei med fransk touche: Franske og britiske preferanser i EUs sikkerhets – og forsvarspolitikk', *Internasjonal Politikk*, 64(4), pp. 487–507.
21. 'Londres s'éloigne de Paris sur l'Europe de la Défense', *Le Figaro*, (13 November 2006).
22. Moravcsik (1993). 'Preferences and Power in the EC: A Liberal Intergovernmentalist Approach', *Journal of Common Market Studies*, 31(4).

23. David Pilling (28 February 2008). 'Japan's Aid Policy: Doing Less with Less', *Financial Times*.
24. Cimbala and Forster, 2004. Interviews, Brussels, 2007.
25. PM Harper refused to fly the flag at half-mast for the fallen in Afghanistan See: Canada leader accused of trying to de-emphasise danger to troops. *International Herald Tribune*, 24 April 2006. See also debates in Britain and the Netherlands on deployments to ISAF, and also article (3 March 2007) 'Canada: Accentuating the Positive', *The Economist*, p. 52.
26. *Aftenposten*, (6 December 2008). Interviews, Brussels, February 2007; Interview, MOD, London, May 2007.
27. Author's interview with Norwegian diplomat, 2007.
28. Herve Morin, *Discours de le ministre de la défense*, 10 February 2008, 44. Security Policy Conference, Munich, Intervention, p. 13.
29. B. Kouchner, *Pour une défense europeenne* (11 March 2008) *Le Monde*.
30. 'France Renegotiates African Defence Agreements', *Daily Telegraph*, 3 March 2008.
31. George Friedman (2008). A New French Strategy. Strategic Forecasting, Inc. See also the British press during the official visit of President Sarkozy to France in March 2008. *International Herald Tribune* (14 September 2007). 'French Minister Signals NATO Rapprochement', *International Herald Tribune* (14 September 2007).
32. Vennesson, P. (2003). 'Civil-Military Relations in France: Is there a Gap?', *Journal of Strategic Studies*, 26, 29–42.
33. Rieker (2005). From Common Defence to Comprehensive Security Towards the Europeanisation of French Foreign and Security Policy? NUPI Working Paper 691.
34. Chirac, J. (19 January 1992). Opening speech at the Recontres nationales pour L'Europe, Palais de Congres.
35. Chirac, J. (22 February 1996). *Intervention televisee*, TF1.
36. 'Europe's Closest Friendship Falls Apart', *The Independent* (28 February 2008).
37. Interview, MOD (9 May 2007).
38. Interview, MOD (9 May 2007).
39. *Daily Telegraph* (10 May 2007).
40. *Financial Times* (2 March 2007).
41. 'Britain and France Strike Common Stance', *International Herald Tribune* (21 July 2007), p. 3.
42. Interview. British MOD, 6 May 2007.
43. Interview with former Norwegian ambassador to London. Oslo, 2007. Interview with former Norwegian ambassador to London. Oslo, 2007.
44. 'Franco-British Fraternity Hailed', *Financial Times* (27 March 2008), p. 3.
45. 'Paris Comes to Canada's Aid with Extra Troops', *Financial Times* (8 February 2008); 'Rice urges NATO to add troops in Mideast'. (7 March 2008).
46. See for example: German Foreign and Security Policy: Trends and Transatlantic Implications. CSR Report for Congress (3 October 2007).
47. Interview, MOD; Interview, British diplomat, May 2007, London.
48. When EADS was awarded a Pentagon contract for air tankers in 2008, congressmen and the general American protested wildly. See: Le contrat remporte par EADS passe mal aux Etats-Unis (8 March 2008). *Le Monde*, p. 15.

As arguments about security were presented, EADS announced steps to limit open-market shares: 'EADS bid to restrict foreign ownership'. (7 March 2008). *Financial Times*. p. 1.
49. Interviews, diplomats and military officers, EU, Brussels, February 2007.
50. Interview, MOD, 9 May 2007.
51. TV4 Nyheterna, 'Har ar Sveriges hemligaste soldater', Svenske elitsoldater på uppdrag i Tschad, 3 March 2008 ('Here are Sweden's most secret soldiers').
52. Interview with professor Marina Nuchiari, Torino University and the Italian Military Staff College, Oslo, 5 February 2008.
53. 'Hanging in There', *The Economist* (31 March 2007), p. 35.
54. Hannah Cleaver (27 November 2004). German MPs want answers to army's failures in Kosovo. Press reports from Berlin; Tony Paterson. (9 May 2004). 'German Troops "Hid Like Rabbits" in Kosovo Riots', *The Daily Telegraph*.
55. 'Switzerland ends military mission in Afghanistan' (2 February 2008). *Pak Tribune*. http://paktribune.com. Also interviews with Norwegian military staff stationed in Mazar-el-Sharif, February 2008.
56. Allergra Stratton. (5 February 2008). 'German Soldiers Fatter Than Average Citizen', *The Guardian*.
57. Marina Nuciari. Conversation in Oslo.
58. J. Bittner. (2008). 'Gibt es die NATO noch?', *Die Zeit*, 7, p. 7.
59. 'Germans to the Front?', *The German Times* (March 2008), p. 5.
60. Stefan Kornelis (7 February 2008). 'Mehr Ehrlichkeit', *Sud-deutsche Zeitung*, p. 4.
61. Steffen Hebestreit (9 February 2008). 'Die Siechende Allianz', *Frankfurter Rundschau*, Leitartikel, p. 11.
62. *Die Welt*, 3 February 2008.
63. 'Where the sniping has to stop', *The Economist* (9 February 2008), p. 53; 'Nato-krise um deutsche Soldaten', *Welt am Sonntag*(3 February 2008), p. 1.
64. 'Kampfen, aber nicht daruber reden', *Sud-deutsche Zeitung* (7 February 2008), p. 6. 'Wir kampfen im Norden', *Die Welt am Sonntag* (3 February 2008), p. 4.
65. Front page headline (1 February 2008). *Sud-deutsche Zeitung*.
66. Interview, officers (9 February 2008). Munchen. Interview, diplomat (9 February 2008). Munchen. Klose fordert Kampfeinsatz in ganz Afghanistan (4 February 2008). *Sud-deutsche Zeitung*.
67. John Vincour (12 February 2008). 'Can Germany Muster the Courage to Fight?', *International Herald Tribune*, p. 2.
68. Jan Techau and Alexander Skiba (February 2008). Volles Engagement in Afganistan! Redliche Debatte daheim! DGAP Standpunkt, (Deutsche Gesellschaft fur Auswartige Politik), Berlin. International Herald Tribune (8 February 2008). Editorial.
69. Question from the floor. (9 February 2008). Munich Security Policy Conference, , Bayerischer Hof, Munich.
70. International Herald Tribune. (6 February 2008), p. 3.
71. Eckhardt Lohse, (3 February 2008). Die Augen Links! FAZ, p. 10.
72. I was interviewed extensively by German media on this. Was it a fact that the Norwegians were engaged in war-fighting? The answer is that the 2007–8 QRF was engaged in a five-week long offensive against the Taliban (Operation Yarekate Yolo II) in the North-west as well as in many other operations, and as a curiosity, all under the command of a German general.

216 Notes

As was said, the first time Norwegians soldiers fought since the Second World War, it is under German command.
73. Robert Gates (10 February 2008). The Future Development of Afghanistan. Lecture, Munich Security Conference.
74. The Guardian (7 March 2008), p. 16.
75. Køhler fur einen Tapferkeitsorden (7 March 2008). FAZ, p. 1; Dem tapferen Soldaten, FAZ, (7 March 2008), p. 1.
76. The Guardian (3 March 2008).
77. FPD-representative Hoff: 'For what, where, for which scenario will such a decoration be given? Does the government imply that the army is involved in war-fighting?'
78. 'Bid to Restore the Iron Cross Awakens Germany's Angst', International Herald Tribune (20 March 2008), p. 1.
79. Quoted in The Times, (8 March 2008).
80. Les grands travaux de la defense francaise. (28 October 2007). Interview with Jean-Claude Mallet. Le Monde, p. 14.
81. US Congress. The Future of NATO. Hearing before the Committee on Foreign Relations.
82. Report to the US Congress, 2006: 4 – NATO: From Common Defense to Common Security.
83. 'The Air Force should buy the best tanker'. (8–9 March 2008). Editorial, International Herald Tribune; 'Le Contrat remporte par EDAS passe mal aux Etats-Unis', Le Monde (8 March 2008), p. 15.
84. Comments to author, 2006, by a Nordic defence minister who will remain anonymous because of the sensitivity of the issue.
85. Rynning (2005, p. 174) concludes that 'NATO was drifitng organizationally towards coalition-type operations but was politically undecided around 2000'. Today this route is even clearer, he contends: 'NATO's Only Option for the Future Is One of Coalition-Making' (p. 175).
86. Lillemor Idling. (5 March 2008). Riksdagen forlanger innsatsen i Tschad. TT (Swedish News Agency).
87. 'Silence europeen apres l'arrestation de trois chefs de l'opposition tchadienne', *Le Monde* (10 February 2008), p. 6. When the planned EU force in the border region between Sudan and Chad was to be deployed, insurgents backed by the Sudanese government tried to stage a coup d'état in Chad. French forces evacuated French nationals and awaited the outcome of the attempted coup, opting to keep the corrupt President Idriss Debry rather than allowing Sudanese backed forces to win, although this was only the least of two bad options according to diplomatic sources (Interview, München, 9 February 2008). The Norwegians and Swedes had co-trained an engineering battalion for the planned UN force in Darfur. The battalion was ready to deploy in January 2008. But after having had to accept a UN mandate that China agreed to under great power pressure, the Sudanese president, Omar Al-Bashir, said that Nordic soldiers would be regarded as 'CIA and Mossad-agents'. This was an explicit threat, and the battalion was dismantled. Yet the Swedish part of it was going to be deployed to EUFOR in Chad instead.
88. 'Le deploiement de l'EUFOR pourait reprendre rapidement', *Le Monde* (10 February 2008).

89. Revisiting NATO–EU relations. (10 March 2008). SDA Discussion Paper. Brussels.
90. The author is a member of the Task Force on Belarus, a high-level group of ex-ministers who try to find a way to orient Belarus towards Western democracy. The usefulness of a softer EU approach is clear, but the need to keep the alternative alive is obvious when the regime one deals with, is such a hard case.
91. 'Sarkozy Tests the Consensus At the Core of Europe', *Financial Times* (18 March 2008), p. 9.
92. *International Herald Tribune*, (29 January 2008).
93. Sarkozy, N. Discours de M. le President de la Republique devant le Parlement britannique (28 March 2008).
94. Ibid., p. 7. On dit que le Royaume-Uni et la France ont des conceptions opposées de L'Europe et que l'affrontement entre nos deux pays est une donnée structurelle de la construction européenne. Je ne suis pas d'accord, je pense profondément que nous pouvons la nous allier. Je crois a la nécessite de l'OTAN ... Je crois a l'amitee historique avec les États-Unis d'Amérique et personne ne me fera a cette conviction.
95. 'Gaullist No More?', *The Economist*, (5 April 2008), p. 34.
96. 'Bush Eases Stance on EU Defence Capacity', *Financial Times* (3 April 2008).
97. Ibid., 'Gaullist no more?'.
98. Article with same title by Liam Fox, *The Telegraph* (7 April 2008).
99. 'Bush Eases Stance on EU Defence Capacity', *Financial Times*, (3 April 2008).

Bibliography

Adler, E. and Barnett, M. (1998). *Security communities*. Cambridge: Cambridge University Press.
Aggestam, L. (2004). *A European foreign policy? Role conceptions and the politics of identity in Britain, France, and Germany*. Stockholm: Akademitryck.
Aggestam, L. (2004). Role identity and the Europeanization of foreign policy. In B. Tomra and T. Christensen (Eds), *Rethinking European Union foreign policy*. Manchester: Manchester University Press.
Agrell, W. (2005). Fra forsvarspolitikk til teknologipolitikk – svensk forsvarsindustri hinsides det nasjonale eksistensforsvaret [From defence policy to technology policy – the Swedish Defence Industry beyond National Defence]. In J. H. Matlary and Ø. Østerud (Eds), *Mot et avnasjonalisert forsvar?* Oslo: Abstrakt Forlag.
Allen, D. (2005). The UK: A Europeanized government in a non-Europeanized polity. In S. Bulmer and C. Lequesne (Eds), *The member states and the EU*. Oxford: Oxford University Press.
Andersson, J. J. (2006). *Armed and ready? The EU battlegroup concept and the Nordic battlegroup*. Stockholm: International Peace Research Institute.
Anthony King, 'The Paradox of Multinationality', in Occasional Papers, NATO DEFENCE COLLEGE, no. 23, Rome, October 2007.
Arreguin-Toft, I. (2005). *How the weak win wars*. Cambridge: Cambridge University Press.
Avant, D. (2005). *The market for force*. Cambridge: Cambridge University Press.
Bachrach, P. and Baratz, M. (1962). Two faces of power. *American Political Science Review*, 56, 947–52.
Bailes, A. (2005). *The European Union security strategy: An evolutionary history*. SIPRI Policy Paper no. 10. Stockholm: International Peace Research Institute.
Bailes, A. (2007). *The European Security Strategy: An Evolutionary History*, SIPRI, Stockholm, policy paper 10 February 2007.
Bailes, A. (2008). The EU and 'better world': What role for the Europeans? *International Affairs*, 84(1), 115–30.
Balme, R. and Voll, C. (2005). France: Between integration and national sovereignty. In S. Bulmer and C. Lequesne (Eds), *The member states and the EU*. Oxford: Oxford University Press.
Barbe, E. and Johansson, E. (2008). The EU as a modest 'force for good': The European neighbourhood policy. *International Affairs*, 84(1), 81–96.
Barcelona Report, The (2004). *Barcelona report of the study group on Europe's security capabilities*. Barcelona.
Barnett, M. and Duvall, R. (Eds) (2005). *Power in global governance*. Cambridge: Cambridge University Press.
BBC News (2005). *NATO in a spin over Afghan expansion*. 12 December. http://news.bbc.co.uk/1/hi/world/south_asia/4521318.stm (accessed 21 December 2007).
Beck, U. (2005). On post-national war. *Security Dialogue*, 36(1), 5–26.

Beger, N. and Bartholme, P. (2007). The EU's quest for coherence in peace-building: Between good intentions and institutional turf wars. *Studia Diplomatica*, LX(1): 245–63.

Belkin, P. et al. (2007). *German foreign and security policy: Trends and transatlantic implications*. CRS Report for Congress, 3 October. Washington, DC.

Berge, A. (1914). *Listerlandets kystværn og kaperfart 1807–1814*. [Privateering in coastal Norway, 1808–1814]. Tønsberg: Tønsberg Aktietrykkeri.

Berger, M. (2006). Investigating transatlantic strategic cooperation in the post-cold war era. Unpublished MA thesis, Leiden University, Germany

Biscop, S. (2007). The ambiguous ambition: The development of the EU security architecture. *Studia Diplomatica*, LX(1): 265–78.

Blair wins major test of nuclear deterrent. *International Herald Tribune* (15 March 2007). p. 1.

Blunden, M. (2000). France. In I. Manners and R. Whitman (Eds), *The foreign policies of EU Member States*. Manchester: Manchester University Press.

Bohnen, J. (1997) 'Germany', in Howorth, K. and Menon, A. (Eds.).

Boin, A., Ekengren, M., and Rhinard, M. (2005). The Commission and crisis management. In D. Spence (Ed.), *The European Commission*. London: John Harper Publishing.

Bono, G. (2005). National parliaments and EU external military operations: Is there any parliamentary control? *European Security*, 14(2), 203–29.

Born, H. and Hanggi, H. (Eds) (2004). *The 'Double democratic deficit': Parliamentary accountability and the use of force under international auspices*. Aldershot: Ashgate.

Born, H. and Hanggi, H. (2005). *The use of force under international auspices: Strengthening parliamentary accountability*. Geneva Centre for the Democratic Control of Armed Forces, Policy Paper 7, Geneva.

Bretherton, C. and Vogler, J. (1999). *The EU as a global actor*. London: Routledge.

British Defence Doctrine (2001). London: Joint Warfare Centre, MOD.

Brownlie, I. (1991). *International law and the use of force by states*. Oxford: Clarendon Press.

Buzan, B. and Wæver, O. (2003). *Regions and power: The structure of international security*. Cambridge: Cambridge University Press.

Cameron, F. and Quille, G. (2004). *ESDP. The state of play*. EPC Working Paper 11. Brussels: European Policy Centre.

Camp, S. V. (2005). Can permanent structured cooperation contribute to more efficient military capabilities in Europe? In S. Biscop (Ed.) *E pluribus unum? Military integration in the European Union*. IRRI-KIIB. 21–7. Brussels: Egmont Papers.

Canada leader accused of trying to de-emphasize danger to troops. (26 April 2006). *International Herald Tribune*.

Cassese, A. (1986). *International law in a divided world*. Oxford: Clarendon Press.

Cassese, A. (2005). *International Law*, second edition, 46–8.

Chayes, A. and Chayes, A. (1995). *The new sovereignty. Compliance with international regulatory agreements*. Cambridge: Harvard University Press.

Chuter, D. (1997) 'The United Kingdom', in Howorth, J. and Menon, A. (Eds.), *The European Union and National Defence Policy, Routledge, 1997 – The State and the European Union Series*.

220 Bibliography

Chesterman, S. (2004). Humanitarian intervention and Afghanistan. In J. Welsch (Ed.), *Humanitarian intervention and international relations*. 163–75. Oxford: Oxford University Press.
Cini, M. (Ed.) (2007). *European Union Politics*, Oxford University Press.
Cimbala, S. and Forster, P. (2004). *US, NATO and military burden-sharing*. London: Frank Cass.
Clark, I. (2005). *Legitimacy in international society*. Oxford: Oxford University Press.
Clark, W. (2003). *Waging modern war. Bosnia, Kosovo, and the future of combat*. New York: Persus Books.
Coker, C. (2007). *The warrior ethos: Military culture and the war on terror*. London: Routledge.
Comprehensive Political Guidance, NATO, Adopted at Riga Summit 2006. Annex 1.
Cooper, R. (2004). *The breaking of nations: Order and chaos in the 21st century*. London: Adelphi Papers.
Cornish, P. and Edwards, G. (2005). The strategic culture of the European Union: A progress report. *International Affairs*, 81(4), 801–20.
Dahl, R. (1957). The concept of power. *Behavioural Science*, 2, 201–15.
Darnis, J-P. et al. (2007). *Lessons learned from European defence equipment programmes*, Occasional Paper no 69. Paris: Institute of Security Studies.
Defiant warmonger to the last. *Daily Telegraph*, (10 May 2007). p. 20.
Delcourt, B. (September 2003). The normative underpinnings of the use of force: Doctrinal foundations and ambiguities in the CFSP/CESDP Discourse. Paper presented at the ECPR workshops in Edinburgh.
De Wijk, R. (2004). *The art of military coercion. Why the west's military superiority scarcely matters*. Amsterdam: Mets & Schilt.
Diesen, S. (2004). Det militære paradigmeskiftet og konsekvenser for norsk forsvar. [The military paradigm change and its consequences for Norwegian defence]. *Norsk Militært Tidsskrift*, 8(9), 4–6.
Diesen, S. (2005). Mot et allianseintegrert forsvar. [Towards an alliance-integrated defence]. In J. H. Matlary and Ø. Østerud (Eds), *Mot et avnasjonalisert forsvar?* Oslo: Abstrakt Forlag.
Dobbins, J., McGinn, J. G., Crane, K., Jones, S. G., Lal, R., Rathmell, A., Swanger, R., and Timilsina, A. (2003). *America's role nation-building from Germany to Iraq*. Santa Monica: RAND Corporation.
Duchene, F. (1972). Europe's role in world peace. In R. Mayne (Ed.), *Europe tomorrow: Sixteen Europeans look ahead*. 32–47. London: Fontana.
Dumbrell, J. (2006). *A special relationship*. Basingstoke: Palgrave-Macmillan.
Dunne, T. (2004). When the shooting starts: Atlanticism in British security policy. *International Affairs*, 80(5), 893–909.
Economist, The (2006). French foreign policy: The glory days are passing, 16 December, p. 23.
Economist, The (2007a). *Britain's neglected wars*, 18 August.
Economist, The (2007b). *Military spending: Tarnished glories*, 8 December, p. 44.
EDA (2006). *An initial long term vision for European defence capability and capacity needs*. Brussels: EU.
Eide, E., Kaspersen, A. T., Kent, R., and Von Hippel, K. (May 2005). Report on integrated missions: Practical perspectives and recommendations. Independent study for the expanded UN ECHA core group, NY: United Nations.

Engelbrekt, K. and Hallenberg, J. (Eds) (2008). *The European Union and strategy.* Abingdon: Routledge.
Eriksson, A. (2006). Europeanization and governance in defence policy: The example of Sweden. *Stockholm studies in political science*, 117. Stockholm: Stockholm University.
European Security Strategy, EU Commission, Brussels.
European Council (2003). *A secure Europe in a better world. European security strategy.* Brussels: European Council.
European Council (2005). *Conclusions.* Brussels: European Council, 21–22 November.
Everts, S. et al. (2005). *A European way of war?* London: Centre for European Reform
Everts, P. and Isernia, P. (Eds) (2001). *Public opinion and the international use of force.* London: Routledge.
Findlay, T. (2002). *The use of force in UN operations.* Oxford: Oxford University Press and SIPRI.
Flexible Integration. (1995). Report in the series *Monitoring European integration.* London: Centre for European Policy Research.
Forster, A. (2000). Britain. In I. Manners and R. Whitman (Eds), *The foreign policies of EU member states.* Manchester: Manchester University Press.
Forster, A. (2006). *Armed forces and society in Europe.* Basingstoke: Palgrave-Macmillan.
Forster, A. and Blair, A. (2002). *The making of Britain's European policy.* Harlow: Longman.
Frantzen, H. (2005). *NATO and peace support operations, 1991–1999.* London: Frank Cass.
Gardner, H. (Ed.) (2004). *NATO and the European Union.* Aldershot: Ashgate.
George, S. (1992). *Britain and the European community.* Oxford: Clarendon Press.
George, S. (1994). *An awkward partner. Britain in the EU.* Oxford: Oxford University Press.
Giegerich, B. and Wallace, W. (2004). Not such a soft power: The external deployment of European forces. *Survival*, 26(2), 163–82.
Gourevitch, P. (1978). The second image reversed: The international sources of domestic politics. *International Organization*, 32(4).
Gowan, R. (2005). The battlegroups: A concept in search of a strategy? In S. Biscop (Ed.), *E pluribus unum? Military integration in the European Union*, IRRI-KIIB. 13–17. Brussels: Egmont Papers.
Græger, N. et al. (2002). *The ESDP and the Nordic countries.* Berlin: Institut fur Europaeische Politik.
Grant, C. (2000). Intimate relations: Can Britain play a leading role in European defence and keep its special links to US intelligence? CER Working Paper. London: Centre for European Reform.
Gray, C. (2000). *International law and the use of force (Foundations of public international law).* Oxford: Oxford University Press.
Gruber, L. (2005). Power politics and the institutionalisation of international relations. In M. Barnett and R. Duvall (Eds), *Power in global governance.* Cambridge: Cambridge University Press
Guay, T. R. (2005). Defense industry developments in the US and Europe: Transatlantic or bipolar? *Journal of Transatlantic Studies*, 3(1), 139–57.
Hanggi, H. and Tanner, F. (2005). *Promoting security sector governance in the EU's neighbourhood.* Chaillot Paper 80. Paris: Institute for Security Studies.

Hansen, A. (2006). *Evolution of planning for civilian crisis management missions from EUPM onwards*. Oslo: Norwegian Defence Research Institute.

Haugevik, K. M. (2005). Britain and the ESDP. 1998–2004. MA thesis. Department of Political Science, University of Oslo.

Haugevik, K. M. (2006). *Internasjonal Politikk*, 65(4), 2006

Heier, T. (2006). Influence and marginalisation: Norway's adaptation to US transformation efforts in NATO, 1998–2004. PhD thesis, Department of Political Science, University of Oslo.

Held, D. and Koenig-Archibugi, M. (2004). *American power in the 21st century*. Cambridge: Polity Press.

Hendricksen, W. (2005). The Bush doctrine of pre-emptive self-defence. MA thesis, Faculty of Law, University of Oslo.

Henriksen, D. (2006). Demokratisk underskudd i NATO under Kosovokrigen [Democratic deficit in NATO during the Kosovo War]. *Norsk militært tidsskrift*, 12.

Herbst, J. (2004). Let them fail: State failure in theory and practice – implications for policy. In R. I. Rotberg (Ed.), *When states fail: Causes and consequences*. Princeton, NJ: Princeton University Press.

Heusgen, C. (2005). Is there such a thing as a European strategic culture? *Journal of Common Market Studies*, 2(1), 29–33.

Hill, C. (2004). Britain and the ESS. Unpublished paper.

Hoffmann, S. (1972). Obstinate or obsolete? The fate of the nation-state in and the case of Western Europe. *Daedalus*, 95.

Howorth, J. (2003). ESDP and NATO. Wedlock or deadlock? *Cooperation and Conflict*, 38(3), 235–56.

Howorth, J. (2005). From security to defence: The evolution of the CFSP. In C. Hill and M. Smith (Eds), *International relations and the European Union*. Oxford: Oxford University Press.

Howorth, J. (2005b). The Euro-Atlantic security dilemma: France, Britain, and the ESDP. *Journal of Transatlantic Studies*, 3(1) 39–50.

Howorth, J. and Keeler, J. T. S. (Eds) (2003). *Defending Europe: The EU, NATO and the quest for European autonomy*. Basingstoke: Palgrave-Macmillan.

Howorth, J. and Menon, A. (1997). *The European Union and defence policy*. New York: Routledge.

Hyde-Price, A. (2004). European security, strategic culture, and the use of force. *European security*, 13(4), 323–43.

Hyde-Price, 2008. A realist perspective on ethical power Europe. *International Affairs*. 84(1), p. 29.

ICISS (2001). *The responsibility to protect*. Report of the International Commission on Intervention and State Sovereignty, Ottawa: International Development Research Centre.

Johnston, I. (1995). Thinking about strategic culture. *International Security*, 19(4), 32–64.

Jones, S. G. (2007). *The rise of European security cooperation*. Cambridge: Cambridge University Press.

Juhasz (2001). Forfatter Årstall Trykt. In Philip Everts and Pierangelo Isernia (Eds), *Public opinion and the international use of force*. London: Routledge.

Kagan, R. (2003). *Of paradise and power: America and Europe in the new world order*. New York: Knopf.

Kaldor, M. et al. (2007). 'Human Security as a new strategic narrative for Europe' *International affairs*, 83, 2 pp. 273–288.
Kassim, H. et al. (2001). *The national co-ordination of EU policy*. Oxford: Oxford University Press.
Kennedy, D. (2006). *Of law and war*. Princeton, NJ: Princeton University Press.
Khol, R. (2005). Ongoing cooperation between Europe's armed forces. In S. Biscop (Ed.), *E Pluribus Unum? Military integration in the European Union*, Egmont Papers no. 7, 5–13. Brussels: Royal Institute for International Relations.
King, G. and Murray, C. (2001). Rethinking human security. *Political Science Quarterly*, 116(4), 585–610.
Koenig-Archibugi, M. (2004a). International governance as a new *raison d'etat?* The Case of the EU CFSP. *European Journal of International Relations*, 10(2) .
Koenig-Archibugi, M. (2004b). Explaining government preferences for institutional change in EU foreign and security policy. *International Organization*, 54(1), 137–74.
Kotsopoulos, J. (2007). *Studia diplomatica*, 40 (1), p. 230
Krahmann, E. (2003). Conceptualising security governance. *Cooperation and Conflict*, 38(1), 5–26.
Laffan, B., O'Donnell, R., and Smith, M. (Eds) (2000). *Europe's experimental union: Rethinking integration*. London: Routledge.
Lantis, J. S. (2005). EU strategic culture and US ambivalence. *Oxford Journal of Good Governance*, 2(1), 55–65.
Lindley-French, J. (2004). The revolution in security affairs: Hard and soft security dynamics in the 21st century. *European Security*, 13, 1–15.
Lindley-French, J. and Algieri, F. (2004). *A European defence strategy*. Report from the Venusberg Group, Guterloh: Bertelsmann Foundation.
Manigart, P. (2001). Public opinion and European defense. Unpublished manuscript. Royal Military Academy, Belgium.
Manners, I. (2002). Normative power Europe: A contradiction in terms? *Journal of Common Market Studies*, 40(2), 235–58.
Manners, I. (2008). The normative ethics of the EU. *International Affairs*, 84(1), 45–60.
Matlary, J. H. (2004). How important is a UN mandate? *Journal of Military Ethics*, 3(2), 129–41.
Matlary, J. H. (2005). Internasjonaliseringen av militærmakten: makt eller avmakt? [The Internationalisation of Military Policy: Power or Importence?] In J. H. Matlary and Ø. Østerud (Eds), *Mot et avnasjonalisert forsvar?* 185–244. Oslo: Abstrakt Forlag.
Matlary, J. (2006). *Values and weapons: From humanitarian intervention to regime change?* Basingstoke: Palgrave-Macmillan.
Matlary, J. H. and Østerud, Ø. (Eds) (2007). *Denationalisation of defence: Convergence and diversity*. Aldershot: Ashgate.
Mayer, H. (2008). Is it still called Chinese whispers? The EU's rhetoric and action as a responsible global institution. *International Affairs*, 84(1), 61–80.
McCormick, J. (2007). *The European superpower*. Basingstoke: Palgrave-Macmillan.
Merk, R. (2006). Census counts 100,000 contractors in Iraq. *The Washington Post*, (5 December).

Miskimmon, A. (2004). Continuity in the face of upheaval – British strategic culture and the impact of the Blair government. *European Security*, 13(3), 273–99.

Moravcsik, A. (1993). Preferences and power in the EC: A liberal intergovernmentalist approach. *Journal of Common Market Studies*, 31(4)

NATO (2007). *The NATO response force*, Document from the official website of the NATO, updated 14 December. http://www.nato.int/issues/nrf/index.html (accessed 20 December 2007).

Naumann, K. (2005). Military needs of a strategic culture in Europe. *Oxford Journal of Good Governance*, 2(1), 21–5.

Naumann, K. and Ralston, J. (2005). *European defense integration. Bridging the gap between strategies and capabilities*. Washington, DC: Centre for Strategic and International Studies.

Neumann, I. (2002). Diplomatiet. In I. Neumann (Ed.), *Global Politikk [Global politics]*. Oslo: Cappelen .

Neumann, I. and Heikka, H. (2005). Grand strategy, strategic culture, practice. *Cooperation and Conflict*, 40(1), 5–23.

Niblett, R. (2007). Choosing between America and Europe: A new context for British foreign policy. *International Affairs*, 83(4), 627–41.

Norway (2004). *Styrke og relevans. Strategisk konsept for Forsvaret* [Strength and relevance: Strategic concept for the armed forces]. Oslo: Ministry of Defence.

Norway. Forsvarsdepartementet (2004). *Relevant force – strategic concept for the Norwegian armed forces*. Oslo: Ministry of Defence.

O'Hanlon, M. (2004). The American way of war. In S. Everts, L. Freedman, C. Grant, F. Heisbourg, D. Keohane, and M. O'Hanlon (Eds), *A European way of war?* London: Centre of European Reform.

Posen, B. (2003). Command of the Commons. *International Security*, 28(1), 5–46.

Prime Ministers Office, Canada (2005). *A role of pride and influence in the World*, Canada's International Policy Statement. Ottawa: Department of International Affairs.

Public servants (Editorial). *Financial Times* (4 July 2007).

Putnam, R. (1988). The logic of two-level games. *International Organisation*, 42(3), 427: 60.

Quille, G. (2004). The ESS. A framework for EU security interests? *International Peacekeeping*, 11(3), 422–38.

Reichberg, G. (2007). Preventive war in classical just war theory. *Journal of History of International Law*, 9, 5–34.

Rieker, P. (2003). Europeanisation of Nordic security. The EU and the changing security identities of the Nordic states (Dr. polit. thesis, University of Oslo).

Rieker, P. (September 2004). *Conflicts and cooperation: Reinterpreting French–US Relations and French foreign policy After 9/11*. Paper presented at the 5th Pan-European Conference in The Hague.

Rieker, P. (2006). From common defence to comprehensive security: Towards the Europeanisation of French foreign and security policy? *Security Dialogue*, 37(4), 509–28.

Rifkind, M. "The Special relationship between the US and the UK – is it special?", in Ziegner, G. (2007) *British Diplomacy. Foreign secretaries reflect*, Politico's, London, pp. 97–113

Ripsman, N. and Paul, T. V. (2005). Globalisation and the national security state: A framework for analysis. *International Studies Review*, 7, 199–227.
Rotberg, R. I. (Ed.) (2004). *When states fail: Causes and consequences*. Princeton, NJ: Princeton University Press.
Ruggie, J. G. (Ed.) (1993). *Multilateralism matters: The theory and practice of an institutional form*. Columbia, NY: Columbia University Press.
RUSI, (2005) Royal United Services Institute, UK.
Rynning, S. (2001). Shaping military doctrine in France. *Security Studies*, 11(2), 86–116.
Rynning, S. (2003). The EU: Towards a strategic culture? *Security Dialogue*, 34(4), 479–96.
Rynning, S. (2005). *NATO renewed: The power and purpose of transatlantic cooperation*. Basingstoke: Palgrave-Macmillan.
Rynning, S. (2006). The ESDP: Coming of age? In F. Laursen (Ed.), *The treaty of nice: Actors, preferences, bargaining and institutional choice*. Leiden and Boston, MA: Martinus Nijhoff Publishers.
Salmon, T. C. and Shepherd, A. (2003). *Toward a European army. A military power in the making?* Boulder, CO and London: Lynne Rienner Publishers.
Sandholz, W. (1992). *High-tech Europe. The politics of international cooperation*. Berkeley, CA: The University of California Press.
Schake, K. (2003). The US, ESDP and constructive duplication. In J. Howorth and J. T. S. Keeler (Eds), *Defending Europe: The EU, NATO and the quest for European autonomy*. Basingstoke: Palgrave-Macmillan
Schmitt, B. (2003). *The EU and armaments: Getting a bigger bang for the euro*. Chaillot Papers 63. Paris: Institute for Security Studies.
Schmitt, B. (2005). *European capabilities action plan (ECAP)*, Institute for Security Studies, September. http://www.iss-eu.org/esdp/06-bsecap.pdf (accessed 21 December 2007).
Schmidt, P. (2005). Bowling by the same rules? EU–US relations and the transatlantic partnership. *Journal of Transatlantic Studies*, 3(1), 123–38.
Singer, P. W. (2003). *Corporate warriors. The rise of the privatized military industry*. Ithaca: Cornell University Press.
Shaping Europe's defence debate – A study by the SDA for the French Ministry of Defence, (November 2007). Brussels: EU.
Sjursen, H. (Ed.) (2007). *Civilian or military power? European foreign policy in perspective*. Abingdon: Routledge.
Sköns, E. (2005). Omstruktureringen av vesteuropeisk forsvarsindustri – mark edskreftenes logikk [Restructuring Western European defence industry – the logic of the market forces]. In J. H. Matlary and Ø. Østerud (Eds.) *Mot et avnasjonalisert forsvar?* Oslo: Abstrakt Forlag.
Smith, M. (2004). *Europe's foreign and security policy: The institutionalization of cooperation*. Cambridge: Cambridge University Press.
Smith, P. (2005). *The utility of force: The art of war in the modern world*. London: Allen Lane.
Syren, H. (2005). Från nationellt til flernationallt forsvar? Ett svensk perspektiv. Lecture at conference Felles sikkerhet i Norden: fra splittelse til samarbeid? [From national to multinational cooperation? A Swedish perspective]. 2005-konferansen. Oslo, 29 October.

Thomson, R. et al. (Eds) (2006). *The European Union decides*, Cambridge University Press

Toje, A. (2005). Introduction: The EU strategic culture. *Oxford Journal of Good Governance*, 2(1), 9–17.

Toje, A. (2006). American influence on EU security policies, 1998–2004. Unpublished PhD thesis, University of Cambridge.

Transforming NATO: A political and military challenge, NATO Secretary-General's Annual conference. (2005). Brussels: Royal United Staff Institute.

Treacher, A. (2003). *French interventionism: Europe's last global player?* Aldershot: Ashgate.

Ulriksen, S. (1996). *Desentralisert militær integrasjon? Forsvarspolitikk i Vest-Europa etter den kalde krige*, [Decentralised military integration? Defence policy in Western Europe after the Cold War] NUPI-rapport 208. Oslo: NUPI.

Ulriksen, S. (1997). Sannhetens øyeblikk? Europeisk forsvarsindustri – forening eller undergang? NUPI-notat 582. Oslo: NUPI.

Ulriksen, S. (2003a). Det militære Europa [The military Europe, in.... A Different Super-power]. In P. Rieker and S. Ulriksen (Eds), *En annerledes supermakt? Sikkerhets – og forsvarspolitikken i EU*. Oslo: NUPI.

Ulriksen, S. (28–29 August 2003b). Military Europe: Capabilities and constraints. Paper presented at the conference Fra konvent til konstitusjon. Europas utvikling og norsk forskning. Centre for European Studies: Kristiansand.

Ulriksen, S. (2004a). Requirements for future European military strategies and force structures. *International Peacekeeping*, 11(3), 457–73.

Ulriksen, S. (2004b). Operation Artemis: The shape of things to come? *International Peacekeeping*, 11(3), 508–25.

Ulriksen, S. (2007). European Military Forces: Integration by default. In Matlary, J. H. and Østerud, Ø. (Eds), *Denationalisation of defence: Convergence and diversity*, Ashgate, UK.

United Nations (2 December 2004). *A more secure world: Our shared responsibility*, Report by the Secretary-General's High-level Panel on Threats, Challenge and Change. (A/59/569) New York, United Nations.

United Nations Reform Panel (2004). *A more secure world: Our shared responsibility*, Report of the Secretary-General's High-Level Panel on Threats, Challenges, and Change, New York: United Nations; also available online at http://www.un.org/secureworld/report3.pdf

van Camp, S. (2005). Can permanent structured cooperation contribute to more efficient military capabilities in Europe? In S. Biscop (Ed.), *E Pluribus Unum? Military integration in the European Union*, Egmont Papers no. 75–13. Brussels: Royal Institute for International Relations.

van Creveld, M. (1999). *The decline of the state*. Cambridge: Cambridge University Press.

Vedby-Rasmussen, M. (2006). *The risk society at war. Terror, technology, and strategy in the 21st Century*. Cambridge: Cambridge University Press.

Wagner, W. (2005). *The democratic legitimacy of ESDP*. ISS Occasional Paper no. 57. Paris: EU Institute of Security Studies.

Wagner, W. (2006). The democratic control of military power Europe. *Journal of European Public Policy*, 13(2), 2000–216.

Wallace, W. (2005). Is there a European approach to war? Unpublished paper.

Wallace, W. (2005a). Foreign and Security Policy. In H. Wallace, W. Wallace, and M. A. Pollack (Eds), *Policy-making in the European Union*. Oxford: Oxford University Press.

Wallace, W. (2005b). Is there a European approach to war? Working Paper, Conference, The price of peace, 9 May.

Weaver, K. (1996). The politics of blame avoidance. *Journal of Public Policy*, 6(4), 371–98.

C. Weber and S. Haddad (2007). French Military Doctrine. In Yost, D. S. (Ed.) *NATO and international organizations*. NATO Defense College, Forum Paper 3.

Weiss, T. (2005). *Military-civilian interactions: Humanitarian crisis and the responsibility to protect*, second edition. New York: Rowman and Littlefield.

Wegge, N. (2003). Med Brussel som utgangspunkt? [From the Vantage-point of Brussels?] IFS report. Oslo: Institute of Defence Studies

What is human security? (2004). *Security Dialogue*, 35(3). Special Section.

Wheeler, N. (2000). *Saving strangers: Humanitarian intervention in international society*. Oxford: Oxford University Press.

Wither, J. (2005). *Expeditionary forces for post modern Europe: Will European military weakness provide an opportunity for the new condottieri?* Camberley: Conflict Studies Research Centre.

Wulf, H. (2005). *Internationalizing and privatizing war and peace*. Basingstoke: Palgrave-Macmillan.

Yost, D. (2003). The US–European capabilities gap and the prospects for ESDP. In J. Howorth and J. T. S. Keeler (Eds), *Defending Europe: The EU, NATO and the quest for European autonomy*. Basingstoke: Palgrave-Macmillan.

Yost, D. S. (Ed.) (2007). *NATO and international organizations*, NATO Defense College, Forum Paper 3.

Ziegner, G. (Ed.) (2007). *British diplomacy. Foreign secretaries reflect*, The LSE Lectures. London: Politicos.

Index

actorness, of EU, 203, 204
ad bellum decision-making, 62
Afghanistan, 3, 20, 37, 65–6, 74, 126, 129, 148, 151, 152, 156, 158, 181, 185, 207
Africa, 58, 65, 102, 105, 117, 125, 134, 189
Aggestam, L., 115
Agrell, W., 132
Airborne Warning and Control System (AWACS), 144, 150
Amsterdam Treaty, 42, 43, 107–8, 120–1, 134
Annan, K., 18, 126
Artemis, Operation, 46, 57, 58, 61, 125, 126, 128, 147, 160, 162, 175, 192
AWACS, *see* Airborne Warning and Control System

Bachrach, P., 90
Balkans, 58, 160
Baratz, M., 91
Barbe, E., 85
Barcelona Report, 44, 45
Barnett, M., 86, 89, 90, 91
battlegroups, 48–9, 63, 64, 72, 111, 125–30, 142, 175, 176
  military integration in, 173–4
Berlin Plus, 55, 60
Berlusconi, S., 92–3
Biscop, S., 180
Blair, T., 66, 92, 100, 112–14, 117, 141, 160, 199, 205, 207
Bohnen, J., 165
Bono, G., 143
Born, H., 143
Bosnia, 24, 44, 46, 57, 99, 104, 135, 144, 177
Britain
  ESDP policy, 6, 72, 79, 97, 111, 112, 115, 116, 119, 125, 170, 171

  EU policy, 70, 98, 111, 170, 191, 196, 201
  foreign policy, 114, 116
  great game, 110–17
  military operation, 51, 93, 105
  motivation, 80, 100
  national interests, 74
  power, 89–90
  public opinion, 100, 161
  security policy, 31, 74, 79, 107, 117
  special relationship, 71
  strong governments, 159–62
Brown, G., 2–3, 75, 100, 116, 119, 209
Bunia, 57, 125, 135
Bush, G. W., 37, 92
Buzan, B., 36

CFSP, *see* Common Foreign and Security Policy
Chad, 20, 117, 135, 192–3
Chayes, Abraham, 86
Chayes, Antonia, 86
chocolate summit, 136
Chuter, D., 111
Cimbala, S., 92
civilian headline goals (2008), 53
civilian power, 84, 144
Civil-Military Cell, 55, 56
Clark, W., 22
coalition of the willing, 8, 90, 98, 180
  pooling of sovereignty, in ESDP, 188; capability, 204; coercive diplomacy, 195–202; EU as arena or actor, 190–2; EU strategic culture, 202–4; *in bello* decision-making matter, 192–5; legitimacy, 204–6
coercive diplomacy, 63, 71, 90, 195–202, 203
cold war, 19, 20, 33, 89, 132, 139, 201

Commission, *see* European Commission
Common Foreign and Security Policy (CFSP), 9, 40, 82, 83, 120–1, 129
Concordia, Operation, 57, 147, 160, 162
Constitutional Treaty, 69, 121, 134
constructivist approaches, 79–83
Contact Group, 135
Cooper, R., 44, 117, 203
Copenhagen Criteria, 43, 202
Council of Defence Ministers, 128
crisis management, 15, 20, 53, 58, 61, 70, 108, 129, 176, 203
Crisis Response Coordination Team, 56
Crisis Room, 54–5
Cyprus, 61, 99

Dahl, R., 90–1
Darfur, 35, 110, 117, 189, 193
DCI, *see* Defence Capabilities Initiative
de Gaulle, 75, 104, 105, 106, 163
De Wijk, R., 206
Defence Capabilities Initiative (DCI), 50, 59, 184, 185
Denmark, 52, 63, 89, 112, 129
de-territorialisation, of security policy, 23–5, 200
Diesen, S., 16
directoire, 135, 170, 196, 197
DR Congo, 20, 24, 46, 57, 72, 117, 125, 126, 174, 188, 189
Duvall, R., 86, 89, 90, 91

ECAP, *see* European Capabilities Action Plan
EDA, *see* European Defence Agency
EDC, *see* European Defence Community
EGF, *see* European Gendarmerie Force
enhanced cooperation, 121, 123, 188, 210
entente cordiale, 116, 119
EPC, *see* European Political Cooperation

Eriksson, A., 101
ESDP, *see* European Security and Defence Policy
ESS, *see* European Security Strategy
EU Military Committee (EUMC), 56, 128
EU Military Staff (EUMS), 55, 56, 128
EUFOR, 189, 192
EUMC, *see* EU Military Committee
EUMS, *see* EU Military Staff
Europe puissance, 106
European Capabilities Action Plan (ECAP), 20, 49–50
European Commission, 43, 53, 54, 56, 58, 121, 132, 190
European Council, 43, 49, 121
European Defence Agency (EDA), 9, 51–3, 65, 68, 70, 174, 178, 186, 203
   defence industry pooling, 130–4
European Defence Community (EDC), 198
European Gendarmerie Force (EGF), 53–4
European Parliament, 42, 121, 132, 190
European Political Cooperation (EPC), 40, 83
European Security and Defence Policy (ESDP), 1, 40
   decision-making, 61–7, 120
   exercising power in, 89–94
   institutional capacity building, 54–5
   integration: in battlegroups, 173–4; through procurement and planning, 174–6
   legitimacy for use of force, 41–6
   military capabilities, 46–9
   military capacity, 169, 176–84
   military integration, in Europe, 171–3
   operations, 57–8
   planning Cell instead of headquarter, 55–6
   political dynamics at work in, 83
   political process, 84–7
   pooling of sovereignty, 188; capability, 204; coercive

European Security and Defence
  Policy (ESDP) – *continued*
    diplomacy, 195–202; EU as
    arena or actor, 190–2; EU
    strategic culture, 202–4; *in
    bello* decision-making matter,
    192–5; legitimacy, 204–6
  principles, 44
  realist models of, 77–9
European Security Strategy (ESS),
  43–4, 50, 53, 62, 115, 202
European Union, 5, 196
  as arena or actor, 190–2
  decision-making, 61–7
  French model for, 206–12
  legitimacy for use of force, 41–6
  military capabilities, 46–9
  and NATO, relationship between,
    60–1, 72–3, 103
  operation, 57–8, 140
  politics, 2
  soft power, 34, 84–6, 196
  strategic culture, 202–4
  see also individual entries
European Union Police Mission
  (EUPM), 57
expeditionary warfare, 66, 67, 166,
  178

failed state, 32, 36, 208
Finland, 5, 63–4, 89, 184, 189
follow on stabilisation forces, 127
foreign policy prerogative (FPP), 2,
  66, 74, 75, 141, 143, 157, 161, 164,
  169, 200
Forster, A., 166
Forster, P., 92
FPP, *see* foreign policy
  prerogative
France, 5, 71, 77
  ESDP policy, 6, 72, 97, 108, 119,
    170, 171
  EU policy, 98, 108, 124, 170, 191,
    196, 201
  great game, 101–3
  military operation, 51, 93, 105
  national interests, 74
  NATO policy, 70, 104, 106, 110, 119,
    141, 163

power, 89–90
public opinion, 162, 163
security policy, 31, 74, 101,
  107, 117
strategic thinking, 80, 103;
  evolution of, 104–10
strong governments, 162–4
Frantzen, H., 29

Germany
  constitutional court, 150
  ESDP policy, 165, 207
  EU policy, 72, 150, 151
  military operation, 151
  national interests, 74
  NATO policy, 120, 150, 154, 155,
    165, 207
  power, 77, 78
  public opinion, 152
  security policy, 74, 110, 157, 207
  weak governments, 149–59
Gourevitch, P., 4
great game, 6, 73, 97
  battlegroups, 125–30
  EDA and defence industry
    'pooling', 130–4
  grand strategy in Europe, 99–101
  main political dynamic, 120–5
  unilateral to multilateral force
    deployments, 117–20
great power game, 6, 31, 73, 74, 77,
  88, 89–90, 105, 139, 174, 190,
  196, 211
Guay, T. R., 77, 130

Hanggi, H., 143
Haugevik, K. M., 79
Headline Goal 2010, 50–1
Headline Goal Task Force (HTF), 50
Helsinki European Council, 49
Helsinki Headline Goals, 48, 129
High Representative, 52, 121
high-intensity warfare, 176
Hill, C., 101, 114
Hoffmann, S., 69
Howorth, J., 113
human rights, 35, 42, 43, 44, 195
human security, 34–5, 41, 44,
  45–7, 205

humanitarian intervention, 20, 30, 35, 65, 208
Hyde-Price, A., 22

identity, 80, 81
in bello decision-making, 62, 192–5
institutional capacity building, 54–5
integration, 2, 68–9, 124, 170, 179, 180
  in battlegroups, 173–4
  through procurement and planning, 174–6
  see also military integration; political integration
internal conflict, 21, 136
International Commission on Intervention and State Sovereignty (ICISS), 35
international organisations, 7, 19, 30, 34, 73–4, 86–7, 92, 93, 107, 119, 145, 212
International Stability and Assistance Force (ISAF), 10, 30, 31, 34, 36, 38, 65–6, 89, 151, 153, 185–6
interoperability, 21, 177
Iran, 135, 196, 199
Iraq, 3, 41, 57, 66, 108, 114, 126, 135, 161, 192, 196, 210
ISAF, *see* International Stability and Assistance Force
Italy
  defence policy, 146
  foreign policy, 146
  public opinion, 147
  weak governments, 146–9

Johansson, E., 85
jointness, 134
Jones, S. G., 77

Kagan, R., 68, 176
Kaldor, M., 44
Kennedy, D., 22, 26, 27
Kinshasa, 57, 135
Koenig-Archibugi, M., 6, 139
Kortenberg, 56
Kosovo, 24, 44, 100, 177, 203
Krahmann, E., 19

L'Europe de la Défense, 101, 103, 204, 208
Laeken European Summit (2001), 49
Laffan, B., 18
legitimacy, 3, 22–3, 38, 89, 91, 109, 149, 201, 202, 204–6
  for use of force, 41–6
  see also multilateral legitimacy
Lisbon Treaty, 62, 69, 75, 102, 109, 121

Maastricht Treaty, 42
Macedonia, 46, 57, 60
Manners, I., 82
McCormick, J., 85
Merkel, A., 116, 155
military capabilities, 18, 46–9, 101, 119, 122, 180, 193, 198
military command structure, 59–60
military force, 1, 25, 65, 71, 87, 152, 191, 199–201, 203, 205
  deployment of, 18, 66, 86, 143
  right authority to, 23, 33
  scope for, 31
  state may lose monopoly on, 26–9
  Western use of, 29, 38
military integration, 65, 70, 138, 141, 142, 179, 183, 205, 207
  in Europe, 171–3
  and political integration relationship between, 30
military modernisation, 48, 178, 179, 180, 206
military tool, 15–16, 28, 46, 92, 100, 135, 179, 197
  deployment of, 18, 22–3, 32
  in integrated missions, 18–19
Miskimmon, A., 116
mission civilicatrice, 82
Mitterrand, F., 78, 107, 162, 163
Moravcsik, A., 4
multilateral legitimacy, 6, 31–6, 171, 204
multilateral security policy, 7–8
  see also new national interests

Napoleonic paradigm, 16, 17, 24, 26, 27
national caveats, 30, 31, 38, 185

NATO, 20, 22, 88, 137, 192
  and the EU, relationship between, 60–1, 72–3, 103
  military transformation, 48, 59, 127, 179, 184
  operation, 140
  political crisis in, 185
  political reinvigoration of, 179
  political transformation of, 179
  Response Force (NRF), 59, 127, 129, 172, 176, 185
  role, 58–60, 70, 104
Naumann, K., 29
new national interests, 68, 140
  constructivist and institutionalist approaches, 79–83
  ESDP: exercising power in, 89–94; realist models of, 77–9
  indirect power, 86–9
  in security policy, 73–7
  soft power, 84–6
New Public Management (NPM), 18, 28
Niblett, R., 115
Nice Treaty, 43, 121
normative power, 82, 84
North Atlantic Council (NAC), 59
North Sea Strategy, 177
Norway, 64, 89, 97, 154, 158, 175, 183
Norwegian Strategic Concept, 25

Operation Enduring Freedom (OEF), 36, 90
optional wars, 3, 4, 41

parliamentary powers, 147, 149
Paul, T. V., 210
PCC, *see* Prague Capabilities Commitment
peace dividend, 169
peace support operations (PSOs), 20, 21, 53, 70, 71, 137, 192, 200, 205
permanent structured cooperation, 62, 69, 72, 121, 122–3, 125, 126, 203
pooling of sovereignty, 2, 67, 105, 106, 138, 142
  in ESDP, *see* European Security and Defence Policy
Posen, B., 77, 176

post cold war, 1, 16, 31, 32, 33, 34, 47, 97, 105, 127
post-national security policy, in Europe, 15, 92
  de-territorialisation, 24–5
  internationalisation, driving forces of, 29–31
  legitimacy power, 89
  multilateral legitimacy, 31–6
  nation-state to service-state, 17–19
  non-state actors, implications for, 23–5
  security interests, return of, 36–9
  state may lose monopoly, on military force, 26–9
  territorial threat to diffuse risk, 19–23
Prague Capabilities Commitment (PCC), 20, 59
Prague summit, 59
Precision Guided Missiles (PGM), 182
private military companies (PMCs), 18, 24, 28
public opinion, 3, 22, 66, 157, 158, 162
Putnam, R., 2, 4, 5, 74, 139

qualified majority voting (QMV), 121

Ralston, J., 29
Rapid Reaction Force (RRF), 50, 61, 65, 185
realism, 77, 87, 90
relevant military capacity, 85, 101
responsibility to protect (R2P), 32, 34, 36, 47
Revolution in Military Affairs (RMA), 48, 101
Rieker, R., 80
Rifkind, M., 114
Riga NATO summit, 31, 59, 185
right authority, to military force, 23, 33
Ripsman, N., 210
robust operation, 40
RRF, *see* Rapid Reaction Force
rule of law, 43
Rules of Engagement (ROE), 146, 150
Rynning, S., 163

St. Malo declaration, 47, 68, 110, 112, 141
Salmon, T. C., 129
Sandholz, W., 82
Sarkozy, N., 6, 105, 116, 119
security actor, 23, 33
Security Council, 33
security interests, return of, 36–9
security service, 27–8
self-binding, 93, 139, 140, 165, 173
  see also executive multilateralism
'service-state' model, 18
SHAPE, *see* Supreme Headquarters Allied Powers Europe
Shepherd, A., 129
Smith, R., 4, 16, 46
soft power, 34, 84–6, 196
soft security, 201
Solana, J., 44, 52, 204
sovereignty, 35, 106, 186
special relationship, 71, 111, 113, 114
state, definition of, 16
state-to-state wars, 18, 21, 31, 32, 35, 200
'stick and carrot' tools, 43
strategic actor, 202, 203
Strategic Concept, 185
strategic thinking, 22, 137, 201
Supreme Headquarters Allied Powers Europe (SHAPE), 56, 61
Sweden, 5, 63, 64, 89, 97, 112, 135, 189

Taliban, 36–7, 148, 154
territorial threat, to diffuse risk, 19–23
terrorism, 32, 61, 65, 108
Thatcher, M., 78

Thessaloníki European Council, 50, 51
Thomson, R., 170
Treacher, A., 19
Treaty of the European Union (TEU), 40, 83, 121, 146
Turkey, 61, 99
two-level game, 4, 5, 67, 75, 93, 98, 138–43
  domestic political processes, 143–5
  strong governments, 159, 165–6
  weak governments, 146, 164–5

Ulriksen, S., 29, 105, 126, 172, 173, 176, 179
United Nations, 18, 32, 33–4, 205
  High Level Report, 182
  mandate, 22, 34, 41, 62, 66, 157, 202, 210
  Secretary-General, 192
United Nations Security Council (UNSC), 9, 32, 33, 65, 71, 211
United States, 37, 54, 68, 71, 79, 87, 102, 131, 152, 174, 176, 185, 196, 197
UNPROFOR, 114
UNSC, *see* United Nations Security Council

van Creveld, M., 28
Vedby-Rasmussen, M., 15
Venusberg report, 20, 178

Wæver, O., 36
Wagner, W., 143
war on terror, 41, 65
wars amongst the people, 16, 46
Wheeler, N., 23
Wulf, H., 30